Better Homes and Gardens®

vegetable fruit & herb gardening

WILEY

John Wiley & Sons, Inc.

Better Homes and Gardens® Vegetable, Fruit & Herb Gardening

Contributing Writer and Project Editor: Megan McConnell Hughes
Contributing Designers: Sundie Ruppert, Lori Gould
Editor, Garden Books: Denny Schrock
Editorial Assistant: Heather Knowles
Contributing Copy Editor: Terri Fredrickson
Contributing Proofreaders: Susan Lang, Peg Smith
Contributing Indexer: Ellen Sherron
Contributing Photographers: Marty Baldwin, Scott Little, Dean Schoeppner, Denny Schrock
Contributing Photo Researcher: Susan Ferguson

Meredith® Books
Editorial Director: Gregory H. Kayko
Editor in Chief, Garden: Doug Jimerson
Editorial Manager: David Speer
Art Director: Tim Alexander
Managing Editor: Doug Kouma
Executive Director, Sales: Ken Zagor
Director, Operations: George A. Susral
Business Director: Janice Croat
Imaging Center Operator: Trena Rickels

John Wiley & Sons, Inc.
Publisher: Natalie Chapman
Associate Publisher: Jessica Goodman
Executive Editor: Anne Ficklen
Assistant Editor: Charleen Barila
Production Director: Diana Cisek
Manufacturing Manager: Tom Hyland

This book is printed on acid-free paper.

Published by John Wiley & Sons, Inc., Hoboken, New Jersey
Published simultaneously in Canada

Note to Reader: Due to differing conditions, tools, and individual skills, Meredith Corporation assumes no responsibility for any damages, injuries suffered, or losses incurred as a result of following the information published in this book. Before beginning any project, review the instructions carefully and, if any doubts or questions remain, consult local experts or authorities. Because codes and regulations vary greatly, you should always check with authorities to ensure that your project complies with all applicable local codes and regulations. Always read and observe all the safety precautions provided by manufacturers of any tools, equipment, or supplies, and follow all accepted safety procedures.

***Better Homes and Gardens* Magazine**
Editor in Chief: Gayle Goodson Butler

Meredith National Media Group
President: Tom Harty
Executive Vice President: Doug Olson

Meredith Corporation
Chairman of the Board: William T. Kerr
President and Chief Executive Officer: Stephen M. Lacy

In Memoriam: E.T. Meredith III (1933–2003)

Photo Credits
Photographers credited may retain copyright © to the listed photographs.

Howard F. Schwartz, Colorado State University, bugwood.org: 114C, 116C

Gerald Holmes, Valent USA Corporation, bugwood.org: 115R

For general information on our other products and services or for technical support, please contact our Customer Care Department within the United States at (800) 762-2974, outside the United States at (317) 572-3993 or fax (317) 572-4002.

Wiley also publishes its books in a variety of electronic formats. Some content that appears in print may not be available in electronic books. For more information about Wiley products, visit our web site at www.wiley.com.

Library of Congress Cataloging-in-Publication Data

LOC information available upon request
ISBN: 978-0470-63856-9
Printed in the United States of America

10 9 8 7 6 5 4 3 2 1

grow your favorite fruits, vegetables, and herbs right outside your door. The inspiring images and easy-to-follow planting, growing, and harvesting advice on the following pages will yield a bountiful harvest and months of scrumptious, garden-fresh meals.

table of contents

p.6
FROM GARDEN TO TABLE
Explore the many benefits of homegrown produce.
8 Grow your own
10 What to grow
14 Getting started

p.16
EDIBLES IN THE LANDSCAPE
From backyard vegetable gardens to fruit trees as front yard accents, edibles are at home throughout the landscape.
18 Site selection
20 Traditional garden
22 Edible landscaping
26 Small spaces

p.28
GROWING PRODUCE IN POTS
Container gardens make it possible to harvest fresh food outside your door.
30 Anywhere gardens
32 Container design
34 Plant a pot
38 Container care

p.42
CLIMATES AND SEASONS
Let climate and seasons guide your planting for a bountiful harvest.
44 Know your zone
46 Edibles and climate
50 Extend the season

p.54
GOOD EARTH
Fertile, workable soil produces the tastiest fruits, vegetables, and herbs.
56 All about soil
60 Nutrients
66 Soil solutions

p.70
PLANTING TIME
Starting plants from seed or transplants is easy with these growing tips.

72 How to start
74 Planting indoors
78 Planting outdoors
82 Seedling care

p.84
WATER SMART
Provide plants with the water they need to thrive while conserving the valuable resource.

86 When to water
88 Ways to water
92 Water smart

p.94
GARDEN PESTS
Prevent and manage common garden pests with easy tips and the pest encyclopedia.

96 All about pests
106 Pest prevention
110 Pest encyclopedia

p.122
ALL ABOUT PRUNING
Spur fruiting trees and shrubs to produce abundantly with a few basic pruning practices.

124 Getting started
126 Fruit trees
130 Brambles
132 Small fruits

p.134
GARDEN PLANS
Use these easy-to-follow planting plans to create your homegrown feast.

136 Container gardens
140 Inground gardens
144 Herb gardens

p.146
VEGETABLE ENCYCLOPEDIA
Each entry describes when and how to plant, how to manage pests, and harvest tips. Favorite vegetables, such as tomatoes and peppers, are highlighted as well as lesser-known plants.

p.214
FRUIT ENCYCLOPEDIA
Hardy tree fruits, citrus, and fruiting shrubs are covered in this in-depth guide to growing fruit.

p.254
HERB ENCYCLOPEDIA
Culinary herbs are productive and easy to grow. The encyclopedia covers planting basics and shares tips for using herbs in the kitchen.

276 Zone map
278 Frost Maps
279 Resources
280 Index

from garden to table

Dinner is right outside your door. Grow your own nutrient-packed vegetables, fruits, and herbs.

p.8

GROW YOUR OWN

Dig into the encompassing benefits of growing your own food. From the ultimate in fresh flavor to the assurance of pesticide-free production, backyard edibles bring goodness to the table.

p.10

WHAT TO GROW

With hundreds of easy-to-grow fruits, vegetables, and herbs available at the garden center, a big hurdle is deciding exactly what to grow in your garden.

p.14

GETTING STARTED

This book is stocked with all the garden-smart info you need to grow great produce. In these pages you'll find a rundown of what you can expect so you can get on with eating your first tomato!

Grow your own

With a backyard garden, you know all kinds of things about the vegetables, fruits, and herbs you harvest to create meals for your family. To begin, count on intense flavor. Produce tastes best when it is fresh—plucked from the vine when it is perfectly ripe and eaten soon after. Your homegrown tomatoes will be sweeter than those from the supermarket, and just-picked lettuce will be deliciously tender and flavorful. If you're not careful, the best of your harvest will not make it to the table as you delight in a gardenside snack.

When the field-to-table distance is mere feet instead of hundreds of miles, putting together a spur-of-the-moment meal is as easy as stepping out the door, harvesting what is ripe, and combining the produce with some kitchen staples. A mesclun salad topped with slivers of baby radishes and a handful of sweet peas is the perfect starter for a springtime supper. A backyard garden can infuse your breakfast, lunch, and supper with fresh flavor from midspring through fall. Can and freeze your produce and you can easily eat from the garden 12 months a year.

A neat and tidy way to grow fruits, vegetables, and herbs, raised beds not only look good, but they are good for plants too. These quick-draining garden plots promote healthy, vigorous plants.

Nutrient boost

More often than not, backyard garden produce boasts more nutrients than supermarket counterparts. Research shows that the shorter the time between when a fruit or vegetable is harvested and when it is consumed or preserved, the more nutrients it contains. So a pepper that is harvested in South America and arrives on your grocery store shelf four or more days later has notably fewer valuable nutrients than the glossy green fruit you plucked from your garden 20 minutes before supper was served.

Along with harboring more nutrients, homegrown produce has fewer chemicals. In fact, a chemical-free produce patch is easy to accomplish with a few pest-free strategies. A backyard orchard, herb garden, and vegetable patch give you the piece of mind that you are providing your family produce without traces of chemicals that are commonly used on large-scale farms.

Go for color

Garden produce is more than just delicious. If you eat enough fresh fruits and vegetables, they will have a powerful affect on your health. University researchers are continuously studying the benefits of a diet rich in fruits and vegetables, and research has led to a new way of thinking.

Aim to eat produce in a rainbow of colors, instead of focusing on eating a particular number of fruit and vegetable servings each day. Researchers have found nutrients and powerful antioxidants vary by color, and by eating many different colors of produce you harness maximum benefits. Use the chart below to plant a rainbow in your garden this year.

Midsummer is ripe with colorful produce. Easy-to-grow tomatoes, peppers, and cucumbers are especially productive. Share your nutrient-rich harvest with friends.

Eat a rainbow

RED	ORANGE AND YELLOW	GREEN	BLUE AND PURPLE	WHITE
RED APPLE	YELLOW APPLE	GREEN APPLE	BLACKBERRY	CAULIFLOWER
BEET	APRICOT	ARTICHOKE	BLUEBERRY	GARLIC
RED CABBAGE	BUTTERNUT SQUASH	ASPARAGUS	EGGPLANT	ONION
CHERRY	CANTALOUPE	AVOCADO	FIG	PARSNIP
RED GRAPE	CARROT	GREEN BEAN	PURPLE GRAPE	POTATO
RED PEPPER	CORN	BROCCOLI	PLUM	TURNIP
RED POTATO	LEMON	BRUSSELS SPROUT	PRUNE	
RADISH	MANGO	CUCUMBER		
RASPBERRY	NECTARINE	GREEN GRAPE		
RHUBARB	ORANGE	HONEYDEW MELON		
STRAWBERRY	PEACH	KIWI		
TOMATO	PEAR	LETTUCE		
WATERMELON	YELLOW PEPPER	LIME		
	PUMPKIN	GREEN ONION		
	RUTABAGA	PEA		
	SWEET POTATO	GREEN PEPPER		
		SPINACH		
		ZUCCHINI		

Eating your garden produce

Think of your edible garden as your sweetly convenient personal produce section.

Your garden will not have pineapple and fresh green beans year-round like your supermarket, but it can offer fresh produce at different times throughout the year.

Deciding what to grow in your edible garden is as simple as making a grocery list. Recall recent trips to your local grocery. What was in your cart as you were leaving the produce section? Make a list of the vegetables, fruits, and herbs you commonly buy. Perhaps carrots, tomatoes, apples, lettuce, garlic, and potatoes top your list. Good news—you can grow all of these foods in a home garden. If bananas, oranges, and kiwi are popular with your family, you can grow these fruits, too, if you live in a warm climate.

In addition to growing the fruits, vegetables, and herbs that you commonly eat, a backyard garden is a low-cost opportunity to try new foods. For just a dollar or two you can introduce your friends and family to edamame, leeks, or garden-fresh cauliflower. Don't worry if you're unsure about the particulars of growing something, the encyclopedia section at the back of this book is stocked with all the information you need to grow produce.

Another way to approach the subject of what to grow in your edible garden is to think about what kinds of cuisine your family enjoys. Are Italian dishes a popular menu item? Do you frequent a favorite Mexican restaurant? Or is your refrigerator full of take-home boxes from a local Asian establishment? Specific fruits, vegetables, and herbs combine to lend these cuisines their telltale flavors. Plant an Italian-theme garden and make your own fresh spaghetti sauce with homegrown herbs and vegetables.

Year-round produce

When deciding what to grow, also think about how you will consume your produce. Most likely you'll eat most of it fresh, but if you take a few extra hours throughout the growing season, you can turn a summertime harvest into a year-round smorgasbord.

Freezing and canning are popular food preservation methods that capture the flavor of fresh produce. Turn a bushel of apples into many pints of applesauce or freeze a few cups of blueberries for use in a midwinter blueberry crumble. For canning and freezing tips and techniques, pick up a copy of the book *Better Homes and Gardens® You Can Can.*

Opposite: **A small garden plot can yield a wide array of produce. Carrots, cucumbers, onions, and radishes are among the vegetables that are the easiest to grow.**

Plant an extra row

In addition to filling your table with fresh produce, your backyard garden can also supply valuable nutrients to people in need. Consider adding an extra row of potatoes, peppers, tomatoes, or other favorite vegetables and donating the produce to your local food bank. Fresh fruit is often in short supply. Plant an extra row of raspberries or another apple tree and share the bounty. Contact your local homeless shelter or soup kitchen to learn about its specific food needs and how you and your garden can meet those needs.

Edibles by cuisine

Make your garden the first place to shop for your favorite fruits, vegetables, and herbs. Whether your family has a penchant for Italian, Asian, or Hispanic dishes, your garden will supply many of the integral ingredients to give your meals gourmet taste at homegrown prices. Trim your grocery bill by growing pricey herbs or costly vegetables for a fraction of the cost you would pay at the supermarket. Choose your cuisine du jour and plan a backyard feast.

1 Asian-inspired garden

It can be tough to find a large selection of Asian vegetables and herbs in the supermarket. So grow your own with this list of edibles. Plant your edible Asian garden in full sun and well-drained soil.

Basil ('Thai')
Cilantro
Cucumber ('Suyo Long' and 'Orient Express')
Edamame
Eggplant
Onions ('Ishikura' and 'Evergreen Long')
Pepper ('Thai Hot', 'Thai Dragon', and 'Jalapeño')
Spinach
Stir-fry greens mix that includes a combination of mustards and bok choi
Snow peas
Yard-long beans ('Kaohsiung')

Italian-inspired garden

Grow your own fresh vegetables and herbs to make a perfect pasta sauce and other mouthwatering dishes. The plants listed here thrive in full sun and well-drained soil. If you don't have space for an expansive garden, grow your favorite vegetables and herbs in pots.

- Arugula
- Basil
- Fennel
- Garlic
- Onion ('Italian Red Torpedo')
- Oregano
- Parsley (Italian flat-leaf)
- Pepper ('Sweet Cherry' and 'Italian Long')
- Thyme
- Tomato ('Viva Italia', 'Roma', and 'Costoluto Genovese')
- Zucchini ('Costata Romanesco')

Mexican-inspired garden

Add homegrown heat to your next Mexican dish with a batch of homemade salsa. It's a cinch to grow all of the basic salsa ingredients in your own garden. These plant recommendations include a host of spicy peppers. In fact, 'Black Pearl' and 'Calico' are so hot that they should be used only in moderation.

- Cilantro
- Garlic chives
- Onion ('Super Star')
- Pepper ('Jalapeño', 'Sweet Pickle', 'Black Pearl', and 'Calico')
- Tomatillo
- Tomato ('Better Boy' and 'Golden Jubilee')
- Sweet Corn

Getting started

Direct-seed beans in a raised bed garden after all danger of frost has passed. Get a jump-start on the season with pepper transplants. And dress up the bed with flowering annuals such as marigolds and alyssum.

In a few short weeks, your empty balcony or forlorn patch of turf will be the site of a fruitful garden. Use *Vegetable, Fruit & Herb Gardening* as a resource for need-to-know answers throughout the growing season or read each chapter and build a foundation of practical knowledge. From site selection to when to harvest the first red tomato of the season, the following pages are packed with everything you need to know to plant and care for vegetables, fruits, and herbs.

Site selection and preparation

One of the most important tasks in creating any garden is to choose the appropriate site. All plants have particular soil and sun requirements, and the following pages will help you match your site conditions with vegetables, fruits, and herbs that will thrive in those conditions. Once you determine the site, it's time to create the best growing conditions possible. Removing sod for a garden bed and choosing soil for a container garden are just two of the site preparation tasks covered.

Planting
Whether you start plants from seeds or transplants purchased at your local nursery, you'll find tips and techniques to ensure young plants put down roots. Get a jump on the gardening season by starting seeds indoors with the help of the indoor seed-starting section.

Care and maintenance
Timely weeding, watering, and pest control will promote a bountiful harvest. Look for timesaving tips for accomplishing these garden chores, as well as environmentally friendly pest control techniques.

Harvest
Picking vegetables, fruits, and herbs at optimum ripeness allows you to capture the fruits' maximum sugars and valuable nutrients. You'll find harvest tips throughout the book.

Encyclopedias of edibles
The most popular vegetables, fruits, and herbs are covered in detail in the encyclopedias. Each entry has specific planting advice, care tips, harvest information, and cultivar recommendations, along with colorful photos.

TEST GARDEN TIP

Restrain yourself

If you are planting a vegetable garden for the first time, make sure to plant no more than you can use or take care of. It's easy to get caught up in the fun of planting without thinking about the time you'll need to weed, water, and harvest.

Vegetables require a steady supply of moisture to be productive. Apply water to the base of the plant and avoid wetting the foliage to cut down on disease problems.

edibles in the landscape

Plant your favorite foods in a traditional plot, create an edible front yard garden, or turn your balcony into a buffet—the choice is yours.

p.18
SITE SELECTION

The perfect combination of sun, rich soil, and ample moisture sets the scene for a lush edible garden. Learn how to choose the best site for your fruits, vegetables, and herbs.

p.20
TRADITIONAL GARDEN

Perk up your traditional edible garden with these tips for adding structure, color, and form. In short order your edible garden will become a backyard destination.

p.22
EDIBLE LANDSCAPING

Make the most of your growing space by adding fruits, vegetables, and herbs to shrub borders, perennial beds, and your front yard.

p.26
SMALL SPACES

Pack a bountiful garden into a small space with the use of containers and other space-saving garden techniques. Add valuable growing space to your courtyard, patio, or balcony with these ideas.

Choose the best site

Choosing a site for growing edibles is a little like choosing a home. If your dwelling satisfies your basic need for shelter, you're more likely to be happy and productive. Apply the same principle to choosing a site for growing vegetables, fruits, and herbs and they'll reward you with armloads of produce. When choosing a home for your edibles, keep these tips in mind.

Sweet sun

Choose a site that receives 8 to 10 hours of sun a day. While some leafy vegetables will thrive in less light, most edible plants need 8 or more hours of sunlight a day.

Opt for direct light. Sunlight filtering through a tree canopy does not provide plants with the same light qualities as direct sunlight. Choose a growing spot where plants do not have to compete with trees and shrubs for sunlight.

Rich soil

Make nutrient-rich soil a priority. Plant roots harvest nutrients necessary for fruit and foliage production from the soil. Choose a site with nutrient-rich soil; color is often a good indicator of soil nutrient content. Dark brown or black soil often has the most available nutrients.

Look for a quick-draining site. Waterlogged soil will quickly suffocate plant roots. Choose a site that drains quickly after a rain. Avoid depressions and swales where water collects. A relatively level spot promotes good drainage and is also easier to plant and care for than an undulating site.

Plan to make amends. Even the best garden soils benefit from a rejuvenating layer of compost. Whether you garden in a pot or a backyard plot, plan to give your soil a boast by incorporating organic amendments every year or two.

Water wonders

Locate your garden near a water source. Whether you choose to hand water with a watering can or hose or install a simple drip irrigation system, the proximity of a water source is important. In general, vegetables require more frequent irrigation than herbs. Fruit trees require minimal watering after establishing a deep root system.

Pay attention to soil texture. A soil's texture often determines how well it will hold water and then share that water with a plant. The best soil for an edible garden crumbles easily in your hand when you gently squeeze it.

Opposite: **Lettuces and herbs thrive in this patio-side raised bed garden. The garden's close proximity to the house simplifies watering and harvest.**

Beware of black walnut trees

Black walnut trees are unfriendly planting companions for many edibles. These trees secrete a substance called juglone through their roots into nearby soil. Juglone is also present in the plants' leaves, twigs, and hulls and can leach into the soil as the plant parts decompose.

Some plants are very sensitive to juglone and quickly wilt and die in its presence. Tomato, pepper, cabbage, eggplant, and potato are the most sensitive edibles. Melon, squash, bean, carrot, and corn all show good resistance to juglone, as do peach, cherry, nectarine, and plum trees.

Your best line of defense is to steer clear of planting near black walnut trees. The greatest concentration of juglone is under the canopy of the tree. A mature tree's toxic zone extends about 50 feet from the trunk of the tree.

Plant a traditional vegetable garden

Planted in rows, a traditional garden is easy to weed by running a small tiller down the length of the rows every two weeks.

A traditionally designed edible garden is usually rectangular, but don't let the simple shape stop you from lending your produce garden some creative flair. Grow pole beans up a collection of twig towers or edge the garden with a border of knee-high zinnias. Traditional vegetable gardens are as unique as the people who tend them.

A good choice for a large sunny yard, a traditional garden is firmly rooted in function. A row-style planting scheme makes it easy to water and weed young plants and harvest produce. End-of-the-season garden chores are as simple as removing all the leaves, stems, and plant debris. Then it's a cinch to spread compost over the swath of open ground and till it in.

The size of a traditional edible garden depends on the types and amounts of vegetables, fruits, and herbs you wish to grow and how much time you have for garden chores. The best size garden is large enough to be enjoyable and offer space to plant a variety of vegetables but small enough not to be a burden. If you are just starting out, begin with a simple 10×10-foot plot. Both manageable and productive, a 100-square-foot garden offers many opportunities.

Design know-how

Combine a geometric plot and a few rows of plants and you're well on your way to designing a traditional edible garden. Amplify your garden's production while simplifying plant care with these traditional garden design tips.

Honor spacing suggestions. In your exuberance to pack as many tantalizing vegetables into a defined space, it's easy to downsize plant spacing recommendations to squeeze in just one more row of heirloom carrots. Resist, resist. An exceptionally dense planting scheme may look great on paper and even appear possible at planting time, but plant growth will prove otherwise. Densely planted gardens are difficult to weed and water effectively, more susceptible to pest problems than well-spaced counterparts, and frustrating to harvest.

Plan for paths. An easy access route through the garden is essential for quick maintenance and hassle-free harvest. Aim to create paths that are at least 2 feet wide and blanket them with a weed-inhibiting layer of organic mulch.

Cluster annuals. For easy cleanup and soil preparation at the beginning and end of the season, plant annuals together in one contiguous area while grouping perennials and woody plants in another space. This arrangement allows blueberries, sage, and other long-lived plants to grow undisturbed when you annually prepare soil for the vegetables.

Think about maintenance practices. If you plan to run a small tiller between rows to eliminate weeds, allocate ample space—at least 3 feet between rows. Plan for easy watering by planting water-loving plants, such as raspberries and blueberries, together near a convenient water source.

Productive and pretty

Make a traditional edible garden a backyard focal point. Whether the garden is visible from your kitchen window or the dining table on your back patio, if it is easy to see when you gaze into the backyard, you're more likely to stay ahead of the weeds and remember to gather produce as soon as it is ripe. Dress up an edible garden with these pretty and productive landscape elements.

1

2

3

4

5

1 **ARBOR**
Frame the garden entry with an arbor cloaked with pole beans or kiwi. Or add color with the blooms of climbing roses, clematis, or morning glories.

2 **FENCE**
Surround the garden with a low decorative fence. A simple picket, rustic twig, or stately stone fence will define the garden border and maybe even keep pests away.

3 **FLOWERS**
Wake up a sleepy green vegetable garden with edible flowers. Try nasturtiums, calendula, sweet violets, and lavender.

4 **OBELISK**
Add height with an obelisk. Made of wood, stone, or a mixture of materials, an obelisk will quickly become a focal point. Train sweet peas or climbing edibles up the sturdy structure.

5 **TREES**
Use dwarf fruit trees to unite the edible garden with the surrounding landscape. Plant trees along the garden perimeter or one on each corner.

Grow edibles in your landscape

Invite edibles into beds and borders.

If a traditional vegetable garden isn't your style or your lot is short on space, consider an edible landscape. Plant fennel near your foundation and border your patio with peppers. Not only does an edible landscape make it possible to grab a snack as you mow your front lawn or harvest a handful of beans as you grill a steak, but it also maximizes growing space, filling your table with homegrown produce.

Get started designing your edible landscape by taking stock of your current yard. Look for lackluster nonedible plants that can be replaced with edibles. Instead of enclosing your backyard with a traditional hedge, consider a row of blueberries. Springtime flowers, summer fruit, and colorful fall foliage make blueberries an excellent landscape plant.

When adding trees to your lot, go with edibles. Although it might not grow as large or live as long as a maple or an oak, an apple, peach, or pear tree will provide food for your family, friends, neighbors, and wildlife. Avoid planting fruit trees near patios, driveways, and walkways because they are bound to drop fruit, creating a mess on paved surfaces.

Annual excitement

Carrots, radishes, squash, and other annual edibles make excellent landscape plants too. For year-round good looks, pair these short-lived plants with shrubs or perennials. Perennial edibles such as raspberries, sage, thyme, and many other herbs are good choices, but so are traditional landscape plants such as boxwood, daylilies, and junipers.

The key to success is matching plants with their preferred growing conditions. Don't plant vegetables in the dry environment under your home's eaves, and beware of shade cast by nearby plants and buildings.

Some edibles have a tendency to take on a shabby appearance at the end of the season. For example, the foliage of potato plants dies down as the tubers mature, and foliar diseases occasionally plague tomatoes. Plant these productive but not-so-pretty plants in a backyard planting bed while reserving prominent planting space for eye-catching vegetables like lettuce, peppers, eggplant, and all kinds of herbs.

Plan for change

An edible landscape is constantly evolving. Shade will increase as shrubs and trees mature, casting dappled light on what was once full-sun planting spots. Water will also become scarce in the soil surrounding maturing woody and perennial plants.

At the beginning of every growing season, take a few minutes to walk through your landscape and look at how the evolving growing conditions are meeting the needs of your fruits, vegetables, and herbs. Look for changing sun-shade patterns, low-water areas, poorly drained spots, crowded garden beds that need expansion, and plants that need division.

Opposite: **Lettuce, cabbage, and kale are neatly contained in a tidy planting bed bordered by a boxwood hedge.**

Front-yard worthy Neat and tidy growing habits, minimal pest problems, and bountiful production make these edibles perfect for garden beds. Don't hesitate to plant them in a prominent place. Their consistent good looks will add edible decoration to your landscape.

VEGETABLES	FRUITS	HERBS
ARTICHOKE	APPLE	BASIL
BEET	APRICOT	CHIVES
BROCCOLI	BLUEBERRY	LAVENDER
CARROT	CHERRY	LEMON VERBENA
CHARD	GRAPE	OREGANO
KALE	KIWI	PARSLEY
KOHLRABI	MANGO	ROSEMARY
LEEK	PEACH	SAGE
LETTUCE	PEAR	THYME
ONION	PLUM	
PEPPER	STRAWBERRY	
RADISH		
RHUBARB		
TOMATILLO		

Plant an orchard

There is an apple cultivar for nearly every climate. When grafted to a dwarfing rootstock, these productive trees are at home even in the smallest urban landscapes.

Don't be intimidated by the word "orchard." It might conjure up an image of acres and acres of apple trees or a massive mango grove, but a backyard orchard can be as simple as a couple of cherry trees. Integrate the fruit trees into an existing shrub bed and they instantly become landscape plants. Whether you choose to grow two or three fruit trees or a half-acre orchard, here are a few particulars to keep in mind as you plan for a sweet harvest.

Site specifics

Selecting a site for a fruit tree involves taking stock of the planting site's current conditions and predicting the site's future conditions. Fruit trees, like most vegetables, require full sun for good growth and fruit production. When selecting a planting site, pay close attention to nearby trees, which may cast shade on the young fruit tree in 5 or 10 years as the plants grow and mature.

Fertile, well-drained soil is essential. Like most edibles, fruit trees will grow poorly, if at all, in heavy clay soil.

Above left: **Most sweet cherries, like many fruit trees, generally require pollination from another cultivar.**

Above right: **Plant care and pollination are often simplified when several different fruit trees are planted together in a small backyard orchard.**

Ensure pollination

Several types of fruit require more than one variety for pollination and subsequent fruit production. These plants set fruit only when they receive pollen from a nearby plant of a different variety. These types of plants are called self-sterile and include some peaches, apricots, and crabapples and most apples, pears, plums, and sweet cherries. 'Royal Ann' sweet cherry, for example, must be within 100 feet of another cherry tree with compatible pollen that blooms at the same time as 'Royal Ann' or it will not produce any cherries.

The fruit encyclopedia section explains the exact pollination needs for every tree fruit. You'll even find suggested cultivar pairings, which makes it easy to select which fruit trees to grow.

Care and maintenance

When given regular care, fruit trees will produce bushels of fruit three to five years after planting. Deep watering is essential during the first year after planting. To encourage strong root growth, plan to soak the tree's root zone every week or two during the first year after planting. Drought conditions will require more frequent watering. Prevent competition for moisture by removing weeds and grass from underneath the tree's canopy. Spread a 4- to 6-inch-thick layer of mulch under the tree, keeping it away from the trunk.

Plan to prune fruit trees every two to three years to ensure a strong branching structure that will support the developing fruit.

ASK THE GARDEN DOCTOR

I have a small yard. Can I grow fruit trees?

ANSWER: Even the smallest yard usually has space for a fruit tree. For years, scientists have been working to select and produce small, productive fruit trees for the home landscape. A standard-size apple tree can grow from 20 to 40 feet high and spread 25 to 40 feet. Dwarf apple varieties, by contrast, can be held to a height of about 10 feet with a 10-foot spread. Expect similar results from dwarf apricots, cherries, nectarines, oranges, peaches, and plums.

Check the fruit encyclopedia for a list of dwarf cultivars for most fruit trees. When shopping at the nursery, check the plant tag for information about the tree's height and spread.

Take advantage of small spaces

Even the smallest growing spots can host a vibrant edible garden.

Edibles will thrive on a 5-foot-square balcony, in a sunny front entryway, or in a miniscule backyard plot. Vegetables, fruits, and herbs prefer spacious plots, but they have the potential to be just as productive in tight quarters, especially if you provide ample water and nutrients. Make the most of your limited planting space with these ideas.

Embrace containers

Filled with quick-draining soil and bathed with ample sun, a container will play host to nearly any edible plant. Station a pot of popular culinary herbs such as basil, thyme, and sage outside your kitchen door for exceptionally fresh flavor. Stock a collection of containers with all the ingredients for salsa; tomatoes, peppers, onions, and cilantro are a cinch to grow in pots.

You can even grow small fruit trees in containers. Choose a hardy dwarf cultivar and a large pot and you'll be harvesting fruit on your patio in a few short years.

Add height

Maximize space by growing plants up instead of out. A vining cucumber takes much less space when it is trained on a trellis rather than allowed to sprawl on the ground. Instead of growing a row of green beans, send plants skyward by planting a pole bean cultivar.

Choose petite cultivars

In recent years researchers have worked hard to select small or dwarf cultivars of many edibles—from fruit trees to tomatoes—that will thrive in ever-shrinking landscapes. These petite cultivars are often nearly as productive as their full-size relatives. The vegetable, fruit, and herb encyclopedias at the back of this book include small cultivars for small spaces.

Practice succession planting

Succession planting is all about maximizing planting space. It is a planning and planting process that allows the garden space to be continuously in production from spring to fall. For example, follow a fast-growing spring crop of arugula, radishes, spinach, or peas with a summer crop of bush beans, cucumbers, or eggplant in the same planting space. Then tuck cool-season plants such as broccoli and lettuce into open areas among the summer vegetables for a late fall or winter harvest.

Take advantage of intercropping

This technique pairs fast-maturing crops with those that are slower to grow so valuable garden space won't lie empty. Intercrop by sowing lettuce or cilantro seeds in the spaces between tomato plants. By the time tomatoes take up their full space and are fruiting, the lettuce or cilantro is finished producing.

Plant a community garden plot

Community garden plots offer urban residents an expanse of open soil perfect for growing prized edibles. Along with providing coveted growing space, a community plot will connect you with local gardeners.

Reserve prime, full-sun space near your home for frequently harvested edibles such as herbs, cherry tomatoes, and lettuce. Plant other favorite crops in the more expansive community plot.

Above left: **Delineated by flagstones set on edge, this tiny raised bed garden is carved out of a busy courtyard garden.**

Above middle: **A good example of intercropping, rows of lettuce flank tiny kale plants. After the lettuce is harvested, there will be plenty of space for the kale to grow and mature.**

Above right: **Petite tomato and pepper cultivars make it possible to grow many of these summer treats in a small space.**

Opposite: **Garden anywhere with containers, even on a gravel patio. Here, tomatoes, peppers, and herbs are planted in galvanized buckets dressed up with a colorful coat of paint.**

growing produce in pots

Whether you garden on a half acre or 4 square feet on a patio, growing edibles in containers makes it possible to harvest favorite foods outside your door.

p.30
ANYWHERE GARDENS

Use culinary container gardens to harvest homegrown produce no matter where you live.

p.32
CONTAINER DESIGN

Some plants grow better than others in the tight confines of a container garden. Check out these tips for choosing the best containers and cultivars for your potted edible feast.

p.34
PLANT A POT

The best potting soil paired with healthy, vigorous plants sets the scene for a bountiful harvest. Learn all about the characteristics of good potting soil and how to plant your container garden.

p.38
CONTAINER CARE

Simplify watering chores and grow pest-free, productive container gardens that are a treat for the taste buds and the eye with these quick and easy care ideas.

Grow edibles anywhere

Containers filled with tomatoes, peppers, alpine strawberries, lettuce, and herbs turn a deck into a productive edible garden.

Containers make it possible to grow juicy tomatoes, spicy peppers, and sweet strawberries almost anywhere.

Turn a barren front walkway into an edible symphony of texture and color by lining it with pots of edible plants. Add taste to a desolate courtyard with containers brimming with produce and herbs.

Not only do edible container gardens offer tasty fruits, vegetables, and herbs, but they are also valuable landscape elements. Lend privacy to a patio by grouping three to five large container gardens to form a living screen. Frame an entry by flanking it with containers of neatly trimmed dwarf apple trees. Use an edible container garden to dress up a lackluster section of a perennial border or shrub garden. When planted in bold containers, a portable garden is an instant focal point that can be moved around the landscape as needed.

Container gardens are especially useful where inground gardening is not possible. Balconies, decks, and housing association covenants often limit gardening, but containers make it possible to harvest a sprig of rosemary and a handful of parsley at a moment's notice.

Don't be confined to ground level when planning your edible container garden. Go vertical. Hanging baskets and window boxes will help you make the most of every square inch of growing space.

Seek sun

Just like an inground edible garden, container gardens generally need 8 to 10 hours of direct sun for good growth. Rooftop gardens and south- and west-facing locations usually offer ample sunlight. Gardening on the north or east side of a building or in the shade of a tree limits the number of edibles you can grow but doesn't eliminate edible gardening. Instead of growing sun-loving tomatoes and peppers, grow spinach, lettuce, and herbs that tolerate partial shade. The encyclopedia section details the sunlight requirements for all edibles.

Water is another necessary ingredient in a container garden location. Water should be easily accessible as container gardens require watering at least daily, if not twice a day, on the hottest days of summer. A nearby spigot makes filling up a watering can or delivering water with a hose a quick and easy task.

TEST GARDEN TIP

Sturdy support

Hanging baskets and window boxes make great container gardens, but these sky-high gardens can become very heavy as the fruit ripens. Use sturdy supports or brackets, attached to wall studs where possible, to anchor baskets and boxes.

Herbs are especially easy to grow in containers. Grillside seasoning is easy with an enamelware container filled with rosemary and two types of thyme.

Design a container garden

Think of a container garden as a petite version of an inground garden.

Combine rich, well-drained soil with ample sunlight and healthy plants and you'll be rewarded with luscious produce. In a container garden, just as in an inground garden, grow the edibles you commonly use in the kitchen and introduce your taste buds to new flavors by setting aside some space for new plants.

Pot-friendly plants

Hundreds of vegetables, fruits, and herbs grow well in containers. They are typically short, stocky, and exceptionally good at withstanding strong winds and rigors of growing in a confined area. Researchers are constantly working to develop cultivars for container gardens.

Container-friendly tomato plants often produce slightly smaller fruit than their inground counterparts, but they are just as prolific and gems at standing tall when laden with many pounds of fruit. Bush forms of the traditional vining cucumber make it possible to grow these summer staples on your patio without a trellis.

Some plants, though, are not well suited to containers. Corn, melons, and several varieties of squash require vast amounts of space or extensive trellising to grow in containers. Purchase these crops at your local farmer's market and use the container space to grow other container-friendly plants instead.

Herbs are exceptional container plants. Grow your favorite herbs right outside your door for fast harvest. Basil, parsley, thyme, and oregano are popular culinary herbs and will thrive when grown together. Grow rosemary in a pot and enjoy its fragrance and flavor year-round in cold climates when you move it inside for winter.

Fruit trees require more effort than easy-to-grow vegetables and herbs, but the results are well worth it. In a container it's possible to grow 'Improved Meyer' lemons in Michigan and peaches in North Dakota because their mobility makes it easy to move them to shelter when cold weather comes (or wheel them to a shady spot if desert heat is your challenge).

Container considerations

Choose the largest container possible for your edible garden. The larger the container, the more soil moisture it will retain and the less frequently you'll need to water. With that concept in mind, it is possible to choose a container that is too large if you intend to move it during the growing season. Pots at least 10 inches across can hold herbs, green onions, lettuces, and other small crops. For tomatoes, peppers, and other large plants, choose a pot that holds 5 to 15 or more gallons of soil.

Almost any type of vessel can be converted into a container garden. Tubs, buckets, and half barrels work well as do a variety of items from flea markets and salvage yards. Garden and home centers offer hundreds of colorful ceramic, plastic, and concrete options. The key to a perfect pot is drainage holes in the bottom. Without drainage holes, water will collect in the soil, displacing necessary oxygen and eventually suffocating plant roots.

Opposite: **A collection of herbs, Swiss chard, and bush-type cucumbers spill out of stone containers. The obelisk provides support for vining cucumbers.**

Take five **Tomatoes, peppers, and herbs are some of the most popular edibles for container gardens. Here are five great tomato and pepper cultivars and five herbs that are easy to grow in pots. Count on these plants to be deliciously prolific and well-behaved.**

TOMATOES
- 'BUSH BIG BOY'
- 'PATIO'
- 'PIXIE'
- 'SALADETTE'
- 'SMALL FRY'

PEPPERS
- 'BELL BOY'
- 'GYPSY'
- 'JALAPEÑO'
- 'RED CHERRY'
- 'SWEET BANANA'

HERBS
- BASIL, 'MINIMUM'
- PARSLEY, CURLY AND FLAT-LEAF
- THYME
- OREGANO
- SAGE

Start with soil

Soil is a plant's lifeline. It helps make water, nutrients, and air available to plant roots. Great soil is essential to plant growth and fruit production. It pays to invest in good-quality potting soil that will sustain plants from planting time until the first frost, or for years in the case of fruit trees and perennial herbs. Before planting your edible containers, use these tips to search out the best soil for a rich harvest.

The ideal soil will not come from your yard—garden soil is too heavy, compacts too easily, and drains poorly in pots. Instead, the best soil is formulated to drain well but still hold moisture; it is light enough to use in a portable container but heavy enough to keep the pot from toppling over in a strong wind.

For convenience, use an all-purpose potting mix that includes a blend of ingredients, such as peat, vermiculite, perlite, sand, and bark, suited to most potted plants.

The best soil for edible container gardens is a quality potting soil. A soil-based potting mix provides nutrients and drainage necessary for healthy plants.

Look for a soil-based mix that is made with sterilized loam. It is a dense soil that will hold moisture and nutrients well. The package will tell you if it is soil-based or a soilless mix (made primarily with peat, coir/coconut husk, bark, wood chips, or sawdust), which will be lightweight and dry out too quickly for most edibles.

Compost is a valuable addition to a soil mix. Many prepackaged mixes contain compost and the package label will list percentage of compost by volume in the mix. Compost contains nutrients plants need for growth but because it releases those nutrients slowly over time, additional fertilizing is often needed for a continuous harvest of edibles.

Customize a potting mix by incorporating compost made in your own backyard, slow-release fertilizer, and water-holding polymer crystals, which will lessen feeding and watering but not eliminate the chores. Be sure all purchased soil additives are labeled for use with edible plants.

Go organic with an organic soil-based mix. There are many on the market. Look for one that is specially formulated for edibles; it will likely contain more valuable nutrients than general mixes.

Densely planted containers like this rely on nutrient-rich potting mixes, such as those that contain slow-release fertilizers to sustain fast growth.

The drain game

Every container must provide drainage, giving excess water an escape route. Placing pot shards in the bottom of a container is no longer recommended—this technique hinders drainage instead of improving it. Try one of these methods instead.

1 SCREEN
If a container's drainage hole is large, cover it with screening, newspaper, or a coffee filter to prevent soil from leaking out.

2 GRAVEL
If a container has no drainage hole and you prefer not to drill one in it, create a drainage area using a 2-inch layer of gravel.

3 LINER
When lining a container with landscape fabric or plastic, cut several drainage holes in the liner for water to escape.

Plant your container garden

Do you have ten minutes? You have time to plant an edible garden!

Containerized edible gardens are quick to plant and quick to care for thanks to their petite size. Even though you can plant a container faster than you can make a trip to the grocery store, it's important to pay attention to details at this stage to ensure strong, healthy plants. Plant with care now and you'll be shopping for fruits and vegetables on your patio instead of at the supermarket.

Use the last frost date for your area as an indicator of when to plant. Plant cool-season vegetables such as lettuce, spinach, and radishes, and hardy herbs two to three weeks before the last average frost in your region. Wait until after the chance of frost has passed to plant warm-season crops such as tomatoes and peppers. Don't know when your last spring frost date is? Contact your local extension service.

Plant in place if the container will be too heavy to move after it is planted.

Before planting in terra-cotta, soak the container in water. A dry clay pot absorbs moisture from soil.

Fill a container half to three-fourths full with potting mix. Blend in slow-release fertilizer and water-retentive crystals, if desired. Top with plain potting mix.

Place the largest plant in the center of the container for a symmetrical design, off to one side for an asymmetrical balance. Leave adequate space for stakes, particularly around tomatoes, if necessary. Rearrange plants until you're pleased with the display.

Remove one plant at a time from its nursery pot, starting with the largest. To dislodge a large plant from a nursery pot, gently lay the pot on its side and press firmly on it with your foot. Roll the pot to the opposite side and repeat the process. Then slide the plant out of the pot.

To plant, set the plant in the container and add potting mix around the root ball. Set smaller plants in place. Fill in between plants with soil mix without packing it.

If you wish to plant seeds, sow them directly in a container filled with potting mix. Use a water wand or sprinkler can to gently moisten the seedbed before planting. Follow planting instructions on the seed packet.

Leave 2 inches between the top of the soil mix and the container rim for water and mulch.

After planting, moisten the potting mix thoroughly (until water runs out of the pot's drainage hole). Elevate the pot with pot feet or bricks so water can escape freely.

Opposite: **Plant thyme near the edge of a container. As it grows, its vigorous, trailing stems will spill over the side of the pot.**

Just the right size

Size matters when it comes to the perfect container for edibles—if the pot is too small, your tomato plant might topple. If a fruit tree is planted in a massive container, you'll have a tough time lugging it inside at the end of the season. Use these sizes as a guide.

POT SIZE:
1 gallon
(10-inch diameter and at least 6 inches deep)
HERBS
LETTUCE
ONION
SPINACH

POT SIZE:
4 to 5 gallon
BEET
CARROT
CUCUMBER
EGGPLANT
GREEN BEAN
PEPPER
POTATO
TOMATO

POT SIZE:
5 to 7 gallon
DWARF FRUIT TREES

Watering tips

Regular watering is essential to a bountiful container garden harvest.

When set on a timer, a simple irrigation system can take care of your watering chores. It is especially useful for watering edibles, like this lemon verbena, when you are away from home for days at a time.

Unlike their inground counterparts, container-grown edibles can't send out roots to mine for additional moisture because they are confined. So they rely on you to provide ample water, especially on hot, dry summer days when they are funneling all their resources into producing juicy fruit or foliage. Diligent watering, sometimes as often as twice a day, will yield weeks of fresh produce.

Containers usually require watering daily during summer or every two or three days during cooler periods, unless nature handles it for you. Hot, dry weather and small pots can necessitate twice-daily watering.

Plants suffer from too much water as much as from too little. Determine if a container garden needs water by poking your finger into the soil up to the second knuckle. If the soil feels dry, it's time to water. Check pots daily.

Saturate the potting mix thoroughly. You know you have saturated the soil when excess water drains out the drainage hole. Quick, efficient drainage is key. Soil sours, roots rot, and root-killing mineral salts build up in a container that drains poorly.

If a soilless mix dries out completely, re-wet it by standing the pot in a large vessel of water overnight.

Watering early in the day is best. It allows plants to soak up what they need before afternoon heat causes excessive evaporation. Watering in the evening can leave moisture on foliage and promote disease.

Use a watering can to water only a few containers. Group pots and water them all at once. For faster watering by hand, use a hose and watering wand to quickly deliver water to many containers.

Using drip irrigation set on a timer takes the work out of watering. A drip system also saves water by delivering it near plants' root zones with as little evaporation and runoff as possible. Check the system seasonally to make sure the timer works and lines are not clogged or punctured.

Self-watering pots feature built-in reservoirs that deliver moisture to the soil. They require less frequent watering.

Water-holding mats fit into the bottom of hanging baskets and other containers, wicking moisture into the soil.

TEST GARDEN TIP

Early riser

The best time to water plants is in the early morning. Daytime sun and wind will quickly dry leaves, thwarting the development of fungal diseases. Take 10 minutes before you leave for work to thoroughly soak your container gardens.

Watering wands are a fast, gentle way to water container gardens. A sturdy, long-handle wand makes easy work of watering tough-to-reach hanging baskets too.

Grow a healthy container garden

As long as they are watered regularly, container gardens are undemanding.

Vigorously growing plants, especially flowering ones like these edible yellow calendula, require regular nutrients. For no-hassle fertilizing, use a soil mix that includes slow-release fertilizer.

An investment of 10 minutes a week to mulch, stake, feed, and tidy a trio of edible container gardens will reap produce all summer long.

Fertilize

Choose organic fertilizers when possible. Not only do they enrich the soil, but most also improve soil structure. Organic fertilizers include compost, well-rotted manure, fish emulsion, and kelp products.

Gradual-release fertilizer blended into a potting mix before planting offers an easy way to fertilize container plants continuously. The coated granules release nutrients slowly, usually over three to nine months. Many packaged potting soils designed for edible plants include a gradual-release fertilizer in the mix. If your mix does not, you can blend in one according to package directions.

Water-soluble plant food is an alternative. Make a solution of plant food and water, sprinkle it on the soil, and reapply it regularly throughout the growing season.

Plants show signs of nutrient deficiency particularly in their foliage, alerting you to their need for fertilizer. Clues include pale or discolored leaves, weak or slow growth, and small leaves and flowers.

Mulch

Mulch prevents soil from washing out of pots and splashing on foliage when you water plants. It also insulates soil and plant roots, helping them stay cooler during the hottest days of summer.

Organic mulches, such as cocoa shells and chipped or shredded bark, decompose gradually and add nutrients to the soil mix.

Spread a 1- to 2-inch layer of mulch on top of the soil after planting. Apply it loosely and evenly; avoid compacting mulch and piling it up around the plant stems.

Tidy up

By late summer or early fall, when some plants are no longer in production and appear bedraggled, it is time to replace them. Swap a tomato plant for an about-to-bloom aster and enjoy a colorful fall bloom show. Or plant a fall crop of spinach.

Potted fruit trees require root pruning every two to three years to maintain healthy, vibrant growth. To root-prune, remove the plant from its container while it is dormant, and shave off an inch of soil and roots at the sides and bottom of the root ball. Return the plant to the same container, adding potting mix to replace the soil you have removed, and water the root zone thoroughly.

Pests and diseases rarely bother edible container gardens but when they do, take action quickly. Disfigured or discolored foliage or fruit and visible insect pests are signs of a potential problem. Diagnose the problem accurately with the help of the Garden Pests chapter beginning on page 94.

Prevent excessive soil moisture evaporation by topping containers with a layer of mulch. Shredded bark is easy to find at garden centers.

Stand tall

Staking top-heavy fruits and vegetables in containers is not necessary, but it will promote a larger harvest and create a more attractive pot garden. Many tomatoes and some peppers and eggplant benefit from staking. Bush-type cultivars and those bred specifically for containers often don't require support. Help wayward plants stand tall with these tips.

Start young Put stakes or trellises in place at planting time to avoid disturbing roots later in the season. Staking at planting also ensures that the supports are in place as soon as plants begin to grow.

Strength is essential Wood dowels, thick twigs, commercial tomato cages, and a variety of found objects all make good plant supports as long as they are sturdy. Choose strong stakes to support tomatoes, which often have several pounds of fruit hanging from their vines.

Secure stems Use small pieces of nylon or cloth to tie plant stems to stakes. Or thread branches through sturdy tomato cages or trellises.

all about climate and seasons

Take cues from climate and seasons when choosing which fruits, vegetables, and herbs to plant and when to plant them.

p.44
KNOW YOUR ZONE

Planting zones are a quick and easy way to determine which plants will grow, produce fruit, and successfully overwinter in your area.

p.46
EDIBLES AND CLIMATE

Climate influences when to plant fruits, vegetables, and herbs. Learn all about nature's cues and you'll reap tasty rewards.

p.50
EXTEND THE SEASON

Get a jump start on the spring growing season or extend your harvest until the snow flies in early winter with these season-extending ideas.

Know your Zone

Even if you have only dabbled in gardening, you have probably run across the term "zone." Perhaps someone has asked you what zone your garden is or shared that they're growing a Zone 7 plant in their Zone 5 garden. So, what is a zone and why is it important?

Whether winter brings snow or just cool temperatures to your plot, gardening zones are based on low winter temperatures. Learn more about your garden's zone on page 276.

Zone defined

In an effort to help gardeners select plants that will survive the winter in their region, the United States Department of Agriculture developed a map that divides North America into zones based on lowest recorded temperatures. Zone 1 is the coldest and includes portions of Alaska and Canada. Zone 11 is the warmest and is primarily in southern Mexico.

Plants are classified by the coldest temperature they can endure. For example, plants hardy to Zone 6 survive where winter temperatures drop to −10°F, while those hardy to Zone 8 die long before it's that cold. These plants may grow in colder regions but must be brought indoors over the winter or replaced each year. Keep in mind that soil conditions, sun and shade, and wind also influence a plant's ability to overwinter.

Plants rated for a range of hardiness zones can usually survive winter in the coldest region as well as tolerate the summer heat of the warmest one. To find your garden zone, check out the zone map on page 276.

Plant for your zone

A plant tag or seed packet will list a plant's zone unless the plant is typically grown as an annual, meaning it grows from seed, bears fruit, and dies in one year. Tomatoes are annual plants. They complete their life cycle in one year. Peppers, eggplant, beans, potatoes, and the majority of other vegetables are annual plants too.

Many herbs, on the other hand, tolerate cold temperatures and overwinter in the garden. Sage, for example, is hardy in Zones 4 to 10. If you live in Zone 4 or above, count on sage to come back year after year. A recurring garden performance like this garners sage the label "perennial." Chives, marjoram, oregano, rosemary, and thyme are all perennial herbs.

Fruit trees and shrubs are also grown as perennial plants. Hardiness zone is particularly important when selecting trees and shrubs. Cold temperatures can injure buds and prevent fruiting while leaving the plant unscathed. The opposite is also true. Some plants, like apples, require a specific amount of cold temperatures to spur fruit development.

Rhubarb is a tough, hardy perennial. It overwinters with ease in Zones 2 to 9. When planted in an ideal site, rhubarb will grow nearly anywhere.

What is a microclimate?

A microclimate is the climate in a small area that is different from the climate around it. The small area might be warmer or colder than a nearby area. Warmer microclimates are favored as they make it possible to grow plants that are not typically hardy in the surrounding region. Your yard likely includes such microclimates. Consider locating tender plants in these microclimates.

Your house and other buildings create microclimates by absorbing heat during the day and radiating it into the landscape at night. The south side of a building is typically the warmest. The west side is also warm.

Balconies and rooftops are unique microclimates because they are above ground level. The elevation sometimes helps them escape frosts that kill tender plants at ground level. Keep in mind that cold, dry winds may mitigate any heat gain.

Fences, walls, and large rocks can protect plants from wind and radiate heat, creating sheltered spots.

Paved surfaces such as patios, driveways, and sidewalks can absorb heat during the day and radiate it into the landscape at night, moderating nighttime temperatures.

Fruit crops and climate

The grapes scrambling up this arbor are hardy to Zone 4, but the apple tree planted in a container behind the stone wall is hardy to only Zone 6. It is moved inside for winter.

Fruit crops are particular when it comes to climate,

but when you satisfy their requirements, they'll produce with abandon. While it is possible to grow the ingredients for a grand fruit salad in your backyard—think bananas, apples, oranges, blueberries—it's not practical. Fruit plants thrive in specific climates and what grows well in one region may fail in another. Learn what fruit crops your climate will support and enjoy your unique backyard fruit salad.

Too cold

Cold is the most common factor limiting the growth of fruit trees and shrubs. Cold temperatures thwart the growth of the plants' roots, stems, and leaves and also bring about a late spring frost that will nip tender buds. The frost may not damage the plant, but it will kill the buds, preventing fruit from forming.

Abiding by zone requirements is key to successful growth and fruit harvest. Only grow fruit crops that are hardy in your zone. For extra protection, choose plants that are hardy to one zone lower than yours. For example, if your garden is Zone 5, plant varieties that have a hardiness rating to Zone 4.

Planting trees and shrubs in a microclimate can protect tender fruit crops. (Learn all about microclimates on page 45.) These special areas of your yard are protected from chilling winds and are often recipients of radiant heat. Screen an orchard from cold northwestern winds by planting it near a dense stand of evergreens. Or plant a peach tree in a courtyard and take advantage of the radiant heat generated by nearby buildings.

Too warm

Most fruit trees also need a specific amount of heat to produce fruit while having a low tolerance of high temperatures. Peaches and nectarines generally require long hot summers to produce high-quality fruit. Apricots, on the other hand, prefer cooler summers and do not reach peak flavor in regions where the heat is ideal for a flavorful peach crop.

Some fruit crops react poorly to warm winter weather too. These crops require chilling, meaning the temperature must be below 45°F for a specified number of hours. Apples, cherries, pears, and peaches all require winter chilling. They languish in tropical areas.

Just right

Don't let these details deter you from planting a couple of fruit trees or a few fruiting shrubs. Most fruiting plants have a wide adaptation to temperature and produce fruit in all but extremely hot- or cold-summer areas. For reliable crops, stick with plants that are hardy in your zone. Also keep in mind that new heat- and cold-tolerant cultivars and species often become available. If you see a new offering, check its hardiness rating. It might be worth trying.

ASK THE GARDEN DOCTOR

How do I protect a tender fruit tree from cold temperatures?

ANSWER: Increase the hardiness of marginally hardy fruit trees with these easy-care practices. First, make all fertilizer applications before mid-June. The tree will absorb the nutrients in a timely manner and not produce tender, new growth at the end of the season when it can be injured by freezing temperatures. Water regularly. A drought-stressed tree is more susceptible to winter injury than a tree growing in moist soil.

Exceptional hardiness

Hardiness varies greatly within a species. A species may be generally classified as hardy to Zone 6, but plant breeders may have developed hardier cultivars that can tolerate the rigors of Zone 4, for example. This exceptional hardiness is becoming common as researchers breed plants for cold tolerance.

Contact your local extension office or garden center to learn about notably hardy cultivars of your favorite fruits. Or do research on the Internet by visiting the University of Minnesota, Cornell University, and Texas A&M University websites and searching the term "hardy fruit."

Vegetables and climate

Corn, tomatoes, and beans are warm-season crops, requiring long, hot days to produce fruit. Cauliflower, on the other hand, thrives in the cool temperatures of spring and early summer.

Relative to climate, vegetables are divided into two groups, cool season and warm season. Working with the idiosyncrasies of their climate, gardeners in most regions can successfully grow both types of crops. A solid understanding of the climate needs of cool- and warm-season crops will help you know when to plant your favorite vegetables.

Cool-season vegetables

Cool-season vegetables grow best when temperatures range between 40° and 75°F. In most areas, they can be planted two to four weeks before the last spring frost. These crops are most often those that develop edible roots, stems, leaves, or buds.

Most cool-season crops don't mind frost. After frost blankets their leaves, they will show little or no signs of damage and continue to grow, unfurling new leaves. Some cool-season crops are frost hardy, meaning they tolerate prolonged freezing temperatures.

Cool-season crops are also unique in that their seeds germinate best in cool soil. The root systems of these plants are shallower and the plants themselves are smaller. Cool-season crops stop producing in early summer when temperatures range above 80°F.

Cool-season crops are typically planted as soon as the soil can be worked in spring. In regions where nights remain cool, you can sow them every two weeks or so for a continuous harvest that extends into fall. This planting method is called succession planting and ensures a bountiful harvest from spring to fall.

In warmer regions, plant cool-season vegetables as early as possible in late winter or spring, and plant seeds or transplants again in late fall for harvest in winter.

There are also cold-hardy vegetables that can survive throughout winter in some regions, especially under an insulating blanket of snow. These include carrots, parsnips, and garlic.

Warm-season vegetables

Warm-season vegetables, such as tomatoes, peppers, corn, and okra, originated in tropical climates. These are the crops that develop edible fruits as opposed to cool-season crops, which usually develop edible roots, stems, leaves, or buds. Warm-season crops are killed by frost and won't perform well if temperatures fall below 50°F. Planting before the soil and air temperatures have adequately warmed in spring has poor results. Wait until about two weeks after the average last frost date in your area to plant warm-season crops.

You can encourage many warm-season crops to continue growing, albeit slowly, into fall by protecting them from frost with row covers, cold frames, and other season-extending devices. But warm-season crops perform best during the height of summer.

Kale and loose leaf lettuce thrive in cool weather. Plant this combination as soon as the soil can be worked in early spring.

Cool-season crops

These vegetables love cool soil and cool temperatures. Plant them in early spring.

ASPARAGUS	CAULIFLOWER	KOHLRABI	POTATO
BEET	CELERY	LEEK	RADISH
BROCCOLI	CHARD	LETTUCE	RHUBARB
BRUSSELS SPROUTS	COLLARDS	ONION	RUTABAGA
CABBAGE	GARLIC	PARSNIP	SPINACH
CARROT	KALE	PEA	

Warm-season crops

Heat makes these vegetables produce fruit. Plant them in the garden after the last chance of frost passes.

ARTICHOKE	MELON	SWEET POTATO
BEAN	OKRA	TOMATILLO
CORN	PEANUT	TOMATO
CUCUMBER	PEPPER	
EGGPLANT	SQUASH	

Get an early start in spring

With a little planning, you can harvest garden-fresh vegetables for six months, nine months, or even year-round if you live in a tropical climate. The majority of gardeners in Zones 3 through 8 can easily increase their garden harvest season by at least one month when they plant early spring vegetables. The same goes for fall—cool-season crops thrive at the end of the season too. Learn about early spring planting here and turn to page 53 for tips on extending the harvest into fall.

Spring ahead: when to plant

Soil temperature is the best indicator of when to plant crops, no matter what climate you live in. Some cool-season crops readily germinate in soil as low as 40°F; others do best when the soil is 50°F. Use a simple soil thermometer (available at garden centers for less than $20) to check soil temperature in early spring.

The workability of garden soil is another factor when planting an early spring garden. Avoid planting in soggy soil that is still full of moisture from snow or spring rains. Wait until the soil dries and can be cultivated. For more tips on soil preparation, see pages 55–69.

What to plant

Cool-season species, such as greens, broccoli, peas, and radishes, thrive in the cool air and soil temperatures in early spring, or in winter in Florida, the Gulf states, and southern California.

For extended cold hardiness, choose varieties with notable frost tolerance. For example, 'Coronado Crown' broccoli tolerates frost better than many other broccoli varieties.

Warm-season crops can be planted indoors. An early start indoors will give warm-season crops a jump start on the growing season.

Opposite: **Spring bulbs are a cue that it is time to plant lettuce, peas, and other cool-season crops. Wait for bulb foliage to emerge and then plant your vegetable seeds.**

Where to plant

Choose a protected planting location if possible. A warm microclimate, such as a south-facing slope, the south side of a building, or a spot that is protected from cold northwestern winds, will be a few degrees warmer than other planting locations, allowing you to get started gardening earlier in the season while protecting crops from late season frosts. Learn more about microclimates on page 45.

Soil covered with dark organic mulch, such as compost or shredded leaves, will warm faster in early spring than bare soil. Plan ahead in late fall and spread a 2-inch-thick layer of organic mulch on the garden in preparation for early spring planting, or add a layer of mulch in late winter and achieve the same results.

Raised beds offer many advantages in spring. Not only do they drain faster than an inground planting bed, but the soil in a raised bed also warms faster. A raised bed is an excellent place to plant early spring produce.

Layer of protection

Even though soil is warm enough to plant cool-season crops, a hard frost could still blanket the area and harm young plants. Covering plants with a sheet or cotton blanket is a simple method for protecting plants from an occasional late spring frost.

A cold frame is simply a miniature greenhouse made of glass or plastic and placed over plants. Cold frames often increase air temperature around plants by 3 to 6 degrees. This small increase in air temperature, combined with warm soil, can bump up the harvest of cool-season produce by two to six weeks. Glass garden cloches have the same effect.

Temperature matters

Purchase a soil thermometer next time you're at the garden center. These cool-season vegetables germinate from seed at the prescribed soil temperatures.

40°F	50°F	60°F
ARUGULA	CHINESE CABBAGE	BEET
FAVA BEAN	LEEK	BROCCOLI
KALE	ONION	BRUSSELS SPROUTS
LETTUCE	SWISS CHARD	CABBAGE
PARSNIP	TURNIP	CARROT
PEA		CAULIFLOWER
RADICCHIO		
RADISH		
SPINACH		

Harvest through fall

Pumpkins and squash signify the end of the summer growing season. Continue harvesting homegrown produce by planting cool-season crops in late summer.

Ripe watermelons and brilliant orange pumpkins

signify the end of the gardening season for many, but the warm days and cool nights of fall are perfect for growing many vegetables. A rich end-of-the-season harvest depends on careful planning and planting when you're in the middle of harvesting tomatoes, peppers, and eggplant. Use this simple late season gardening calendar as a guide and you'll enjoy an additional month or more of fresh produce.

Three months before fall frost

Note: If you don't know the first fall frost date for your area, contact your local extension service or inquire at your local garden center.

Make a list of fall crops you would like to grow. In most regions, cool-season crops such as lettuce, carrots, and radishes are popular fall crops. Gardeners in Zone 8 and above can grow a second crop of tomatoes, peppers, and other warm-season crops.

Select a planting site for your fall crops. The ideal planting site might be home to beans, tomatoes, or another warm-season crop three months before the first fall frost, but if you anticipate that crop to finish producing in about a month, it is a great site for fall vegetables.

Eliminate weeds. Summer weeds can wreak havoc on a fall garden. Their extensive root systems will quickly crowd out seedlings and transplants. Get rid of weeds in preparation for planting. Cover the weed-free area with a 2-inch-thick layer of mulch.

Buy seeds or transplants. Vegetable seeds and transplants can be hard to find in late summer. If plants are not available in your area, the Internet is a valuable option. When choosing varieties, pay close attention to the "days to maturity" label found on most seed packets and plant tags. All vegetables planted in late summer should mature in 80 days or less to prevent the chance of frost damage.

Gardeners in Zones 8 and higher should opt for fast-maturing warm-season plants. 'Bingo', 'Celebrity', and 'Carnival' tomatoes produce fruit in about 75 days.

Two months or so before frost

Spread a layer of compost over the planting site to enrich the soil. After clearing existing plants on the site, spread a 2-inch-layer of compost over the soil.

Plant seeds or transplants about 60 to 80 days before the first expected frost. Use the variety's "number of days to maturity" as a guide. Mesclun greens are ready for harvest in just 40 days, so they can be planted much later than beets, which require about 60 days of growth.

Water regularly after planting. Periods of dry weather are common in late summer and early fall. Aim to provide seedlings and transplants with about 1 inch of water per week.

One month before frost until harvest

Keep frost protection in the form of blankets or sheets on hand to cover plants if temperatures dip below freezing in early fall.

Continue to water regularly to promote healthy plants and fruit production.

Harvest frost-tender plants such as tomatoes, peppers, and sweet corn before frost hits. Most cool-season crops will weather a light frost with ease. In fact, the flavor and texture of carrots and parsnips are distinctly improved by a touch of frost.

Above left: **Leeks are some of the last crops to harvest in the fall garden. Requiring nearly four months to mature, they taste sweetest after they are nipped by a fall frost.**

Above middle: **Harvest all tomatoes if a frost is predicted. Wrap green tomatoes in newspaper and ripen them indoors.**

Above right: **Large storage onions require as many as five months to mature and are often harvested in early fall. They are ready to pull when about half of the bulbs' tops bend over.**

good earth

Every delicious tomato, peach, and carrot begins with properly prepared soil. Invest time and effort in preparing soil and you'll reap edible dividends.

p.56
ALL ABOUT SOIL

The storehouse for nutrients, water, and oxygen, healthy soil promotes healthy plants. Learn about soil components, then size up your own earth.

p.60
NUTRIENTS

Edible plants draw nutrients from the soil to produce stems, leaves, and fruits. Add valuable nutrients with these soil care tips, including instructions for making your own compost.

p.66
SOIL SOLUTIONS

Improve soil structure and nutrient content with these simple techniques. From incorporating compost to building a raised bed, there are many things you can do to improve your soil.

Build soil knowledge

Healthy soil produces healthy plants. The bright color stems of Swiss chard indicate that the soil is nutrient rich and it drains well.

Before adding amendments to your soil, take a couple of minutes

to gather some soil sense. Think of the following discussion as a soil primer. Once you know how soil is formed and its basic components, you'll be ready to get your hands dirty and assess and improve the good earth that is in your backyard.

What is soil?

Soil is simply weathered rocks and minerals combined with organic matter, water, and air. Rain, snow, ice, and varying temperatures pulverize rocks into tiny particles. Different kinds of rocks and the ways that weathering affects them result in the wide variety of soils.

Soils that develop in warm, wet environments weather quickly. In these soils many of the minerals that act as plant nutrients are washed away by frequent rains. Soon the soil becomes acidic and contains a large percentage of iron. The soil takes on a red or yellow color and often needs fertilization in the form of compost or commercial fertilizer for plants to thrive.

Hot, dry environments often produce soil that is low in nutrients too. Since weathering is slow in arid regions and water is scare, salts that are detrimental to plant growth accumulate. Incorporating compost and watering deeply is one way to discourage salt buildup and to infuse nutrients into the soil.

Essential organic matter

Organic matter is the most dynamic component of soil. It may be living or dead, composed of plant or animal material, and easily visible or infinitesimally small. A teaspoon of healthy soil contains an entire universe of microorganisms. The organisms are working to decompose plant and animal parts. When the organic matter finally stabilizes and stops decomposing, the result is humus—a naturally rich, dark, crumbly material that increases soil fertility.

Most often called compost when it is added to the soil, organic matter improves the workability and structure of all soils. It helps break apart clay particles, allowing soil and air to move through the soil. And organic matter improves sandy soil, helping it to better retain water and nutrients.

Soil types

Sand Soils made of sand have the largest particles and the largest amount of pore space—or space for water and air to move through the soil. Sandy soil drains quickly and can be worked shortly after rain. In cold climates, sandy soil is appreciated because it warms faster in spring than clay soil, allowing gardeners to plant vegetables early.

Sometimes water passes through sandy soil so quickly that roots cannot supply plants with enough water. And as water passes through the soil it takes nutrients with it, which is why sandy soil is usually low in fertility.

Silt Tiny rounded soil particles make up silt. Because the small size results in more surface area and smaller pore spaces than in sand, silty soil drains more slowly than sandy soil and retains more nutrients.

Clay Individual clay particles are microscopic. An ounce of soil contains millions of clay particles. The miniscule particles often pack together so tightly that roots have a hard time making their way through the soil. Clay is sticky when wet and can be brick-hard when dry. Even though clay is moisture rich, the water may not be available to plant roots because the clay particles are holding it so tightly. The same goes for clay's holding power on nutrients. Soils with a high percentage of clay are difficult to garden in.

Above left: **Raised bed gardening offers the opportunity to customize your soil. Combine native soil with compost and peat moss for a nutrient-rich, well-drained soil mix.**

Above middle: **Soil rich in organic matter is easy to sink a spade into because it has a crumbly texture.**

Above right: **Whether you make your own compost or purchase a bagged product, an annual application of a 2-inch-thick layer will boost soil nutrients and improve soil structure.**

Size up your soil

When talking about soil, gardeners throw around terms like "well-drained," "loose," and "moderate pH." What do these terms mean in relation to the garden and, most importantly, how does your garden rate? Use the following guide to take a close look at the texture and drainage abilities of your garden spot. If you're inclined to learn more about your soil's nutrient content, check out the soil-testing infomation.

Good soil texture and drainage are key to growing carrots with a uniform shape. Loam or sandy soil is ideal. Grow carrots in a raised bed if your soil is sticky clay.

Texture

Soils are almost always a mixture of sand, silt, and clay. The ideal is a loamy soil, which scientists classify as consisting of 40 percent sand, 40 percent silt, and 20 percent clay. Loam is ideal because it holds moisture and nutrients, yet it has plenty of pore space for air, water, and roots.

Nature, however, is seldom easily classified, and the percentage of sand, silt, and clay can vary widely. Your garden soil may be a sandy clay loam, a silty clay, a loamy sand, or myriad potential combinations.

Testing your soil's texture is as easy as moistening ½ cup of soil with water. Roll it into a ball and try forming it into a ribbon between your hands.

Clay soil *(top left)* If the soil packs together and easily forms a ribbon, the soil is clay or has a high clay component. Soils with a high percentage of clay are sticky and will probably stain your skin. If the soil ribbon feels smooth instead of sticky, it is probably silty clay. If it is gritty, it is sandy clay.

Loam *(middle left)* If the soil ribbon holds together but is looser and tends to crumble, it contains a high amount of silt, sand, or organic matter. It is most likely a loam soil.

Sandy soil *(bottom left)* If the soil will not hold together, breaking apart regardless of how much water you apply, it is a sandy soil. It is gritty and you will feel individual grains.

Drainage

Good drainage. Gardeners everywhere talk about good drainage or creating the conditions for good drainage. What is good drainage? Basically, drainage is how much and how fast water moves through the soil. Soil with good drainage has a good supply of oxygen, which is vital to root and plant health. In short, clay soils drain slowly and sandy soils drain rapidly. To test your soil's drainage ability, grab a shovel and head for the garden.

1. **DIG A HOLE.** Use a spade to dig a hole about 12 inches deep and 8 to 12 inches in diameter in soil that is moist but not soggy.
2. **ADD WATER.** Fill the hole with water. Allow it to drain and refill it 12 hours later, noting the time.
3. **TIME IT.** If the soil drains well, all the water will be gone in 2 to 3 hours. But if it takes 10 or more hours to empty, it is poorly drained and most plants will struggle to survive in that area.

Soil testing

A soil test can pinpoint nutrient deficiencies and excesses and pH values, as well as guide you toward materials that will help correct problems. Soil tests can be time- and money-saving and earth-friendly tools because they point out exactly what amendments are needed, thus eliminating needless fertilizer applications.

Be sure to test your soil if plants are showing poor or stunted growth over the course of the growing season. Also test soil if you are starting a garden in an urban area or near a building where lead paint chips may have contaminated the soil. Another case for a soil test is if you are growing a crop that is pH sensitive, such as blueberries, which prefer acidic soil. All other areas generally do not need regular soil testing.

Find a soil-testing lab in your area for the most accurate results. Most county extension services will perform soil tests or provide referrals to commercial labs.

Preparing a soil test sample is as simple as requesting a test kit from a lab. The kit will likely include a bag to gather your soil sample as well as instructions on how to take an accurate sample. Then you send the sample to the lab and receive a report a few days later. The soil report will include recommendations for improving your soil.

Assess your soil's nutrients

Tomatoes are voracious nutrient consumers, but they are easy to satisfy when the soil is enriched with well-decomposed compost or a slow-release fertilizer.

All plants require several nutrient elements for growth. They source carbon, hydrogen, and oxygen from the atmosphere and water. They mine the soil for nitrogen, phosphorus, potassium, and other important elements. Plants use these elements to fuel their food-making process called photosynthesis.

It's a gardener's job to make sure the reservoir of soil nutrients does not become depleted. One of the quickest ways to deplete a nutrient reservoir in a vegetable garden plot is to remove all the foliage, stems, and shoots at the end of the growing season. Instead of removing dead plant material, consider leaving disease-free plant parts in the garden over winter. The plant parts will decompose and add nutrients to the soil. The natural nutrient reservoir depends on this annual recycling of elements to rebuild stockpiles after a long growing season.

How does your soil rate?

Often soil, especially soil enriched with compost, has all of the mineral nutrients a plant needs for strong growth and fruit development. Loam soils are particularly nutrient rich. Clay soil usually has many nutrients too, but the clay binds to the nutrients so tightly that plant roots cannot access them. Excessively sandy soil, on the other hand, is often lacking nutrients. These valuable minerals quickly wash out of sandy soil.

Stunted growth, poor fruit development, and discolored foliage are all signs of a potential nutrient deficiency. The only surefire way to determine the nutrient content of your soil is to submit a sample for testing. Contact your local extension service for soil-testing information. The test results will include suggested soil amendments if there are deficient nutrients.

There are many ways to boost the nutrient content of your soil. The following pages address several popular, earth-friendly choices including nutrient-rich compost, which you can make in your own backyard.

TEST GARDEN TIP

Too much of a good thing

Some edible plants balk at nutrient-rich soil. Lavender and rosemary are two examples. Originating in the Mediterranean where low-nutrient sandy soils are the norm, when planted in high-nutrient soil these plants tend to produce many floppy, vigorous stems with mild flavor. For intense flavor, plant them in well-drained, sandy loam. If your garden soil doesn't fit this bill, grow the plants in a container.

Plant talk

Plants cannot talk, but they are expert communicators. They use their leaves, stems, and overall growth habit to communicate their general well-being. With a little experience you'll soon be able to spot an unhealthy plant. Sometimes poor growth, discolored leaves, or dead foliage indicates a low nutrient level in the soil.

Here are the symptoms of deficiency of the three major elements: nitrogen, phosphorus, and potassium. If your plants exhibit deficiency symptoms, take a soil test. If the soil test identifies a deficient nutrient, apply a synthetic or organic fertilizer as recommended by the testing lab.

Nitrogen deficiency symptoms: Yellowing leaves beginning with the oldest leaves and then younger leaves. Slow, stunted plant growth.

Phosphorus deficiency symptoms: Unusually dark green or purple foliage. Few flowers or fruits. Slow growth.

Potassium deficiency symptoms: Scorching on the margins of the oldest leaves. Weak stems and shriveled fruit.

Add a layer of compost

Each spring before planting, spread a 2-inch-thick layer of compost over your garden and mix it into the top few inches of soil. It will boost soil nutrients and improve soil structure over time.

Compost's many attributes might make you think it is too good to be true. Compost improves drainage in poorly drained soils, making it possible to garden in clay soil. You can mix compost with clay soil to make it loose and workable over time. It can also help excessively sandy soil hold more water. And don't forget compost's valuable nutrient content. Well-made compost is packed with more nutrients and beneficial microorganisms than many other soil amendments. It's easy to see why compost is affectionately called black gold.

Sure, you can buy compost at many garden centers, but if you have a few feet of space you can make compost that is just as good or better than any brand of packaged compost and recycle organic waste at the same time. Here are a few common composting methods and bins; choose the best for you.

Holding units are a good choice for apartment dwellers and those with limited space. These units do not require turning. Layers of green and brown materials are simply piled in the unit, moistened, and left to decompose. Because holding units are not turned, the decomposing material is not infused with oxygen and the composting process takes as long as two years.

Turning units are designed to promote aeration. These units produce compost in a few months because oxygen is supplied to bacteria working inside the pile. The additional oxygen also cuts down on odor problems.

Turning units may be either a series of bins or a structure that rotates, such as a ball or barrel. Most often materials must be saved until a unit can be filled to the correct level. Once these units are filled and the turning process begins, new materials should not be added.

Heaps do not require a bin or structure. A compost heap is simply a carefully layered pile of compostable material, preferably located in part shade and on top of soil or a pallet if poor drainage is a concern. Do not create a compost heap on cement or asphalt. Contact with soil will provide necessary bacteria for the pile.

Turning a heap is optional, but the composting process will be faster if the pile is turned. Optimally, aim to turn a compost heap every two weeks.

Sheet composting is done in fall. With this method, a thin layer of materials, such as leaves or other landscape debris, is worked into garden soil. By spring, the material will be broken down. Sheet composting requires large amounts of soil nitrogen, making this valuable nutrient unavailable to other plants. For this reason, only sheet compost when the garden is fallow.

Trench composting involves digging a trench 8 to 15 inches deep and filling it with 2-inch-thick layers of green and brown compost material. Top the trench with about 2 inches of soil. Decomposition takes about one year. This method is especially good for vegetable gardens that are arranged in rows. You can alternate planting a row and composting a row.

ASK THE GARDEN DOCTOR

How do I keep pests out of my compost pile?

ANSWER: When adding items to your compost pile, don't add meat, bones, and fatty foods such as cheese, salad dressing, and oils. These foods ferment, cause odors, and can attract rodents. Also avoid adding disease-infected plants to the pile. Although the heat generated from the compost process may kill some diseases, some organisms may survive and be returned to the garden.

Make your own compost

Make a compost heap by spreading a 3-inch-layer of brown material on the soil. Top the brown material with a 3-inch-layer of green material. Continue layering as materials become available and water the pile until it is as moist as a wrung-out sponge. Turn the pile once every two weeks.

1 **BROWN MATERIAL** Leaves, dried grass, small wood chips, twigs, soil, and shredded newspaper contribute valuable carbon and microrganisms to the pile.

2 **GREEN MATERIAL** Fresh grass clippings, kitchen scraps from fruits and vegetables, and garden waste provide compost with valuable nitrogen.

3 **WATER** Add water to the pile to encourage bacteria to grow and decomposition to take place. Turn the pile every two weeks, and you'll have nutrient-rich humus in a few short months.

Boost soil nutrients

Water-soluble fertilizer is a quick and efficient way to deliver nutrients to plants when it is applied using a hose-end applicator like this one.

As edible fruits, vegetables, and leaves are growing, the plants are harvesting nutrients from the soil. It's a gardener's job to replenish the nutrients so the soil can continue to provide all the elements necessary for plant growth.

The nutrients plants use in large qualities that might be deficient are nitrogen (chemical symbol N), phosphorus (P), and potassium (K). If you are starting a new vegetable garden plot or your edibles are showing symptoms of nutrient distress (see page 61), take a soil test and follow fertilizing recommendations. Established gardens with healthy plant growth usually have adequate supplies of phosphorus and potassium, and thus nitrogen is the primary focus of fertilization.

Label lingo

Fertilizers are labeled or described according to the percentage of N, P, and K they contain. Take a look at a fertilizer label and you're likely to see three numbers separated by hyphens, such as 10-10-10, on the front of the package. The first number represents N; this product contains 10 percent nitrogen. The second number represents phosphorus and the third number represents potassium.

More often than not, vegetable gardens benefit from a fertilizer that is high in N and lower in P and K because nitrogen readily dissipates in the soil over time, but P and K are more lasting. Herbs and fruit crops are often fertilized less often and benefit from a balanced fertilizer or one that contains equal amounts of N, P, and K.

Amending soil at a glance

Healthy soil promotes healthy plants. Build healthy soil with these soil amendment tips.

When: Timing depends on the type of amendment and the crop. Synthetic slow-release fertilizers are mixed into the soil before planting. Compost is often mixed into the soil before planting and then again in midseason. The crop you are fertilizing is also important. If a high-nitrogen fertilizer is applied to tomatoes in June, the plants will likely produce plenty of leaves but no fruit. See the encyclopedias beginning on page 146 for fertilizer information.

What: Use products specifically formulated for edible gardens. Do not use lawn fertilizers; they often contain herbicides that will harm vegetable plants. In many cases, low-cost organic options such as compost are your best choices because they supply valuable nutrients while improving the soil structure.

How: Purchased products will have specific directions for application. Strictly follow directions because overapplication or improper timing could damage plants and the environment. In the case of homemade compost, spread a 2-inch-thick layer of well-decomposed compost over the garden prior to planting and till it into the top 6 to 8 inches of soil.

Nutrient sources for edible gardens

1. **SYNTHETIC FERTILIZERS** are available as granular products or liquids. Liquid forms deliver nutrients to plants faster than granular products. There are many different N-P-K combinations and even crop-specific formulations. Synthetic fertilizers are convenient and simple to apply, but do so carefully; overapplication can burn plants.
2. **BLOOD MEAL** is dried, powdered blood collected from cattle slaughterhouses. It has a formulation of 12-0-0 and is a rich source of nitrogen. Apply it carefully; it can easily burn plants. Blood meal is a good source of iron.
3. **COMPOST** is decomposed plant parts. Make it yourself or purchase it in bulk at your local garden center. Most commercial compost has a chemical formulation of 1.5-1-1. Compost not only contains nutrients, but it also has microbes, which improve soil structure and suppress disease.
4. **COTTONSEED MEAL** is a by-product of cotton processing. This product, with a formulation of 6-3-2, poses little danger of burn.
5. **COVER CROPS** are planted in fall or early spring and tilled into soil two to three weeks before planting. Annual ryegrass and oats are two popular cover crops. Formulation varies among crops, but all are high in nitrogen. Cover crops add valuable nitrogen to soil while improving soil structure.
6. **FISH EMULSION** is a partially decomposed blend of finely pulverized fish. The odor can be offensive during application, but it dissipates in a day or two. It has a formulation of 4-2-2. Apply fish emulsion after plants have sprouted, to boast initial growth. The nutrients are quickly available to plants.

Improve soil structure

A layer of straw mulch around plants has many benefits. It prevents weeds, slows soil moisture evaporation, and slowly decomposes, improving soil structure.

Just because your garden soil is excessively sandy or dense clay doesn't mean you have to tolerate poor plant growth or give up gardening altogether. There are many relatively simple things you can do to improve soil structure and nutrient content.

Time is your major investment. Incorporating amendments will take a few hours depending on the size of your plot, and waiting for the soil to radically transform will take years. You'll enjoy some success immediately, but the soil will continue to improve as it weathers. Enjoy greater improvement by adding compost and other amendments annually.

Plant a cover crop. Often called green manure crops, cover crops are grains, grasses, or legumes that grow during the fall and winter and are tilled under in the spring. Their roots penetrate and help loosen heavy-textured soils, allowing better air and water movement in the soil. Cover crops also add valuable nutrients to the soil when they are tilled in—a benefit to both sandy and clay soils.

Plant winter rye or wheat, hairy vetch, or crimson clover in fall and turn it under in spring. For a spring cover crop, plant buckwheat, alfalfa, or oats and turn the crop under two to three weeks before planting edibles.

Add a layer of organic mulch. As mulch slowly decomposes it adds organic matter to the soil. A slow addition of organic matter to clay and sandy soil improves the soil's structure. Mulch also works to mediate the compaction of clay soil and prevent an impenetrable crust from forming on top of the soil.

Incorporate compost. Any composted material that has been reduced to humus is a good soil amendment. Homemade or purchased compost is a good choice, as is rotted animal manure. The key is to add enough compost to make an impact. To make a significant change, the volume of compost must equal one-third of the volume of soil you are amending.

Thoroughly mix in amendments. Working when the soil is not wet, mix the compost, rotted manure, or cover crop into the top 12 inches of soil by hand or with a tiller. It's important to thoroughly combine the soil and amendment for good plant growth.

Essential clay advice

Never add sand. While it might seem logical to mix sand into clay in an effort to break up clay's dense structure, the opposite is true. Clay particles will bind to the sand to form a cementlike compound.

Take advantage of freeze and thaw. When clay soil is relatively dry in fall, plow it and break up any clods that result with a garden rake or fork. Leave the soil as is over winter. The repeated freeze and thaw will break up remaining clods and make the soil more workable. Mix in organic matter in spring to augment the freeze-thaw benefits.

Avoid compaction. Foot and vehicle traffic will quickly compact already dense clay soil, making it even harder to amend. Limit compaction by diverting traffic from the area or spreading a 6-inch-thick layer of organic mulch over the soil.

ASK THE GARDEN DOCTOR

My tomato plants' leaves turned brown after I fertilized them. What happened?

ANSWER: Most likely you overfertilized your plants and the excessive nitrogen scorched the leaves. This can happen to any type of plant, most frequently with liquid or granular fertilizer products. Avoid overfertilizing by carefully following application directions. Aid scorched plants by watering them deeply to wash the fertilizer away from the plants' root systems.

How much compost do you need?

Significantly changing soil structure requires a significant addition of compost or well-rotted manure to the tune of at least one-third of the volume of soil you are amending. For example, to amend a garden to a depth of 12 inches, you need to add 4 inches of amendments. How much material is this? Here's how to calculate using a 10×20-foot garden as an example.

1. **Multiply the width and length to get the area.**
   10 × 20 = 200 square feet
2. **Multiple the area by .33 (one-third of a foot) to get cubic feet.**
   200 square feet × .33 = 66 cubic feet
3. **Divide cubic feet by 27 to get cubic yards.** (Large quantities of amendments are usually sold in cubic yards)
   66 cubic feet / 27 = about 2.5 cubic yards

Build a raised bed

Raised-bed gardening is often the best way to rise above frustratingly sticky clay soil. With a small monetary investment and a few hours of work, you can build a raised bed over poor soil. Sites with slow-draining, clay, or rocky soil are not the only benefactors of this smart garden practice—it's a great solution for smal gardens too.

Edibles can be planted more intensely in a raised bed—ideally spaced just far enough apart to avoid crowding but close enough to shade out weeds—because no space has to be set aside for paths. This intense planting scheme is a good fit for urban and rooftop gardens where planting space is at a premium. Raised beds elevated 2 feet or more also reduce bending and stooping.

Remedy slow-draining soil with an easy-to-build raised bed. Looseleaf lettuce, cabbage, and peas thrive in this well-drained raised bed framed with wood planks.

Construction particulars

Size. To prevent walking in a raised bed, build it no wider than 4 feet. At this width, it's easy to access the bed from either side. Bed length is dependent on the site. Opt for short beds with 2-foot paths in between to eliminate unnecessary steps walking around an extremely long bed. The best beds are 12 to 24 inches tall, which allows adequate rooting space and easy construction. Taller beds require retaining walls with foundations.
Materials. Stone, brick, cement block, and untreated wood make fine building material for raised beds. Several raised bed kits are also available.
Soil. Before filling the raised bed with quality topsoil, loosen the ground level soil by rototilling it or turning it over with a spade. Then mix the native soil with topsoil to fill the raised bed.

Maintenance

Water. Raised beds dry out faster than traditional gardens during the heat of summer. Be prepared to water frequently. Spread a 2-inch-thick layer of organic mulch, such as shredded leaves or finely shredded wood mulch around plants to help hold soil moisture.

Avoid compaction. Never walk on a raised bed. The weight will quickly destroy soil structure.

End of season. At the end of the season, disease-free plant parts can be tilled or spaded into the soil. Mix in additional organic matter to add more nutrients and improve soil structure. Over time soil may improve so much that little if any tilling is necessary.

TEST GARDEN TIP

Outside the box

Instead of using lumber to frame a raised bed, try one of these: large stones set side by side, short stacks of patio pavers, or large logs.

Step-by-step: raised bed

What's not to love about raised-bed gardening? These tidy, efficient gardens rise above slow-draining, compacted soil and reduce the need to bend and stoop as you care for plants. Build a raised bed in an afternoon with these easy instructions.

1

2

3

4

5

6

1 SELECT A SITE AND REMOVE SOD
For ease of construction, choose a level site for the raised bed. Also pay attention to sunlight. Most edibles require at least eight hours of direct sunlight per day. Delineate the edges of the bed with white marking paint and use a sharp spade to skim the sod off the site. If this is your first garden, start small—a 4×4-foot bed will provide plenty of planting space.

2 CONSTRUCT THE FRAME
Build the raised bed frame using a raised bed kit, available at home improvement stores and on the Internet, or make your own using untreated lumber. A simple design involves using 4×4s for the corner posts and attaching 2x6s to form side rails.

3 LOOSEN THE SOIL
Set the course for a well-drained bed by loosening the native soil. Most likely compacted during the construction process, the native soil has the potential to thwart the good drainage of the raised bed by not allowing water to percolate into the ground below the bed. Use a sharp spade to turn soil to a depth of about 8 inches.

4 ADD SOIL
Fill the new bed with topsoil. Mix in a generous amount of compost and other amendments, if a soil test indicates they are necessary. Don't skimp on soil for your raised bed; fill it with high-quality, nutrient-rich soil. Garden centers stock many bagged products that contain ample nutrients and have excellent drainage for raised-bed gardening.

5 MIX IT TOGETHER
Using a small tiller or a spade, combine the topsoil, soil amendments, and a few inches of the native soil to form a uniform mixture.

6 PLANT YOUR GARDEN
Raised beds are perfect for growing plants from seeds or transplants. You can even grow perennial plants, such as blueberries or brambles, in raised beds if you like.

planting time

Soil, seeds, water, and time produce delicious results in an edible garden. Start planting today with tips for growing plants indoors and out.

p. 72
HOW TO START

Most annual vegetable plants are started from seeds or transplants. Learn all about the pros and cons of starting plants from seeds and beginning with transplants.

p. 74
PLANTING INDOORS

A few supplies combined with bright light make starting seed indoors a relatively simple process. Save money and get a jump on the planting season by planting seeds indoors in early spring.

p. 78
PLANTING OUTDOORS

A well-prepared seedbed is key to successfully starting seeds outdoors. Learn about seedbed preparation along with outdoor planting tips.

p. 82
SEEDLING CARE

Transplants and seedlings require a bit of special care as they put down roots. Give your young plants a strong start with these care tips.

Getting started: seeds or transplants?

Gardening is full of choices—from what to plant, to where to plant, to when to harvest.

Starting plants is no different. Plants can be grown from seeds or transplants. If you choose to start vegetables and herbs from seeds, you have the choice of planting the seeds indoors or planting them directly in the garden.

With all these choices, it's easy to become overwhelmed. Don't worry, the next few pages will step you through the process of starting seeds and help you sort out all the choices so you can make the best decisions for you and your garden. Soon the only choice you'll have to make is which to eat first: the perfectly ripe watermelon or tomato.

Starting from seed

Although many vegetables can be bought as transplants at your local garden center or home improvement store or on the Internet, it's fascinating to watch plants develop from seeds.

Starting vegetables and herbs from seed has some practical advantages as well. Seeds offer the greatest selection at negligible cost. They are a practical way to grow a large number of plants for you or to share with friends and family. Some seeds are best sown directly in the soil while others need to be planted indoors for transplanting into the garden later on.

Fruit plants are rarely started from seed. Tree fruits, such as apples, and most berries usually are started from nursery-grown transplants.

Opposite: **Growing plants indoors does not require fancy equipment. Recycle clay pots or create a pot out of newspaper. Degradable peat pots can be planted right in the garden in spring.**

Indoors or out?

Where to plant seeds is mostly a question of timing. Some plants benefit from a few extra weeks of growing time. By starting seeds indoors you give them a jump on the growing season before the soil and air temperatures are warm enough for planting outside. Tomatoes, peppers, eggplant, and several more warm-season crops demand an early start in order to mature and set fruit in many climates. Lettuce, carrots, radishes, and beans thrive when seeded into the garden.

Large seeds that germinate quickly are easier to sow outdoors. Small seeds that germinate slowly or germinate best at a specific soil temperature are easier to manage indoors. Bottom line: Sow seeds indoors or in the garden, whichever better suits your season and temperament. Just follow the planting direction on the seed packet for best results.

Transplants

Some seeds are tricky and time-consuming to start indoors or to sow directly in the garden. Buy these vegetables and herbs as transplants at your local garden center or place an order with a plant company on the Internet and transplants will be shipped to your door at planting time. When shopping for transplants, look for sturdy, short plants that have a strong stem and disease-free, healthy foliage.

Indoors or outdoors

Some plants are easiest to start from seeds planted directly in the garden. Others do best when planted indoors or started from purchased transplants. Here's a suggestion of what to plant where.

Sow in the garden

BEAN	LETTUCE	PEANUT*
BEET	MELON	PUMPKIN
CARROT	OKRA*	RADISH
CHARD	ONION	RUTABAGA
CORN	PARSNIP	SPINACH
CUCUMBER	PEA	SQUASH

*start indoors in Zones 6 and below

Sow indoors or start from transplants

ARTICHOKE*	CAULIFLOWER	LEEK
BROCCOLI	COLLARDS	PEPPER
BRUSSELS SPROUT	EGGPLANT	TOMATILLO
CABBAGE	KALE	TOMATO

*difficult to grow from seeds; best grown from transplants

Start seeds indoors

Peat pellets provide the perfect conditions for starting broccoli and other plants from seeds. When the plants are ready to go into the garden, plant the entire pellet, reducing transplant shock.

Technology has made seed-starting indoors a hobby rather than a necessity for most gardeners. Hundreds of vegetable cultivars are available as small transplants from local garden centers and Internet sources. With a couple clicks of the mouse, a collection of heirloom tomato plants will arrive neatly packaged on your doorstep and ready for planting in the garden.

Even though ready-to-plant seedlings are just a click away, it is still a joy to get your hands in the dirt and plant a few seeds while snow and cold winds blow outdoors. With modern methods and products, starting seeds indoors is simple. Begin by gathering the best materials and devising optimal growing conditions.

Containers

The hallmark of a great seed-starting container is drainage. The container must have holes allowing excess water to drain. As long as a container has drainage holes or you can create drainage holes, it will make a fine seed-starting vessel. Recycle yogurt cartons, egg cartons, and waxed paper cups into nifty little containers. You can even turn newspaper into a pot; do this easily with the help of a paper pot maker, which is available online.

A popular option is peat pots. These small containers are made of pressed organic material, such as compost or peat moss. Seeds are planted directly in the pots, and when it is time to transplant seedlings into the garden, you plant the entire pot without disturbing the roots. The pot slowly disintegrates into the soil. Peat pellets are similar. These little discs expand in water to form a 2-inch-tall cylinder. Plant a seed in the expanded disk, which you then treat like a peat pot.

Soil

The best soil for starting seeds indoors is a mix of peat moss, perlite, and starter fertilizer. Look for a commercial seed-starting mix at your local garden center. Don't use garden soil; it compacts easily, preventing tender roots from expanding.

Light

Most vegetable seeds don't need light to germinate, but once they begin to grow they need adequate light so they don't produce long, floppy stems. Leggy seedlings are weak and won't transplant as successfully as short, stocky plants.

Although a lot of light may seem to pour through your windows in winter, it usually isn't enough for seedlings. An indoor lighting setup that includes fluorescent lights provides more dependable, consistent light. You'll find several simple lighting systems for seedlings online.

TEST GARDEN TIP

Planting holes

The eraser end of a pencil is the perfect size for making small planting holes for many seeds. Lightly press the eraser into the potting soil, drop in a seed or two, and gently sprinkle soil over the planting hole.

Step-by-step: starting seeds

Plant seeds indoors six to eight weeks before you plan to plant them outside. Tomatoes and peppers are some of the most popular edibles to start from seeds. These easy-to-grow plants germinate readily and grow rapidly.

1

2

3

4

1 **CHOOSE A CONTAINER**
Start seeds in any type of container that drains readily. Peat pots and peat pellets are especially easy to use because they can be planted directly in the garden. You can also recycle nursery containers; be sure to clean them well before seeding.

2 **ADD POTTING SOIL**
Unless you are using peat pellets, it is necessary to add potting soil to your container. A seed-starting potting mix is ideal, but you can also use an all-purpose potting soil. Quick drainage is essential and a slow-release fertilizer is a good addition. Use a straight edge, such as a small ruler, to level the potting soil, being careful not to compact it.

3 **PLANT SEEDS AND WATER**
Using your fingers or a piece of cardstock folded into a trough, drop two or three seeds into each pot or pellet. Planting depth depends on the plant. Some seeds are planted ½ inch deep while others grow best when they are planted just ⅛ inch deep. Check the encyclopedia section beginning on page 146 for planting depth recommendations. Using a spray bottle, mist the soil daily until seedlings emerge.

4 **PLACE SEEDLINGS UNDER LIGHT**
After the seedlings germinate, move them to a bright location. Fluorescent lights are ideal. Use two bulbs—one cool white and one warm white—to provide ample light for 14 or so hours per day.

Grow healthy seedlings

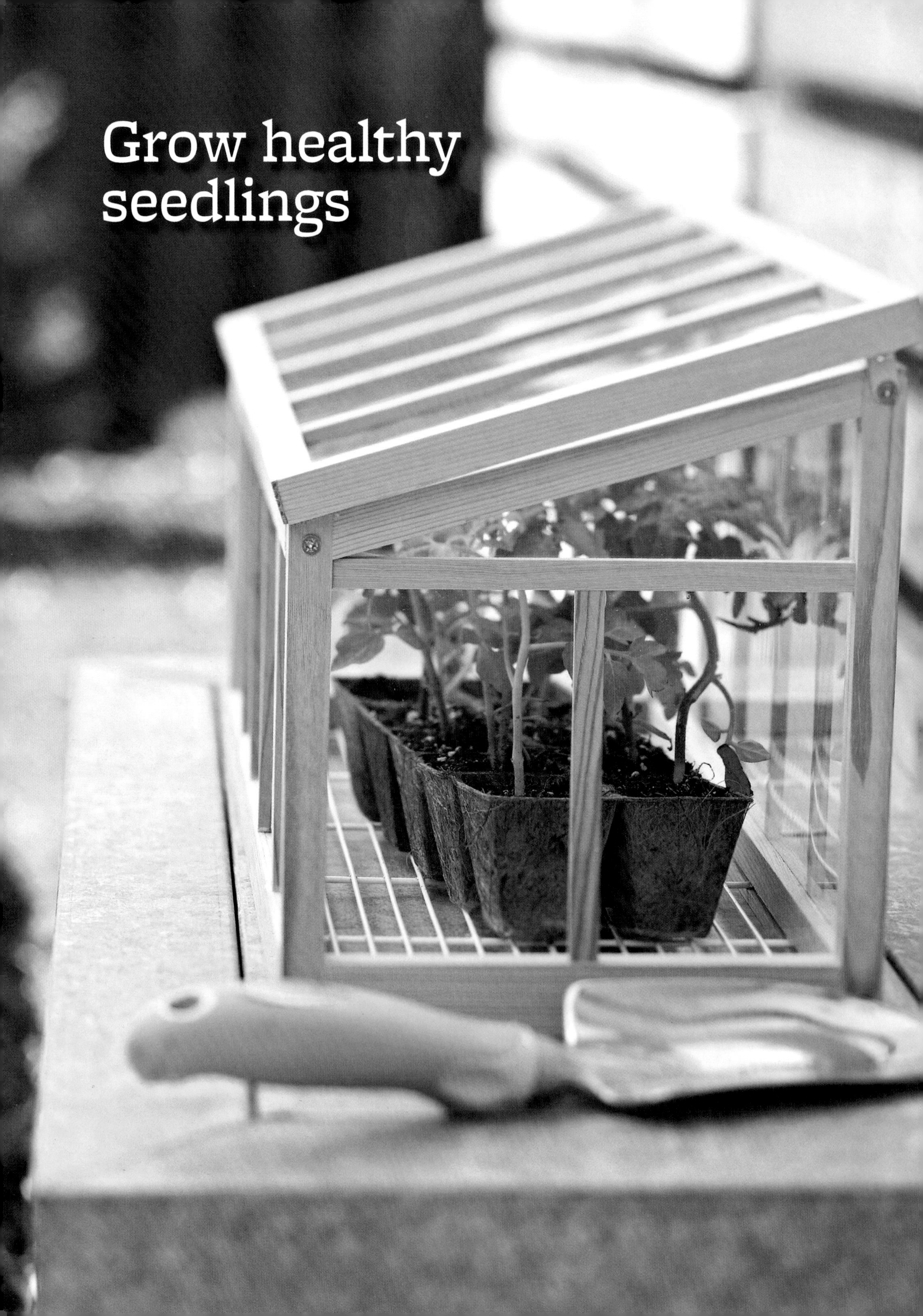

Warm soil and adequate moisture trigger seedlings to germinate in short order.

Follow these tips and you'll have healthy seedlings for transplanting into the garden in a few weeks.

Germination

Seeds tend to need warmer temperatures to germinate than to grow. Most vegetables germinate fast in warm soil. The faster seeds germinate, the less likely they are to rot or be damaged by insects. Under ideal soil temperatures most seeds will germinate within one week. However, some vegetables, such as leeks, may take longer.

Setting pots or seed trays in a warm spot will speed germination. The top of a refrigerator or any place that provides a little extra warmth is all you need. Commercial warming mats, similar to heating pads, are also available.

Spur germination by keeping the soil moist; gently water with a mister or place pots in a watertight container and pour 1 or 2 inches of water in the bottom of the container. Water will naturally travel into the dry soil. Remove the container from the water tray as soon as the top of the soil is moist.

Opposite: **Acclimate seedlings to their new environment by placing them outside for a few hours every day for a week. A simple cold frame will moderate cold winds.**

Light and transplanting

As soon as seeds germinate, move them to a place that has bright light or put them under a bank of seed-starting lights, available online and at home improvement stores.

Once seedlings form a second set of leaves, thin them to one per pot. Use scissors to snip off the weakest seedlings at the soil line. Large plants, such as tomatoes, peppers, and eggplant, might need to be transplanted into a larger pot before planting outside. Figure that once a seedling's height is three times the diameter of the pot, it's time to move it into a larger pot.

Acclimate to the outdoors

One week before you're ready to transplant seedlings into the garden, harden them by acclimating them to outdoor conditions. Find a location that's protected from wind and receives morning sun. Place the seedlings outside, ideally on a cloudy, windless day that's above 50°F, for a few hours, then bring them indoors. Gradually extend the amount of time they are outdoors over a one-week period. By the end of the week, you can leave them outdoors overnight.

Beware of damping off

The biggest hazard in starting seeds indoors is damping off disease. This fungus literally attacks overnight and can wipe out a whole tray of seedlings by morning. The telltale sign of damping off disease is seedlings that have rotted at the soil line. The disease thrives under damp conditions with little air circulation.

To prevent damping off fungus from attacking, don't overwater seedlings. Water until the soil is moist, allowing it to dry slightly between waterings. Also generously space seedlings and encourage good air circulation by placing a fan nearby so it gently moves air around the plants.

Prepare a seedbed

Planting seeds or transplants in the garden begins with preparing the soil.

A potato fork is handy for turning soil and working compost into the top 8 or so inches of soil.

Little preparation, other than adding compost, is needed when vegetables are planted in existing landscape beds to form an edible landscape. New landscape beds and vegetable plots require just a few hours of time, some muscle power, and compost to prep for planting. Here's a quick summary to guide you through the process.

Remove sod. Your soon-to-be vegetable garden is most likely blanketed with turf grass. Begin by skimming away the sod and as many roots as possible. There are several ways to accomplish this. A low-cost option that requires some strength and stamina is to use a sharp shovel to slice under the grass, cutting below the sod's 2- to 3-inch-deep root zone. Be sure to slice deep enough to remove all visible roots and prevent the grass from regrowing as a garden weed.

Sod can also be removed with a sod cutter. Rent this small machine at a home improvement store for the day and use gas power to make quick work of removing sod. Adjust the sod cutter's cutting depth to ensure it removes as much of the sod's root zone as possible.

Toss the sod into a compost pile. It will quickly decompose, turning into compost that can be spread on the garden next spring.

Check soil dryness. Before tilling or turning the soil, check the soil moisture. Tilling wet soil results in hard-to-break clods that will plague you and your plants all season long. To determine when the soil is dry enough to work, press a handful in your fist and squeeze. If the soil readily crumbles, you can till or turn the soil. If water oozes out when you squeeze, it's still too wet. Wait a few more days and check the soil again.

The soil in raised bed gardens often dries more quickly than inground garden soil. If it takes your soil more than a week to dry in spring after a heavy rain, consider gardening in raised beds.

Add compost. It is easier to amend the soil prior to planting. Before planting you have no obstacles in your way, making spreading and mixing in compost a breeze. Spread a 2-inch-thick layer of well-decomposed compost over the garden. Add compost annually in fall or spring and mix it in the soil prior to planting in spring.

Loosen soil. Topsoil in a vegetable garden should be finely textured and free of large clods so sprouts can punch through the soil surface and water can seep into the root zone. Use a tiller or long-handled spade to turn the soil and break up clods. After tilling, smooth the soil with a stiff garden rake, gathering up rocks and large clods as you go.

Soil that crumbles easily in your hand is dry enough to work. Till the soil, mixing in a 2-inch-thick layer of compost to a depth of about 8 inches.

Smother grass

If you have time—four to eight weeks or more—you can kill grass by covering it with sections of newspaper and topping the paper with wood mulch. Cover the grass with newsprint, overlapping sections to create a mat that is at least 10 sheets thick. Top the newsprint with a 4-inch-thick layer of shredded wood mulch. Water the mulch well to prevent the newsprint from blowing. Over time the grass will die and the newspaper will decompose. Till or turn the soil, incorporate compost, and plant seeds or transplants.

Time to plant

Transplants are a quick and easy way to plant your garden. These lettuce and kale transplants will produce edible leaves in just three or four weeks.

The first warm sunny day after a long winter might spur you to begin planting, but hold off. While the air temperature might be warm, the soil temperature is still probably very cool. For most North Americans spring planting occurs sometime between late February and late May.

Plant seeds and transplants of cool-season crops before the last frost date in your area. They'll thrive once the soil reaches about 40°F and is fairly dry. Plant seeds and transplants of warm-season crops outdoors about two weeks after the last average frost day for your area.

Climate often provides exceptions to these guidelines. For instance, if you live in South Florida, you can plant warm-season tomatoes in fall for harvest the following spring. You can't go wrong if you match the needs of the particular crop to the natural climate and weather cycles where you live.

Look to seed packets

Much of the information you need for planting, including the best planting time, is at your fingertips on the back of a seed packet. Seed packets detail plant spacing and planting depth as well as mature plant size. They also give an estimate of how many days from planting time that you can expect ripe produce. This is often listed as "Days to maturity" on the packet.

Seed packets also detail special treatments the seeds might require prior to planting, such as soaking the seeds in water to soften the seed's hard outer covering.

Planting

The most common way to plant seeds is in straight narrow rows. Referring to the seed packet for planting depth, use a hoe or tool handle to make a depression in the loose soil. This will be the planting furrow. To make a straight row, run a plumb line from a stake at either end of the planting bed. Place seeds in the furrow, spacing them as directed on the seed packet and covering them with loose soil, again as directed on the seed packet. Firm the covered row with your hand to ensure seed-to-soil contact and water gently.

Another way to plant seeds is in wide rows, which offer efficiency in small spaces by eliminating pathways. Wide rows should be no wider than 4 feet across so you can comfortably reach the center of the bed. Sprinkle seeds on the wide row bed. Once most of the seeds have germinated, thin any crowded seedlings to proper spacing.

Finally, some vining crops, such as melons and pumpkins, are traditionally grown on mounds of soil called hills. Create a 3-foot-diameter, flat-top mound on heavy soil or just a circle on the ground on sandy soil. Plant five to six evenly spaced seeds per hill, and space the hills based on the individual vegetable you're growing. Thin out all but the strongest two or three seedlings to the proper spacing. Hills give these vining vegetables lots of room to spread and fill in garden beds.

TEST GARDEN TIP

Tasty row marker

Carrots are notoriously slow to germinate. Remember where you planted them by sowing a crop of radishes in the same furrow as the carrots. Radishes spring out of the ground quickly, marking the row. The radishes will be ready for harvest shortly after the carrots germinate.

Tomato planting tips

Tomatoes are usually grown from transplants planted directly in the garden after the last average frost date. When shopping for tomato transplants, look for short, stocky plants. They will withstand strong spring winds more easily than tall, lanky plants. Here are a couple more tomato planting tips.

Stake plants after planting. Whether you use a traditional wire tomato cage or a sturdy dowel sunk into the soil alongside the plant, stake your tomato at planting time to prevent damage to the root ball or foliage that can happen when staking a large plant.

Plant the stem. Tomatoes produce roots along their stems. Bury the stem of an exceptionally tall and lanky transplant to encourage it to produce roots that will anchor the soon-to-be top-heavy plant. Plant the transplant in a 3-inch-deep trench, gently bending the tip of the plant up so that three or four sets of leaves are above the soil and the rest of the stem and root ball are below the soil. The stem will quickly sprout roots.

Seedling care

Nature throws a bevy of diverse weather conditions at tender young seedlings in spring—from sudden snowstorms to scorching heat. More often than not, seedlings will tolerate strong winds, cool temperatures, and occasional heavy rains. There are a few things you can do to moderate weather extremes and encourage fast plant growth.

Be water smart. Seedlings need about 1 inch of water per week for best growth. If it does not rain, water them gently with a watering can or hose fitted with a sprinkling nozzle.

Add a layer of mulch. After seedlings emerge from the soil and develop a second set of leaves or shortly after setting out transplants, spread a 1-inch layer of finely shredded bark, leaves, or other organic mulch around plants. Be sure to keep mulch away from the tender stems. Mulch will help prevent soil moisture evaporation and keep weeds at bay.

Thin plants. Although it might be difficult to discard some of your young seedlings, thinning is necessary for good growth. Well-spaced plants thrive because air can circulate freely, reducing disease, and the stems and leaves can fully expand, allowing for maximum fruit production.

Made of lightweight fabric, a floating row cover protects cold-sensitive peppers from extreme cold and wind. It also prevents insects from damaging plants.

Thin seedlings by cutting off the weakest seedlings at ground level. Use scissors or pruners. Thin established plants by snipping them or gently pulling them, if doing so will not disturb the root system of nearby plants.

Consider row covers. If the threat of extreme cold, wind, or rain has the potential to harm tender seedlings, cover them with a floating row cover. Made of lightweight fabric resembling cheesecloth, floating row covers let sunlight, water, and air through while blocking insects and keeping the transplants slightly warmer.

To use a row cover, simply drape the fabric over the young seedlings and anchor the sides. Or use wire to create half-circle frames. Sink the frames over the plants and drape the cloth over the frames. Floating row covers are so lightweight that vegetables will lift them as they grow.

Some vegetables, such as lettuce and broccoli, can be grown to maturity under row covers. However, if warm temperatures are expected, it's best to open the row covers to cool the plants. Vegetables that are flowering likely need to be uncovered and available to insects for pollination.

Use cloches for warmth. Protect individual plants with mini greenhouses called cloches. You can buy classic glass cloches or fashion your own by cutting the bottom off gallon-size clear plastic jugs. After removing the bottom, make a V-shape slit in the handle's top and set the jug over a plant. Insert a long stick through the handle and deep enough into the ground to keep the jug in place. Don't use the cap. Take the cloche off the plant on days over 50°F to keep excess heat from building up inside, but put it back in the evening if you expect cold temperatures.

Thinning carrots is especially important. A crowded carrot planting will produce small, odd-shaped roots. Thin plants so they are 2 to 3 inches apart.

Tomato tepees

To harvest the first tomato on the block, you'll need to place your seedlings out as early as possible, but you run the risk of a late frost killing plants. To protect the transplants from cold temperatures, place a water-filled frost protector over them. These commercially available plastic sleeves have cells that are filled with water. The water releases heat as it cools at night, significantly warming the enclosed seedling. This kind of system protects seedlings of tomatoes and other warm-season crops down to 20°F. Remove the tepee once the weather is consistently warm.

water smart

Plant roots harvest water from the soil so you can harvest produce from the garden. Water smart to conserve this valuable resource.

p.86

WHEN TO WATER

Plant, soil type, and weather conditions influence a plant's need for water. Decipher these cues and what they mean about when you should water.

p.88

WAYS TO WATER

From a watering can to a sophisticated irrigation system, water flows to plants in a multitude of ways. Choose the best method for your garden.

p.92

WATER SMART

Make the most of natural rainfall and your watering practices with tips for water conservation.

Know when to water

Lettuce and other spring crops generally receive plenty of moisture from rainfall, but if irrigation is necessary, a gentle spray from a garden hose is an easy way to deliver water.

Watering, like most garden chores, is not a one-size-fits-all kind of practice.

How much to water, when to water, and how to water all depend on your garden soil, weather, and the edibles you are growing.

Vegetables and many herbs are short lived and have relatively shallow root systems. Any setback in their growth due to lack of water will negatively influence crop yield. Even if you live in a high rainfall region, keep in mind that natural rainfall alone might not give your new plants adequate water at the right time.

Take cues from the soil

How much and how fast a soil can absorb water depends on its texture, namely the relative amounts of sand, silt, and clay it contains. Clay soils hold the most water for the longest time but absorb it slowly. Rain and irrigation may wash off and not soak into clay soil.

Sandy soils are the opposite. They absorb water quickly, but retain little of it. Most plants in sandy soils need more frequent watering. Mixing compost and other organic matter into clay or sandy soils helps compensate for the weaknesses of both.

Weather considerations

Weather always figures prominently and unpredictably in the watering calculation. Clear, sunny days that are windy will pull much more water from plants and the soil than the same sunny days when the air is calm. Similarly, an 80°F day when humidity is low will place much more water demand on plants than if humidity is high.

Generally, annual plants need about 1 inch of water a week to thrive. If nature delivers 1 inch of water or more, you likely will not have to supplement. If not, plan to water, especially early in the season when the plants are establishing root systems.

Crop considerations

Annual plants, such as most vegetables and many herbs, grow fast and need soil that is consistently moist. Young perennial herbs and young fruiting shrubs and trees also need water frequently compared with the same plants once their roots are established.

Standard fruit trees need a lot of water. If this isn't supplied by rain, deep irrigation is necessary. Dwarf trees may not need as much water, but they do require a constant supply. A newly planted tree has a root spread of up to 2 square feet and needs a minimum of 2 to 4 gallons of water a week. Make appropriate adjustments for rainfall, high temperatures, and soil type.

Once perennial edible plants are established, the differences between plants' water needs become more apparent. Some herbs, such as lavender, have small, waxy, whitish leaves that resist water loss even on hot days. Others, such as mint or lemon balm, have relatively thin leaves through which water passes readily, meaning their roots will need more frequent replenishment, all other things being equal.

TEST GARDEN TIP

Bag it

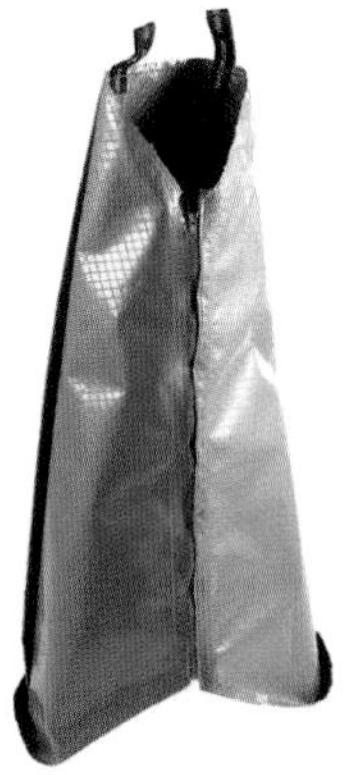

Use water bags, sold as Gator Bags, to prevent runoff when watering newly planted fruit trees. These zippered bags have water reservoirs with holes in the bottom that allow water to seep out of the bag and into the tree's root ball. It takes several hours for a water bag to drain, ensuring all the water percolates into the soil.

Watering cues

There are two ways to know when to water your plants. First, check out the plants themselves. If you watch closely you'll learn to tell when water is needed, and long before the obvious signal—wilting. A water-hungry plant's foliage may take on a dull appearance or stems may not stand as tall and look as vibrant as they do when they are plump with water.

The soil also offers cues to water needs. Scratch the soil 1 or 2 inches below the soil surface. If it is moist, you don't need to water for at least two days. If it is dry, water deeply by soaking the soil to a depth of 6 to 8 inches below the surface.

Ways to water

There are many ways to deliver water to your vegetables, fruits, and herbs. If your garden is like most, you'll likely use some combination of these most common watering methods regularly.

Hand watering: best for container gardens, watering one or two transplanted plants in a large garden, watering seeds after planting This simple method involves watering the garden with a handheld hose, usually with a spray head on the end, or a watering can. It involves no previous soil preparation or equipment installation. It is time-consuming and leads to underwatering because most gardeners do not have the patience to water plants for as long as needed.

Furrow irrigation: best for row-style gardens, large gardens Furrow irrigation works best when you are watering rows of plants; it is often used in large vegetables gardens. Furrows beside plant rows are filled with water and left to soak in. Plant foliage stays dry when furrow irrigation is used, which helps minimize disease development.

If you only have a few tomato plants or a very small garden, hand watering is the easiest way to deliver water to plants during prolonged dry spells.

Basin irrigation: best for fruit trees and shrubs Watering basins are used mainly around fruit trees and shrubs. A ridge of soil is built to contain the water; then the basin that is formed by the ridge is filled with water, either from a handheld hose or a bubbler head on a permanent sprinkler system. A few basins can be filled quickly with water, but if many plants are irrigated by hand in this manner, watering may be time-consuming. Plant foliage stays dry when water basins are used.

Sprinklers: best for large, densely planted gardens Hose-end sprinklers and underground installed sprinklers irrigate a large area at once. They are most effective when used to water heavily planted areas. Sprinklers are wasteful if they are used to irrigate sparsely planted areas. They are also hard to control in windy areas and they wet plant leaves, which may lead to disease problems. They are effective for delivering water over a large area and require less time than most other systems. Due to their drawbacks, choose alternative watering systems if possible.

Drip irrigation: best for any size garden, plants that require constant soil moisture Drip irrigation systems apply water slowly, allowing it to seep into the soil. They are left on for a few hours at a time, often for 4 hours per day. Many types of delivery systems are available. If they are properly operated, drip systems do the best watering job because they keep the soil at a relatively constant state of moisture, without the wet-to-dry fluctuations of other methods. Drip systems work best in light soils and are a perfect solution to watering plants on steep slopes. They do not wet leaves.

Soil basins are particularly effective around fruit trees and shrubs. They hold water, allowing it to seep into the soil.

Low-water edibles

A few edibles are drought tolerant after they have established a strong root system—about eight weeks after planting. For the most part, the vegetables in this group are warm-season plants. Cool-season plants are accustomed to frequent spring rain and balk at dry situations. Many perennial herbs and fruit trees, once established, are drought tolerant.

VEGETABLES
- BEAN
- OKRA
- ONION

HERBS
- CHIVES
- LAVENDER
- ROSEMARY
- SAGE
- THYME

All about drip systems

Easy on the environment and easy on you,

drip irrigation is a smart way to deliver water to thirsty edibles. A water-wise solution for drought-prone regions, drip irrigation prevents runoff by slowly delivering moisture to plant roots. This slow, steady application maintains a delicate balance of air and water in the soil, creating a nearly perfect environment for roots.

Easy to install and adaptable to any size or shape of garden, drip irrigation systems, also called micro-irrigation systems, can be purchased at most home improvement centers. You'll find kits that include necessary emitters, hoses, and other components. You can also purchase individual drip components that will allow you to customize your system or create a customized system from scratch.

How it works

A drip system consists of a combination of hoses, emitters, and basic plumbing fixtures. A hallmark of this type of watering system is its simplicity. It does not need to be trenched into the ground as is the case with sprinkler irrigation. The system's tubing is often laid on top of weed fabric and under mulch to keep it out of sight and to prevent a tripping hazard.

The water source for a drip system is commonly a spigot. A backflow prevention device is attached to the spigot to prevent contaminated water from flowing into the water system. A filter is then attached to trap small particles before they get into the system and clog emitters. A pressure regulator is installed next. This device reduces the household water system to 25 to 30 pounds per square inch. An automatic timer can be installed near the spigot to turn the system on and off.

A ½-inch polyethylene hose, a mainline, transfers water from the spigot to the garden site. The mainline should not exceed 200 feet for consistent water flow. Next, emitter tubing and emitters are attached to the main line. Emitters can be placed every 12 to 24 inches to deliver water to a row-style garden or simply placed as needed in a garden with an irregular design. Drip irrigation systems are easy to reconfigure too. Goof plugs allow you to plug an emitter hole.

Getting started

The first step in installing a drip system is to take stock of your site. Measure the size of your optimal irrigation system by laying out a series of garden hoses in the anticipated location of the drip system. Measure the length of the hoses you used and take the information with you to the home improvement store.

Maintenance

A drip system requires minimal care. During the growing season, periodically check and clean emitters to ensure they are working properly. Remove and clean the filter from time to time. In cold regions, prepare the system for winter by detaching the automatic timer, backflow prevention device, filter, and pressure regulator; store them indoors. Drain the mainline and your system is ready for freezing temperatures.

Opposite: **A very simple drip system consisting of a single drip hose slowly delivers water to tender young lettuce.**

Easy irrigation

There are three basic parts to a drip irrigation system. You can add other features, available at home improvement stores, to customize your system.

Mainline As long as 200 feet, the mainline carries water from the spigot to the garden.

Emitters Place one emitter every 12 to 24 inches in a vegetable garden or water shrubs or small trees using up to three emitters evenly spaced around the plants.

Automatic timer An automatic timer turns a drip irrigation system on and off, handling the watering job for you.

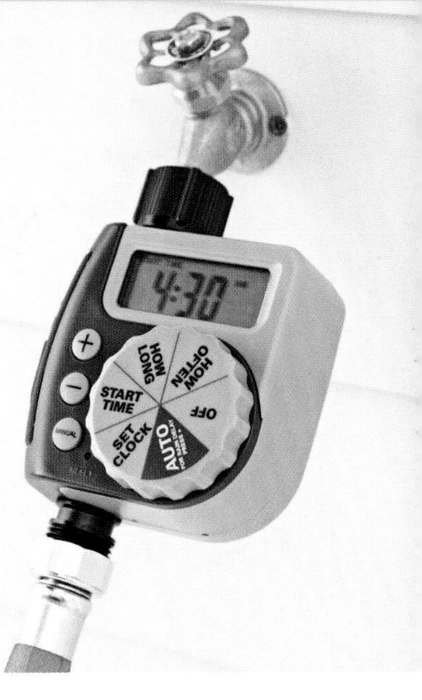

Smart watering practices

Be water smart with these simple tips about when and how much to water.

Supplemental irrigation can prolong the harvest period of lettuce and other cool-season crops in early summer when temperatures rise.

Make the most of every drop with efficient watering practices. These conservation strategies are especially important if your area's water is in short supply or expensive—or both.

Apply 1 inch per week. Most edible plants need 1 inch of water per week. Determine when to water by examining the soil. Gardens with sandy soil must be watered more often than gardens with clay soil. Generally, if the soil is dry 2 inches below the surface, it's time to water. If it is moist, you can delay watering for a couple days.

Water deeply. Your goal whenever you water is to send moisture 6 to 8 inches into the soil to encourage greatest root growth. Well-established edible plants have roots that extend 6 to more than 36 inches deep. By watering deeply, you encourage roots to grow deep into the soil where they can mine their own water. If there is no rain, plan to water your garden deeply about once a week in summer.

Keep foliage dry. Discourage fungal disease from developing by keeping plant foliage dry when watering. Deliver water directly to the root zone.

If you must get the foliage wet, water plants in the morning so they dry quickly in the sun, as opposed to watering at night when the water will stay on the leaves for a longer period of time.

Water conservation

Mulch it. A 2- to 3-inch-thick layer of organic mulch reduces soil moisture evaporation and keeps the soil cooler in summer. In addition, mulch cuts down on weed growth.
Eliminate weeds. Weeds waste water. They compete with plants for water and nutrients. Get rid of weeds as soon as you spot them.
Add organic matter. Mix compost, shredded leaves, and other organic soil amendments into the soil to promote water penetration and retention.
Try closer rows. A small area gardened intensely will produce more vegetables for every inch of water applied than a large garden that is not planted as densely. Most vegetables can be planted closer than the 2- to 3-foot row spacing indicated on seed packets. Radishes, onions, beets, and carrots are easy to grow in rows 1 foot apart. Stake tomatoes and grow cucumbers on trellises for a densly planted garden.
Choose a flat space. For the most efficient water penetration, plant on flat terrain. Planting squash, melons, and other vegetables on hills as described on seed packets, is not the best practice for water conservation. Instead, plant those vegetables in a cluster on flat soil.

TEST GARDEN TIP

Winter hose care

Get a long and useful life from your garden hose by storing it in winter. First disconnect and drain it. Coil hoses once they're drained, and connect the two ends to keep the coil neat. Store hoses flat, not hanging, ideally in a garage or basement where they will not freeze.

Prevent soil moisture loss by spreading a 2-inch-thick layer of finely shredded wood mulch or leaves around young edible plants.

garden pests

Simple prevention strategies stop many garden pests before they cause problems. The following pages are stocked with quick prevention ideas and tips for managing pests if they get out of hand.

p.96

ALL ABOUT PESTS

Get the upper hand in combating pests when you know how, why, and when they populate your garden. Learn more about common insects, diseases, and weeds on the following pages.

p.106

PEST PREVENTION

A well-managed produce garden has few pest problems. Follow these tips for creating a landscape that welcomes beneficial insects and discourages all types of garden pests.

p.110

PEST ENCYCLOPEDIA

Use the encyclopedia to identify garden pests and the damage they cause. Minimize pest damage to your edibles with tips in the management section of each entry.

All about pests

Keep pests at bay by planting a diverse garden. This roving herb planting includes thyme, chives, and bee balm. The cat keeps the vole population in check.

TEST GARDEN TIP
Invite worms

Earthworms are great gardeners. Their tunneling and production of nitrogen-rich excrement keep the soil loose and fertile. They break up clay soils. They balance organic matter in the soil and make nutrients available to plants. Make your garden earthworm-friendly by annually incorporating a 2-inch-thick layer of compost and limiting the use of pesticides.

When you think of the word "pest"

your mind might jump to insect pests—the cucumber beetles and tomato hornworms that munch on juicy produce and succulent leaves and stems. But the term "pest" encompasses more than insects. Diseases, animals, and weeds that cause problems for cultivated plants are also considered pests.

Natural balance

More often than not, insects, diseases, animals, and weeds do not reach pest status because you and nature control their population. The web of relationships in the garden seeks balance. If there is an overabundance of a disease or insect, most likely the environment will change slightly, knocking out the pest population before it becomes a problem.

For example, if aphids are sucking plant sap on tender new growth, watch carefully for a week or so. It is likely that green lacewings or ladybugs will soon appear. Their larvae feed voraciously on aphids, and the plants will probably recover.

Because a healthy garden relies on this intricate interaction between predators and prey, it is essential that you always observe pests in your garden before intervening; don't assume an unfamiliar insect is a pest.

In many cases nothing is required of you when it comes to pest control. Nature will take care of the insect or disease before it becomes a significant problem. Weeds, on the other hand, require more vigorous monitoring and often require action. Since they will readily root in open soil, a 2- to 4-inch-thick layer of mulch will thwart weed seed germination, limiting weed growth most of the season.

Healthy plants

The best thing you can do to prevent pests from gaining the upper hand is to grow healthy plants. Research shows that healthy plants have strong immune systems. They react to pest outbreaks by releasing chemicals that help withstand the attack. The key to growing healthy plants is simple: Provide the sun exposure, soil conditions, moisture levels, and nutrients that the plants require, and they will reward you with vigorous growth.

Healthy plants are easy to grow in healthy soil. Poor soil conditions are among the most common challenges gardeners encounter. The soil around newly built homes and in urban areas can be particularly challenging. Before embarking on a garden adventure, take time to adequately prepare the soil. For soil-amending tips refer to Chapter 5, page 54. If the native soil is unmanageable, build a series of raised beds or garden in containers filled with quality soil. The extra money and time required to garden this way will be well worth it when you are harvesting armloads of delicious produce.

Above left: **Pest-resistant fruit and vegetable varieties make it easier than ever to grow blemish-free food without applying pesticides.**

Above right: **An insect pest is the cause of this foliage damage. Before using a chemical control, take time to accurately identify the pest.**

Integrated pest management

Simple to apply and inexpensive, a layer of weed-free straw mulch applied in spring will suppress weeds until fall.

Integrated pest management (IPM) is a gardening approach that promotes good gardening practices as a way to combat pest problems. The goal of IPM is to solve a problem with the least toxic effect on the environment. Chemical pest control methods are the last option, and rarely used, in IPM.

If a problem does arise, IPM encourages a gardener to look at all the options for control. Blending a variety of plant care and pest control techniques is more effective over the long term than reliance on pest control chemicals alone. IPM uses common sense gardening practices, most of which you probably do already. Here are the steps of IPM.

Prevent problems. Healthy plants and sound gardening techniques and habits are the first steps in an effective home garden IPM program. Provide plants with the sun exposure, moisture, and nutrients they require for strong, healthy growth.

Identify symptoms and pests. As you work in the garden, look for signs of stress or disease, such as yellowing, wilting, puckering, discoloration, and holes in or chewed edges on foliage. Look around to try to identify the cause. For tiny insects, such as mites, aphids, and the crawler stage of scales, hold a piece of white paper under a leaf and tap the leaf. Then look for specks crawling on the paper. You'll find that a magnifying glass is helpful.

Use reference books and university Internet sources to accurately identify what you find. Often you'll find that the pest is short lived or the damage it causes is inconsequential and no control tactics are needed.

Monitor the situation. If you think a plant has a pest, watch to see what changes take place over the following days or weeks. Are the edible parts of the plant damaged? Does the entire plant or just a portion of the plant show signs of decline? Has another insect arrived on the scene, perhaps to consume the first? Is the damage cosmetic and not harming the plant?

Depending on the type of insect, the damage, the weather conditions, and your goals for the plant, you may not need to intervene at all.

Decide if control is required. Only a small percent of insects are potential pests. Determine if the damage is sufficient to warrant control.

Choose control methods. Choosing which (if any) control methods to use is the backbone of an effective IPM program. A successful solution integrates all factors, including the pest, plant, growing conditions, weather, gardener's needs, potential control methods, and cost. This is where you can have a significant impact on your surroundings by starting with the least toxic control methods before advancing to other options, using chemical pest controls as a last result. The following pages detail many effective non-chemical controls for insects, diseases, and weeds.

Keep records and evaluate results. This final step is sometimes neglected. However, because insects are usually seasonal, your records will help you make changes in your plant care routine. Jot down the type of insect, what plant it was on, the type of damage (if any), weather conditions, the time of year, and control methods and their effectiveness.

Accurate identification of a pest is essential for managing it. Keep an inexpensive magnifying glass nearby for identifying pests.

Promote healthy plants

A key component of integrated pest management is to start with healthy plants. Robust, vigorously growing plants will withstand pest problems with greater ease than plants that are struggling to survive. Promote healthy plants with these tactics.

Choose insect- and disease-resistant plant varieties. The encyclopedias at the back of this book highlight varieties with notable pest resistance.

Buy healthy, sturdy transplants with well-developed root systems. Wind, intense rain, and cold temperatures work against transplants in spring. Vigorous, well-rooted transplants will withstand difficult conditions.

Buy plants from reputable growers or grow your own plants from seeds. Diseases and insects are easily transferred from the greenhouse to the garden.

All about insects

A chemical control product might eliminate a troublesome pest, but it might also harm beneficial insects like this monarch butterfly. Choose nonchemical control methods whenever possible.

In nature a balance of predators and prey and a healthy environment usually keep insect pests under control. Occasionally the balance is thrown off, causing pest populations to grow. Weather—unusually mild winters or rainy summers, for example—is a common cause.

When insect pest populations appear to be on the rise and threatening your crops, take a hard look at the damage. Are the pests feeding directly on the harvestable parts of the plant? If so, they might warrant control. Many insects feed on nonedible plant parts. In most cases these pests do not need control. In fact, they might serve a useful purpose by attracting predatory insects that will then feed on more damaging insect pests in the future. When control is necessary, here are the three main ways to outmaneuver pests in your garden.

Physical

Use physical controls to prevent insects from accessing plants or to remove insects that reach plants.

Your fingers Remove leaves that are heavily infested with insects or larvae. Handpick larger insects such as beetles, tomato hornworms, or cabbage loopers. Toss the infested foliage and insects into a bucket of soapy water before discarding them.
Water Dislodge insects from infested plants with a sharp blast of water from a hose. Be sure to spray the entire plant, including the undersides of foliage. This works well against small insects, such as white flies and aphids, as well as spider mites. Repeat treatment as often as needed.
Barriers Floating row covers are lightweight woven materials that keep flying insects such as leafhoppers and moths from landing on plants to feed or lay eggs. Cardboard collars around seedlings prevent cutworms from reaching and chewing through stems.
Traps Commercial sticky traps attract insects such as leafhoppers, flea beetles, and whiteflies. Note that many insect traps perform best as monitoring devices, alerting you when pests arrive in the neighborhood; they are less effective at killing sufficient numbers to make a noticeable dent in pest populations.

Handpicking insects and dropping them into a container of soapy water is a simple way to knock down a pest population.

Biological
Biological control is what nature does all by itself. Beneficial or predator insects carry out most biological control by dining on pest insects. Some common beneficial creatures include assassin bugs, green lacewings, ladybugs, praying mantis, predatory mites, and spiders. Beneficial parasites, such as nematodes, use garden pests as hosts, eventually killing the pest.

You can augment nature's efforts by making your garden inviting to beneficial insects. Create a vibrant community of beneficial organisms in the soil by regularly mixing compost into the planting area. Avoid using pesticides, which kill beneficial insects along with the pests. And include predator-friendly plants in your garden (see the box below).

Chemical
Chemical controls are typically used as a last resort, after a combination of other control strategies have failed and you have determined that the damage warrants intervention. There are many types of pest control products, including organic options.

No matter what type of chemical control you use, it is vital to select the appropriate product for each situation. Grabbing any can on the shelf is likely to do more harm than good if the product is not formulated for the particular plant and pest. If you have a choice, select a target-specific product that acts against a limited number of species.

Calling all beneficial insects
The adults of many beneficial insects require a diet of carbohydrate-rich nectar and pollen. Herbs in the parsley family are among the most attractive plants to various beneficial insects. Plant several clusters of cilantro, dill (shown at left), fennel, and parsley around your garden to beckon beneficial insects. After they take up residence in your garden, they'll get to work eliminating troublesome pests.

All about diseases

Healthy, disease-free transplants, like this lettuce seedling, are a great way to combat disease problems. For added protection, choose a cultivar with notable disease resistance.

Diseases are caused by fungi, bacteria, and viruses.

These tiny, often microscopic organisms are responsible for plant problems that range from powdery white film on foliage to fungus-riddled, mushy fruits.

Diseases are caused by fungi, bacteria, or viruses. Fungi are miniscule organisms that live on plants, causing visible symptoms. Insects, water, and wind are typical ways they spread. Bacteria are single-cell organisms that live on various kinds of organic matter. Unable to survive in the open, they live inside plants and are transferred plant to plant by insects, water, and hands. Viruses are the smallest of the three and the most difficult to control. They are usually spread by insects, though some are spread by seeds and tools.

Generally for a disease to occur, organisms must be transported to a susceptible host. This is often done unintentionally. After the disease is transported to the host, the perfect environmental conditions must be in place for the disease to thrive.

Your best line of defense against diseases is prevention. Embrace these practical garden hygiene and prevention tips and diseases will have trouble getting a toehold in your garden.

Select a great site. Establish your garden in a sunny location with well-drained soil and good air circulation. Look beyond the site and note the vegetation. Remove weeds not only from the garden area but also from surrounding areas because weeds harbor many disease organisms.

Plant resistant varieties. Whenever possible, choose varieties of plants bred to be resistant to debilitating diseases.

Cultivate deeply. Whether by hand or with equipment, cultivate as deeply as possible in order to completely bury remnants of the previous crop or any disease organisms that are attached to them. Tilling to a depth of 10 to 12 inches is optimal.

Control weeds. Certain weeds, particularly those botanically related to the fruits and vegetables in your garden, may harbor viruses or other diseases that could move into your garden with the aid of insects that feed on both plants.

Start disease-free. Nursery transplants, seeds, and potato starts, for example, can all carry disease, meaning problems are guaranteed before you start. Shop at a reputable nursery for healthy, disease-free transplants and certified disease-free seed potatoes.

TEST GARDEN TIP

Stop and smell the basil

Spend time in your garden inspecting your plants. You'll spot problems while they're small and easy to manage. Try this: Spend five minutes in the garden on your way to the mailbox every day.

Always rotate

The simple practice of rotating crops, or planting them in a different location every year, will help minimize pest problems. A rotation strategy confuses pests. Many insects and diseases overwinter in the soil and spring forth the following year to attack plants in the same location. If their preferred host plants are not in the immediate vicinity, the pests are much less likely to reach problem status.

Crop rotation is especially critical for members of the cabbage family (broccoli, cabbage, and related plants) and the tomato family (tomato, pepper, eggplant, and related plants). Members of this group should not be planted in the same space more than once every three years.

All about weeds

Pulling weeds when they are young and before they set seed or ramble out of control saves hours of weeding later in the season.

Whether it's purslane in the parsley or crabgrass in the carrots, most gardeners would agree that weeds are the most frustrating and time-consuming garden pests. Efforts to eliminate weeds from the outset pay off. Spending one or two years diligently removing every weed before it makes seeds can reduce the need for future weed control because fewer weeds will sprout.

Weeds are divided into two categories. The first includes weeds that produce enormous quantities of seeds. These weeds are often easy to kill, either with weed control products or with a hoe, but new ones keep appearing. Weeds in the second category are hard to kill, often because they have persistent underground parts that can sprout into new plants. A few especially troublesome weeds, such as dandelions, have both of these characteristics.

War on weeds

Attention to detail and a small investment of time will go a long way in the fight against weeds. First, when removing weeds by hand or using a tool, work to remove as much of their roots as possible. Use a small trowel or taproot weeder to pry pesky roots out of the ground.

Next, dedicate a few minutes every other day to weeding. Beginning in early spring, spend just five minutes in the garden before you go to work or at the end of the day, pulling weeds. Regular weeding like this will keep weeds small and easy to pull and prevent weeds from setting seed and creating hundreds of new seedlings.

Weed control products are rarely used in food gardens. Toxicity to crops, difficulty in applying chemicals accurately, and the potential for toxic residues are the main reasons for avoiding them.

Work to prevent weeds and you'll nearly eliminate the weed war. Weed prevention begins in early spring before weeds have a chance to get a strong foothold in the garden. Follow these prevention strategies.

Mulch, mulch, mulch. An organic mulch, such as grass clippings or shredded bark, is one of the easiest ways to suppress weeds. Mulch fights weeds by shading the soil. Most weed seeds need light to germinate. A 2-inch-thick layer of mulch blocks light and prevents weed seed germination.

Prevent disease by maintaining a 2- to 3-inch mulch-free zone around the base of plants. Moist mulch in contact with stems, twigs, and trunks creates a portal for fungi and bacteria to enter the plant.

Plant a cover crop. Cover crops provide many benefits, among them reducing weeds. Because they grow fast, cover crops outcompete weeds in the struggle for light and nutrients. Once the cover crop is cultivated and near the soil surface, it acts as a mulch to shade the soil and to prevent germination of weed seeds.

Cover crops can also suppress weeds chemically. Some plants release natural chemicals, either while they are growing or while they are decomposing, which prevent the germination or growth of other plants. Researchers have effectively used cover crops of wheat, barley, oats, rye, sorghum, and sudangrass to suppress weeds.

Cover crops can be planted anytime during the growing season. Plant a small area with a cover crop when the edible crop finishes its growing season. For example, remove lettuce and spinach when weather warms in early summer and plant a cover crop in their place to prevent weeds from taking hold.

ASK THE GARDEN DOCTOR

I have little time to weed. Are there any crops that are nearly weed free?

ANSWER: Some vegetable crops take care of many weed chores for you by shading the soil so much that they prevent weed seeds from germinating. Squash, beans, pumpkins, cucumbers, melons, and corn suppress weeds well after they establish a dense canopy of foliage.

Handy tools

Your hands are likely the best all-purpose weeding tools, but when you need a little more power to pry up deep-rooted dandelions or scuffle out a large patch of lamb's quarters, turn to one of these reliable tools.

Oscillating hoe The stirrup-shape blade of this long-handle garden weeder is sharp on both sides. Eradiate weeds by moving it back and forth in the soil. It is a pro at severing the roots of seedlings and young weeds.

Taproot weeder Many kinds of taproot weeders (at right) are available on the market. These short-handle tools with a fork at the business end, work as a fulcrum, giving you leverage to pull the entire root of an obstinate weed.

Garden smart to prevent pests

Combat poor draining or rocky soil by growing edibles in raised beds. When filled with nutrient-rich compost and topsoil, raised beds produce healthy plants that fend off pests with ease.

Above left: **Harvest vegetables after the morning dew has dried, typically by midmorning, to avoid spreading disease.**

Above middle: **A layer of cocoa bean mulch prevents soil and disease-causing organisms from splashing onto the leaves of young pepper plants.**

Above right: **Greens and rhubarb, along with other spring crops, are best planted and harvested in cool weather. In spring they have better flavor and are less likely to succumb to pests.**

The old adage "an ounce of prevention is worth a pound of cure" rings true when you are working to minimize pest trouble in the garden. More often than not, it is much easier to prevent an insect from taking hold or disease from infecting plants than it is to eliminate the pest once it has invaded the garden. These simple tips and techniques will discourage pests from calling your garden home and send them packing if they do try to take up residence.

Plant crops and varieties that are well suited to the soil and climate in your garden. Your local extension service or garden center might be able to provide area-specific plant and variety recommendations.

Choose pest-resistant varieties when possible. Plant breeders have developed many crop varieties that withstand pest damage and even discourage pests.

Water plants in the morning so they have time to dry before evening. A drip irrigation system is especially beneficial because it prevents foliage from getting wet when watering.

Space plants properly to prevent overcrowding. Often a too-dense planting scheme causes weak growth and reduced air movement, resulting in increased insect and disease problems.

Keep weeds out. Weeds often harbor pests and compete with crops for nutrients and water. Organic mulches are extremely effective for weed control and soil improvement.

Spread a 2- to 4-inch layer of mulch to keep soil from splashing onto leaves, which may bring soilborne diseases in contact with the plants. Mulch also conserves valuable soil moisture.

Rotate your garden plot if you can. Do not grow the same kind of produce in the same place each year. Plant related crops (such as broccoli, cabbage, Brussel sprouts, and cauliflower, which are all in the cabbage family) in one site only once every three years.

Stay out of the garden when the plants are wet with rain or dew to prevent spreading disease.

Avoid injury to plants. Broken limbs, cuts, bruises, cracks, and insect damage are often sites for infection by disease-causing organisms.

Remove and dispose of infected leaves from diseased plants as soon as you observe them. Remove severely diseased plants before they contaminate others.

Plant warm-season crops after the soil has warmed to avoid problems with seed and root rot and to promote vigorous growth. A general guideline is to plant warm-season crops two weeks after the last average frost date.

Inspect plants for egg clusters, beetles, caterpillars, and other insects as often as possible. Handpick as many pests as you can. Avoid sprays until the population of insects has reached a critical threshold level.

Enlist the aid of birds in pest control. Overall, they do more good than harm in the garden. Consider planting trees and shrubs with fruits that attract birds.

Encourage beneficial insects. Naturally occurring predators and parasites are found throughout the landscape. Learn to properly identify these species and avoid using pesticides around them.

Pest Detective

Garden pests and environmental challenges can cause a staggering range of symptoms—from wilted foliage to rotting fruit, or no fruit at all. If you run into befuddling pest problems in your garden, use these tips to sleuth your way to the root of the trouble.

Use the general categories—poor plant growth, damaged foliage, damaged fruit, no fruit, or plant death—to begin defining your plant problem and finding a solution. Remember, many plant problems cause only cosmetic damage, and little or no control is necessary for the plants to be productive.

If you are still stumped after exploring the options presented here, contact your extension office. They will often be able to put you in touch with an area horticulturist who can help identify the problem and share management strategies.

Poor plant growth

IS THE PLANT GROWING IN OPTIMAL CONDITIONS FOR THE SPECIES? Learn more about sunlight and soil requirements for each species in the encyclopedias beginning on page 146.

IF POOR GROWTH IS ACCOMPANIED BY YELLOW FOLIAGE, NITROGEN DEFICIENCY COULD BE THE SOURCE OF THE TROUBLE. See nitrogen deficiency, page 116.

IF SEEDS FAIL TO GERMINATE AND SEND UP SHOOTS, DAMPING OFF COULD BE THE CAUSE. See damping off, page 115. Another cause might be old seeds. Most seeds are viable for at least two to three years but some, such as onions, lettuce, and parsnips, regularly fail to germinate if they are more than one year old.

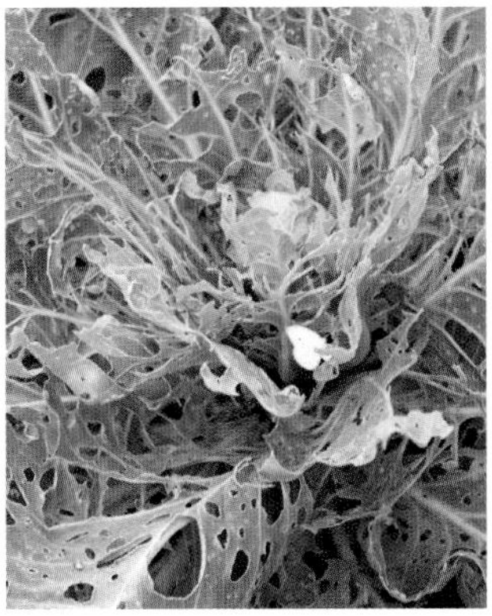

Damaged foliage

DO THE LEAVES HAVE DEAD SPOTS? OR ARE ENTIRE LEAVES DEAD? If so, go to the disease gallery on pages 114–117 and identify the problem. Anthracnose is a possible culprit.

DOES THE FOLIAGE HAVE CHEWING OR BITE MARKS? If so, see the insect pests on pages 110–113 and identify the pest.

ARE THE LEAVES DISCOLORED OR DO THEY HAVE ODD MARKINGS? If so, see the disease-causing pests on pages 114–117 and squash bug entry on page 113.

ARE THE LEAVES DISTORTED, PERHAPS CURLED OR PUCKERED? If so, see the disease-causing pests on pages 114–117, aphid on page 110, and leafhopper on page 112.

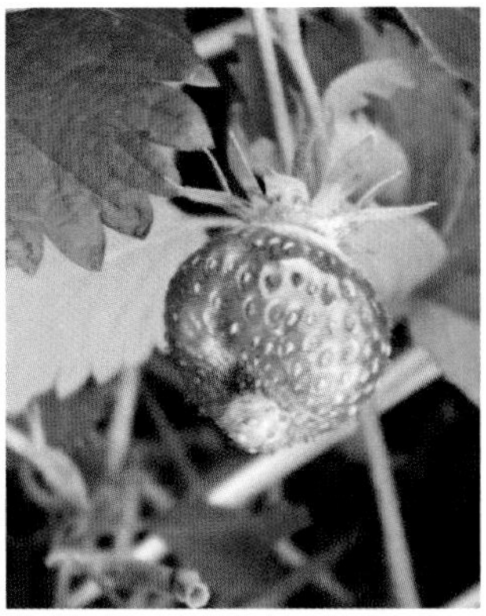

Damaged fruit

DOES THE FRUIT HAVE CHEWING OR BITE MARKS? If so, see the insect pests on pages 110–113 and the animal pests on pages 120 and 121.

DOES THE FRUIT HAVE LESIONS OR SPOTS ON THE SKIN OR FLESH? If so, see the disease pests on pages 114–117.

No fruit

VEGETABLE PLANTS: WAS THE PLANT EXPOSED TO EXTREME TEMPERATURES? If so, see Blossom drop, page 114.

FRUIT TREES: WAS THE PLANT EXPOSED TO FREEZING TEMPERATURES DURING OR AFTER BLOOM? If so, see the appropriate entry in the fruit encyclopedia, beginning on page 214, for more information.

DOES THE PLANT REQUIRE A POLLINATOR FOR FRUIT PRODUCTION? See the appropriate fruit or vegetable entry in the encyclopedias, beginning on page 146.

Plant death

WAS THE PLANT A SEEDLING OR YOUNG TRANSPLANT? If so, see Damping off on page 115.

DID THE PLANT SUDDENLY WILT BEFORE DEATH? If so, see cucumber beetle on page 111 and squash bug on page 113. Fusarium or verticillium wilt could also be the cause; prevent these fungal diseases by planting resistant varieties.

Insect pests

Aphid

Among the most common pests in the garden, aphids do little damage in small numbers, but their population can build rapidly to damaging numbers. They use their piercing mouthparts to puncture plant tissue and remove sap and cell contents.

PLANTS AFFECTED: Nearly every plant in the garden.

DAMAGE: Leaves turn yellow and may be curled, distorted, and puckered. Plants may be stunted and produce few fruits.

SIGNS: Aphids exude a sticky substance called honeydew, which ants feed upon. This is the reason ants are often present where there is an aphid infestation. Black sooty mold is often found growing on the honeydew.

PREVENTION AND MANAGEMENT: Wash aphids off plants with a strong spray of water. Encourage beneficial insects, many of which feed on aphids. Plant herbs and flowering plants in the landscape to attract beneficials. Spray plants with insecticidal soap, or if it is safe for the plant, apply horticultural oil.

Borer

These larvae of beetles or moths tunnel into stems, twigs, and branches, disrupting the transportation of water and nutrients throughout the plant. Squash vine borer is a serious pest of vine crops, and many other borers affect tree and cane fruits.

PLANTS AFFECTED: Cane fruits, corn, fruit trees, pumpkin, squash.

DAMAGE: Holes or tunnels in the trunk or branches. Bark near tunnels may be dead. Foliage on a branch or at the top of the tree is sparse or nonexistent. Affected branches die eventually. Sudden wilting is common on vine crops.

SIGNS: Sap or sawdust may be present near the holes. Cut into the affected branch or stem and you might find the wormlike pest.

PREVENTION AND MANAGEMENT: Maintain plant health by watering and fertilizing regularly. Cut out and destroy all dead or dying branches. Inspect vining vegetables for borers. If you find damage, slit the vine open with a sharp knife to remove the borer, then cover that area with soil. Toss the borer in a bucket of soapy water.

Cabbageworm

Cabbageworms and cabbage loopers munch crops in the cabbage family and lettuce foliage and are prevalent in spring. Established plants can tolerate some damage, but young seedlings or transplants may be killed by a severe infestation.

PLANTS AFFECTED: Broccoli, Brussels sprouts, cabbage, cauliflower, collards, kale, lettuce.

DAMAGE: Leaves have many round or irregular holes.

SIGNS: Green worms up to 1 inch long with light stripes down their backs feeding on leaves. Masses of brown or green pellets may be found between leaves. Clusters of yellow bullet-shape eggs on the undersides of leaves. White moths flying around plants; these are the adult form of cabbageworm.

PREVENTION AND MANAGEMENT: At the end of the season, remove infested plants from the garden to prevent pests from overwintering. If white moths are hovering near plants, cover the crop with row covers. Spray or dust plants with bacterial *Bacillus thuringiensis (Bt)* while the caterpillars are small.

Colorado potato beetle

Both larvae and adult Colorado potato beetles devour the leaves and stems of potatoes, tomatoes, and related crops. They are most damaging to potatoes; the defoliation reduces yields and may even kill the plant.

PLANTS AFFECTED: Eggplant, pepper, potato, tomato, tomatillo.

DAMAGE: Chewed leaves and stems. Damage occurs quickly and can be severe.

SIGNS: Adults are yellow-orange beetles with black stripes. Larvae are fat, red, and wormlike. They may have two rows of black dots. Look for clusters of yellow-orange eggs on the undersides of leaves.

PREVENTION AND MANAGEMENT: Choose an early maturing variety and plant earlier or later than normal to avoid peak beetle activity. Rotate crops, planting a new crop as far away from the previous year's crop as possible. Handpick adults, larvae, and eggs. Destroy them by dropping them in a bucket of soapy water. Colorado potato beetles are becoming resistant to most insecticides. Spray plants with *Bacillus thuringiensis tenebrionis* or Neem when the larvae are very young.

Cucumber beetle

Cucumber beetles chew holes in aboveground plant parts, and their white grub larvae destroy roots and stems below the soil line. It is important to control cucumber beetles because they carry two serious diseases that kill cucurbits: mosaic and bacterial wilt.

PLANTS AFFECTED: Cucumber, melon, pumpkin, squash.

DAMAGE: Plants wilt and die. Damage occurs fast, sometimes overnight. Holes in leaves, leafstalks, and stems.

SIGNS: ¼-inch-long black and yellow striped or spotted beetles.

PREVENTION AND MANAGEMENT: At the end of the season, remove infested plants from the garden to prevent pests from overwintering. Rotate crops, planting a new crop as far away from the previous year's crop as possible. Cover plants with row covers; uncover them when they begin to bloom. Spread a 2-inch-thick layer of mulch around crops to deter egg laying and to limit larvae climbing from soil to fruits. Handpick adults and destroy.

Cutworm

As their name indicates, cutworms cut down young plants at their base. Cutworms are most problematic in early spring when they attack young, tender plants. They rarely cause problems later in the season.

PLANTS AFFECTED: Many plants, including asparagus, bean, cabbage, carrot, corn, lettuce, pea, pepper, potato, tomato, and tomatillo.

DAMAGE: Young plants chewed off at the ground.

SIGNS: 1- to 2-inch-long gray or black worms near the base of damaged plants. The worms coil when disturbed.

PREVENTION AND MANAGEMENT: Cultivate the soil thoroughly in late summer and fall to expose and destroy cutworm eggs, larvae, and pupae. Place a cardboard collar around each individual seedling, as shown above, to prevent the cutworm from reaching the stem. Dust the soil around each seedling with diatomaceous earth.

Insect pests

Japanese beetle

The Japanese beetle is prevalent and destructive in all states east of the Mississippi River. There are also infestations in California, Iowa, Missouri, and Nebraska. Beetles devour plant foliage, reducing yield and killing perennial crops if the damage is severe over a period of years. Beetle populations are unpredictable from year to year. A heavy infestation one year might be followed by a light infestation the next year.

PLANTS AFFECTED: Many different plants, including fruit trees, fruiting shrubs, beans, corn, strawberry, and tomato.

DAMAGE: Leaves that have been chewed between the veins, giving them a lacy appearance.

SIGNS: Metallic green and bronze, ½-inch-long beetles with a white fringe near their wings.

PREVENTION AND MANAGEMENT: Watch for beetles daily, picking those that you see and dropping them in a bucket of soapy water. Most Japanese beetles overwinter in turfgrass, so treating your lawn for grubs may help.

Leafhopper

Leafhoppers attack plants by piercing foliage and drawing out plant sap. Plants may become weak and produce few, if any, fruits.

PLANTS AFFECTED: Many types of leafhoppers affecting many vegetables and small fruits, including apple, grape, and potato.

DAMAGE: Boldly apparent white stippled or puckered foliage.

SIGNS: Slender, wedge-shape insects that are usually green, yellow, or brown. They run sideways and jump when a plant is touched.

PREVENTION AND MANAGEMENT: Clean up and compost plant debris in fall after harvest to prevent leafhoppers from overwintering. Eliminate nearby weeds. Use floating row covers to protect plants. Promote beneficial insects by planting a diverse selection of vegetables, fruits, and herbs and limiting the use of pesticides. Ladybugs and lacewings consume leafhopper eggs and larvae. Diatomaceous earth and insecticidal soap will reduce populations.

Scales

Scales are common tiny pests on citrus trees and, to a lesser degree, on other fruiting trees and shrubs. Scales do not affect vegetable plants or nonwoody fruits. They damage plants by piercing cells and removing sap.

PLANTS AFFECTED: Fruit trees, fruiting shrubs.

DAMAGE: Leaves turn yellow and drop. Fruit drops before it is mature.

SIGNS: Crusty, waxy, or smooth bumps up to ¼ inch in diameter on the trunk, stems, foliage, and sometimes fruit. Some species exude honeydew. Black sooty mold often grows on honeydew.

PREVENTION AND MANAGEMENT: Scales attack weak plants. Water and fertilize as needed to promote healthy plants. Promote beneficial insects. Some ladybugs and parasitic wasps attack scales. Spray plants with horticultural oil.

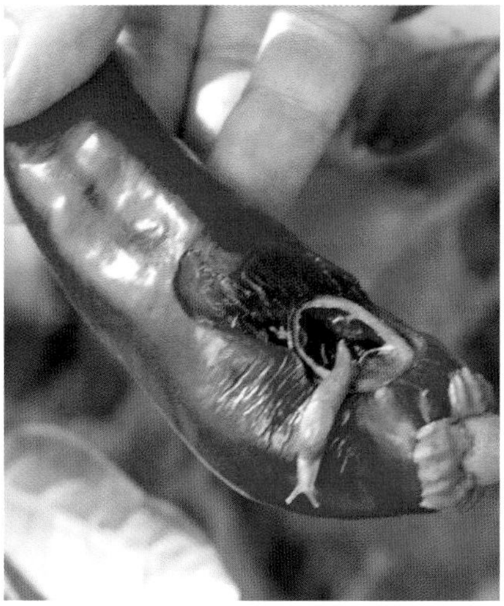

Snails and slugs

Thriving in moist, shaded places, snails and slugs feed on a wide variety of plants. They are similar except that snails have a hard shell they can retreat into and slugs do not. Both are most active at night.

PLANTS AFFECTED: Many plants, including artichoke, citrus, strawberry, and tomato. Snails and slugs target seedlings and herbaceous plants and are serious pests to ripening fruit that is close to the ground.

DAMAGE: Stems sheared off. Leaves riddled with holes. Ripening berries marked with holes.

SIGNS: Slugs and snails leave a trail of silvery slime. The young are petite versions of their parents.

PREVENTION AND MANAGEMENT: Avoid spreading mulch more than 2 inches thick; deep mulch is an optimal snail and slug habitat. Inspect the garden for them at night by flashlight and remove them by hand. Traps are also effective; inquire about traps at your local garden center. Surround garden beds with strips of copper. Sprinkle diatomaceous earth around seedlings.

Squash bug

Squash bugs pierce plant parts and kill or injure plants by sucking sap from cells. Young plants are especially susceptible.

PLANTS AFFECTED: Cucumber, pumpkin, squash.

DAMAGE: Leaves wilt and become black and crisp.

SIGNS: Bright green to dark gray or brown, flat-back bug about ½ inch long. Brick red egg clusters on the undersides of leaves.

PREVENTION AND MANAGEMENT: Clean up and compost plant debris in fall after harvest to prevent squash bugs from overwintering. Rotate crops, planting a new crop as far away from the previous year's crop as possible. Plant varieties that are resistant to squash bug. Handpick and crush adults and eggs. Trap squash bugs by laying boards on the ground and destroying bugs that congregate under them during the day.

Wireworm

Wireworms feed by drilling holes into the base or roots of plants. They are most common in soil where lawn grass was previously grown, in poorly drained soil, and in soil that is high in organic matter.

PLANTS AFFECTED: Many plants, including beet, carrot, corn, pea, potato, and turnip.

DAMAGE: Stunted plants. Slow, if any, plant growth.

SIGNS: Hard, jointed, shiny, cream- to rust-color worms in the soil.

PREVENTION AND MANAGEMENT: Plant after the soil is fully warmed as larvae are more active in cool soils. Use carrots and potatoes as traps. Place a carrot or half a potato in garden soil as though it were growing. Check it every other day or so and discard any wireworms attached to it. Some beneficial nematodes will partially control wireworms.

Common diseases

Anthracnose

Anthracnose is a fungal disease that is spread by water. Tiny spores land on fruits, vegetables, and leaves and can render a bountiful harvest into a rotted mass of foliage or fruit in a few days during hot, humid weather. Anthracnose is relatively easy to prevent by employing smart garden practices.

PLANTS AFFECTED:

Vegetables: bean, cucumber, eggplant, melon, rutabaga, squash, tomato, turnip.

Fruits: brambles, mango, strawberry.

Herbs: cilantro.

DAMAGE: Distinct dead spots on stem, leaf, or fruit. Dead spots are often yellow at first and then turn black. They have a water spotlike appearance and are often depressed or sunken.

PREVENTION AND MANAGEMENT: Mulch plants to limit disease spread. Avoid overhead watering. Rotate crops. Clean up end-of-season plant material. Remove and destroy infected plant parts; do not compost them.

Bacterial blight

Most common in moist, humid weather, this bacterial disease is easily controlled by not working around wet plants.

PLANTS AFFECTED: bean, celery, corn.

DAMAGE: Bright yellow or brown spots on the leaves. Spots often have a distinct yellow border. The spots may enlarge and kill the leaf. Long reddish lesions may girdle the stem of some plants. Water-soaked spots are common on the fruits.

PREVENTION AND MANAGEMENT: Plant disease-free seeds. Don't touch or work around wet plants. Rotate plants by planting in an area only once every three years. Clean up end-of-season plant material. Spray *Bacillus subtilis*.

Blossom drop

Caused by environmental facotrs rather than a disease, blossom drop is grouped here with diseases for convenience. Some plants drop their blossoms when nighttime temperatures dip below 58°F or rise above 85°F. Without blossoms, the plants cannot be pollinated and produce fruit. Sometimes blossom drop occurs after the plant has been pollinated and the fruit has begun to set; if it isn't completely fertilized at the time the blossoms drop, rough and misshapen fruit result. Plants remain vigorous, with lush foliage.

PLANTS AFFECTED: bean, pepper, tomato.

DAMAGE: Blossoms suddenly drop off the plant.

PREVENTION AND MANAGEMENT: Use row covers to raise night temperatures. Promote healthy plants by supplying them with approximately 1 inch of water per week.

Blossom-end rot

Another plant problem caused by environmental conditions, blossom-end rot is caused by a lack of calcium in the soil. Exceptionally dry conditions can make calcium unavailable to plants. Excessive amounts of high-nitrogen fertilizer can do the same thing.

PLANTS AFFECTED: cucumber, pepper, squash, tomato, watermelon.

DAMAGE: Begins as a small water-soaked spot on the fruit opposite the stem. As the spot develops it becomes dark brown to black, sunken, and leathery.

PREVENTION AND MANAGEMENT: Provide plants with at least 1 inch of water per week. Spread a 2-inch-thick layer of mulch around plants to conserve soil moisture. Do not cultivate too close to plants; cultivation can damage roots and lead to blossom-end rot. Avoid using high-nitrogen fertilizers and fresh manures; well-decomposed compost is a good choice.

Damping off

This fungal disease causes sudden collapse of seemingly healthy seedlings or failure of seeds to germinate. It is easily prevented by good seed-starting practices.

PLANTS AFFECTED: Most plants that are started from seed.

Vegetables: beet, broccoli, cabbage, corn, kale, tomato.

Herbs: fennel, parsley, sage.

DAMAGE: Sudden collapse of seedlings. Failure of seeds to germinate.

PREVENTION AND MANAGEMENT: Plant when the soil is at the optimum temperature for the crop. Presoak seeds to speed germination. Use sterile potting mix and containers. Allow the soil to dry between watering. Encourage air circulation near seedlings.

Downy mildew

Downy mildew is a fungus that thrives in cool, wet conditions and high humidity.

PLANTS AFFECTED:

Vegetables: beet, broccoli, cabbage, cucumber, lettuce, lima bean, melon, onion, pumpkin, radish, rutabaga, spinach, squash, turnip, watermelon.

Fruits: blackberry, grape, strawberry.

Herbs: cilantro, French tarragon, horseradish, sage.

DAMAGE: Yellow or brown spots appear on the lowest leaves. Spots gradually expand. White mold appears on the undersides of leaves. Leaves may curl, turn brown, and die.

PREVENTION AND MANAGEMENT: Water plants in the morning so they can dry before nightfall. Promote good air circulation around plants by thinning to proper spacing and abiding by plant spacing recommendations. Spray *Bacillus subtilis.*

Common diseases

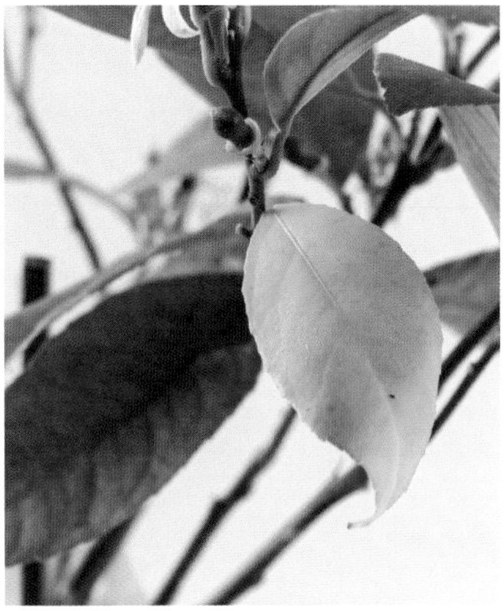

Fire blight

A fungus that is most common in spring when the weather is moist, fire blight is spread by insects and wind. Prevention is the best defense against this destructive disease.

PLANTS AFFECTED: apple, apricot, blackberry, cherry, pear, plum.

DAMAGE: All the leaves on a branch or twig wilt and turn black. The leaves remain on the branch, giving it the appearance that it was burnt. Slightly sunken areas are common on branches and the main stem.

PREVENTION AND MANAGEMENT: Plant resistant varieties. Remove dead stems 8 inches beyond the symptom, and disinfect pruners with bleach between cuts. Spray plants with *Bacillus subtilis*.

Mosaic

A frustrating virus, mosaic is spread by aphids and cucumber beetles. Control large populations of aphids and cucumber beetles and you will reduce the chances of plants being infected by mosaic.

PLANTS AFFECTED:

Vegetables: bean, beet, celery, cucumber, lettuce, melon, pepper, pumpkin, rutabaga, spinach, squash, tomato, turnip.

Fruits: blackberry, peach.

DAMAGE: Mottled yellow, slightly puckered, deformed leaves. Stunted growth on all parts of the plant.

PREVENTION AND MANAGEMENT: Plant resistant varieties. Remove and destroy infected plants. Control aphids and cucumber beetles; see insect pest entries for control methods. Control weeds; mosaic lives in many kinds of weeds. Include a variety of vegetables, herbs, and fruits in the landscape to attract beneficial insects.

Nitrogen deficiency

Nitrogen deficiency is an environmental problem occurring in poor soil. Poor or slow plant growth is an indication of nitrogen deficiency as is yellowing foliage.

PLANTS AFFECTED: all vegetables, fruits, and herbs.

DAMAGE: Lower leaves turn yellow while the upper leaves remain green. Lower leaves eventually turn brown and die. Plants are slow growing.

PREVENTION AND MANAGEMENT: Incorporate a 2-inch-thick layer of compost into the garden every year to replenish nitrogen. Too much compost can cause nitrogen deficiency. Avoid applying more than 2 inches of compost into the soil per season. As soil microbes work to break down the compost, they will tie up available nitrogen making it unavailable to plants. Spray affected plants with a foliar fertilizer.

Powdery mildew

Powdery mildew is a fungus that thrives in both humid and dry weather. The best defense against this disease is to plant disease-resistant varieties.

PLANTS AFFECTED:

Vegetables: bean, cucumber, melon, pea, pumpkin, squash.

Fruits: apple, cherry, grape, strawberry.

Herbs: cilantro, French tarragon, horseradish, mint, sage.

DAMAGE: White patches on leaves. When patches grow together the plant looks as if it was dusted with flour. Stunted or distorted leaves.

PREVENTION AND MANAGEMENT: Plant resistant varieties. Promote good air circulation by spacing and thinning plants appropriately.

Scab

More unsightly than destructive, this fungal disease disfigures leaves and fruits. The fruits are edible after peeling. Trees that lose most or all of their leaves are likely to survive and produce new leaves the following year. However, trees that loose their foliage for several consecutive years due to scab are likely to decline and slowly stop producing fruit.

PLANTS AFFECTED: apple, apricot, avocado, citrus, mango, nectarine, peach, pear.

DAMAGE: Brown, velvety spots on leaves and fruits. Heavily infected leaves turn brown, curl up, and fall off the tree.

PREVENTION AND MANAGEMENT: Remove fallen fruit and leaves. Plant resistant varieties. Apples are commonly troubled by scab, and plant breeders have developed many disease-resistant varieties; search out these tough plants for a long-lasting, healthy apple tree.

Sunscald

Caused by environmental factors, sunscald occurs on fruits when they are suddenly exposed to excessive sunlight and their skin is damaged. Sunscald can also affect tree bark.

PLANTS AFFECTED:

Vegetables: pepper, tomato.

Fruit: bark and fruits of citrus trees and other fruiting trees.

DAMAGE: White or yellow patches on the side of the fruit exposed to the sun. The patches might become sunken and leathery over time. On trees, patches of bark on the trunk or branches darken and die. Cracks and sunken lesions may eventually develop in the dead bark.

PREVENTION AND MANAGEMENT: Limit pruning when fruit is forming. Provide shade if fruits are exposed to sunlight after pruning. Prevent sunscald on tree bark due to intense winter sunlight by wrapping the trunk with paper tape or burlap to the lowest branch.

Common weeds

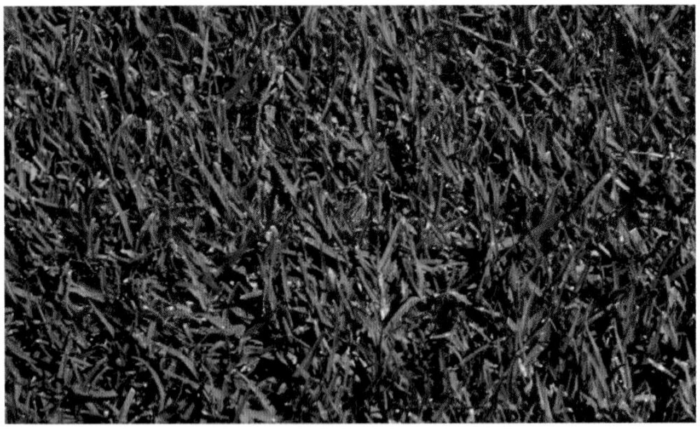

Bermudagrass (*Cynodon dactylon*) is a perennial grass with a vigorous creeping habit. The roots may grow several feet deep, making the plants drought- and heat-tolerant and also difficult to kill. Bermudagrass spreads by seeds as well as above- and belowground stems.

MANAGEMENT: Smother leaves with a heavy layer of fabric or black plastic for several months. Apply glyphosate any time the grass is actively growing. If your garden is surrounded by a Bermudagrass lawn, prevent the grass from creeping into your edibles by burying vinyl edging at least 6 inches deep or by gardening in raised beds.

Common chickweed (*Stellaria media*) prefers damp, shady areas with rich soil. It is a winter annual that grows from seeds sprouting in the fall. The ½- to 2-inch heart-shape leaves are attached to the stem by a slightly hairy stalk. The creeping stems root at their joints wherever they touch the soil. Small, white, starlike flowers bloom in clusters on the ends of the stems from spring through fall.

MANAGEMENT: Hand cultivation and a 2-inch-thick mulch layer together provide most of the control needed.

Crabgrass (*Digitaria* spp.) is an annual weed that grows fast in hot, dry weather. The blades are 2 to 5 inches long and ⅓ inch wide. Seedheads are 1 to 3 inches across (smooth crabgrass) or 4 to 5 inches across (large crabgrass). The seeds remain dormant over the winter and then sprout in the spring. The plants are killed by the first fall frost.

MANAGEMENT: Use a mulch and spread out irrigations, watering only as often as necessary. Frequent cultivation and weed control products that contain acetic acid also can control crabgrass. Use a preemergent weed control product containing corn gluten meal. **Note:** Do not use a preemergent at the same time you are planting seeds in the garden. It will prevent the seeds you sowed, as well as crabgrass, from germinating.

Dandelion (*Taraxacum officinale*) is a rosette-shape perennial with a thick, fleshy taproot that may grow 2 to 3 feet deep in the soil. Its yellow flowers bloom primarily in spring but continue sporadically until frost. Wind carries the seeds. The taproot survives winters.

MANAGEMENT: Pull roots from moist soil. Take care to extract the entire taproot; even a small piece is enough to regenerate the plant. A 2-inch-thick layer of mulch will prevent seeds from germinating and make any that do manage to grow easier to pull.

Lamb's quarters (*Chenopodium album*) grows 1 to 4 feet tall from a short, branched taproot and is common in gardens. The plant is a host for the beet leafhopper, which transmits curly top, a virus disease of beets. Leaves are 1 to 3 inches long with toothed edges. Seeds remain dormant over the winter and sprout in the spring.

MANAGEMENT: Hand pull or remove plants by hoeing. A 2-inch-thick layer of mulch will prevent seeds from germinating. Stop seeds from germinating in a vegetable garden with a preemergent weed control product containing corn gluten meal. **Note:** Do not use a preemergent product at the same time you are planting seeds in the garden. It will prevent edible plant seeds, as well as lamb's quarters, from germinating.

Nutsedge (*Cyperus* spp.) includes two troublesome species—yellow nutsedge and purple nutsedge. Yellow nutsedge is found throughout the United States, and purple nutsedge is primarily a problem in the southeastern United States and coastal California. All nutsedges prefer poorly drained, rich soil. They thrive in frequently watered garden areas. The grasslike, yellow-green leaves grow on erect triangular stems. Seedheads are purple or yellow, appearing from July to October. Nutsedges reproduce by seeds, underground stems, and nutlike tubers.

MANAGEMENT: If there are only a few clumps of nutsedge in your garden, dig up the plants, taking care to dispose of the soil in order to also dispose of the tubers. Glyphosate applied when the plant is actively growing is effective.

Purslane (*Portulaca oleracea*) is a common annual weed in vegetable gardens. It thrives in hot, dry weather. Purslane leaves are ½ to 1½ inches long, succulent, and wedge shape. Small yellow flowers open only in full sunlight from midsummer to frost. The seeds may remain viable in the soil for many years and will sprout in warm weather when brought to the surface during tilling or cultivating. The thick, reddish stems grow vigorously, forming a mat that roots wherever it touches the soil. The stems and leaves store water that enables purslane to survive drought periods.

MANAGEMENT: Because purslane grows low to the ground, an oscillating hoe is often effective, though uprooted plants left in place may reroot. A 2-inch-thick layer of mulch effectively prevents seeds from germinating.

Quackgrass (*Agropyron repens*) is a perennial grassy weed in the northern United States. Its extensive fibrous root system consists of long, yellow-white roots that may grow 5 feet or more in a single growing season. The narrow, bluish green leaves grow on stalks 1 to 3 feet tall. Wheatlike spikes produce seeds from May to September. Seeds may survive in the soil for up to four years, but most germinate in the spring within two years. The underground creeping rhizomes also send up new shoots, increasing the infestation. Quackgrass tolerates any type of soil.

MANAGEMENT: If there are only a few clumps of quackgrass in your garden, dig up the plants. Glyphosate is the quickest way to kill quackgrass.

Animal pests

While animals are intriguing to watch in nature, gardeners don't usually roll out the welcome mat for them in the garden. Deer can mow down a row of lettuce in minutes, and raccoons are known to have a midnight feast in the sweet corn patch.

Gardeners have developed several ways to repel animals, but often the results are inconsistent. They work one year but not the next. Deer in populated areas even learn which dogs to fear and which are harmless nuisances.

Barriers—a fence around the garden to a sheet of hardware cloth laid over a vegetable bed—are usually the most effective ways to control animal pests.

Deer and rabbit populations are so large in some areas that growing an edible garden is almost impossible without a sturdy fence. Don't let animals thwart your gardening efforts; you can erect a sturdy, functional fence around a small area in an afternoon. Garden intensely within the space and your small fenced garden will be more productive than a large unfenced one.

When animal pests need to be removed, traps are usually more effective than poisons. Traps let you see that you have caught the animal. If you don't want to kill the animal in a trap, you can catch it in a live trap and release it in a nearby wilderness area. Local regulations may govern this. Consult your county agricultural commissioner's office about the rules in your area.

Birds of types feed on seeds, seedlings, fruit, and berries in the garden. Birds scratch away at soft soil to unearth newly planted seeds. They peck at seedlings and young leaves. The creatures are especially damaging to berries, grapes, and soft fruit.

MANAGEMENT: Once birds develop the habit of feeding in your garden, you'll probably have to exclude them with wire or fabric cages. If they have not yet developed the habit of feeding in your garden, you may be able to repel them. Set up stakes around the plantings you wish to protect and tie crisscrossing strings between the stakes. Attach strips of aluminum foil to the strings. Birds will not readily fly through the crossing string and will avoid the shiny aluminum. To prevent birds from digging up seeds, lay hardware cloth ($\frac{1}{4}$-inch mesh) over the seedbed. Remove it before the plants are too large to slip through.

Deer can cause severe damage to gardens in rural and suburban areas. They eat many tender fruit, vegetable, and herb plants and browse on the bark, twigs, and leaves of trees and shrubs. They often cause the most damage to woody plants in winter when other food sources are scarce. Males damage trees by rubbing their antlers on the trunks and branches.

MANAGEMENT: The best way to prevent deer damage is to fence out the animals. Deer are strong and agile jumpers; to be effective, a vertical fence must be at least 8 feet high. To protect a single tree, loosely wrap the trunk with a 3-foot-tall piece of chicken wire or a drainage tile that is slit down one side. Look for repellent sprays containing tetramethylthiuram disulfide, egg solids, and hydrolyzed casein protein powder.

Gophers are burrowing rodents that live and feed primarily underground. They eat roots, bulbs, and plants that they pull down into their burrows.

MANAGEMENT: Trapping is the best way to control gophers. Find traps at your local garden center or online. Protect plants where gophers are present by planting them in a cage of hardware cloth. If you garden in raised beds, line the bottom of the raised bed with hardware cloth for added gopher protection.

Rabbits are some of the most damaging garden pests. They are active all year long, mainly during the day. In the summer they feed on tender young plants, especially vegetables. During the winter they gnaw on bark, twigs, and buds. They are especially destructive to young fruit trees in the winter. Rabbits bite off twigs cleanly as if with a knife. They can also clip off twigs on older trees up to 2 feet above snow or ground level.

MANAGEMENT: The best way to keep rabbits out of a vegetable garden is to enclose it with a 1½-inch mesh chicken wire fence. The fence should be 2 feet tall or above the snow level. The bottom should be buried 3 to 4 inches in the soil. To protect a single tree, loosely wrap the trunk with a 3-foot-tall piece of chicken wire or a drainage tile that is slit down one side. Live traps, chemical repellants, cats, and dogs may also be effective.

Raccoons forage at night and are especially fond of sweet corn. These agile climbers also climb trees to feed on fruit, often knocking many fruits to the ground.

MANAGEMENT: Raccoons are intelligent and can be difficult to exclude. Discourage them from raiding your vegetable garden by erecting a 4-foot-tall chicken wire fence, with its top extending 18 inches above the fence post. As the raccoon climbs up to the unattached portion of the fence, its weight will pull the fence down to the ground. Low-voltage electric fences are also popular and effective.

Voles are mouselike with compact, heavy bodies and short legs. They create short, shallow burrows and damage fruit trees by eating bark at or near ground level during winter. When voles gnaw off bark completely around the main stem of a plant, the plant will die.

MANAGEMENT: Limit vole damage by exclusion and habitat modification. Eliminate tall weeds in which they hide and create weed-free strips around fruit trees. Voles will quickly diminish when their habitat disappears. Limit damage in winter by encircling the lower trunk of trees with a 1-foot-tall cylinder made with ¼-inch hardware mesh.

Woodchucks live in underground burrows and feed on tender vegetables in the early morning and late afternoon. Primarily a problem in the North and Northeast, woodchucks also gnaw on tree bark. They do not tunnel for their food but eat aboveground. Woodchucks occasionally contract diseases that they may transmit to humans.

MANAGEMENT: The best way to eliminate damage is to fence out woodchucks. Surround the area you wish to protect with a woven wire fence about 3 feet high. To prevent woodchucks from burrowing under the fence, bend the bottom 12 inches of the wire mesh outward before burying it a few inches deep in the soil.

all about pruning

A few simple pruning practices will ensure your fruiting trees and shrubs produce bushels of fruit year after year.

p.124
GETTING STARTED
Snipping back healthy canes and pruning branches are important parts of maintaining a productive fruit planting. Here's a summary of which plants thrive with regular pruning.

p.126
FRUIT TREES
Prune fruit trees for both size and fruit production with these step-by-step tips that take the guesswork out of pruning.

p.130
BRAMBLES
Raspberries and other cane fruits produce fruit on short-lived canes. When the canes are finished fruiting, it's time to prune.

p.132
SMALL FRUITS
Fruiting shrubs and grape vines are vigorous plants producing many leaves and stems. Keep the foliage in check with pruning to promote good fruiting.

Getting started

Most citrus trees require little pruning other than removing dense growth to open the center of their canopy.

Just as thinning crowded seedlings is part of growing healthy vegetables, pruning and training is part of growing healthy fruit crops. While it might seem counterintuitive that snipping branches off a newly planted cherry tree or sawing limbs off an established heirloom apple will make it produce more fruit, pruning increases fruit production in time.

Don't be overwhelmed by pruning. A backyard fruit tree and shrub planting is a cinch to prune in 60 minutes or less on a crisp winter day. And don't let the fear of pruning stop you from planting fruiting trees and shrubs. Pruning is simply the removal of plant stems and branches to benefit the plant as a whole. More often than not, if you make a wrong pruning cut, there will be few repercussions and the plant will push out new growth in short order.

Why prune

Think of pruning as preventive maintenance. Trees and shrubs will live, grow, and bear fruit without ever being pruned, but experience has shown that good pruning and some training can prevent or remedy many of the problems that arise in fruit growing.

Pruning mature trees can spur them to produce more fruit and improve their fruit quality. Removing branches allows sunlight to filter into the tree canopy, which will promote uniform ripening, increase the fruits' sugar content, and decrease disease problems because fruit and foliage will dry quickly after rainfall. Pruning shrubs has similar benefits.

Annual pruning also keeps the size of a tree or shrub under control. Thoughtful pruning strengthens a tree by encouraging the growth of strong branches that can support mature fruit.

What to prune

Trees All fruit trees benefit from pruning. Dwarf fruit trees naturally retain their short stature, but annual pruning will ensure light can easily reach the center of the tree. Occasional pruning at the top of the tree will limit its height. When to prune fruit trees depends on the type of tree and the climate, but, in general, fruit trees are pruned in the dormant season.

Brambles Raspberries and other cane fruits produce berries on one- and two-year-old canes. When the canes finish fruiting, they die back to the ground. Pruning removes these unnecessary canes and also thins any spindly new growth to promote big berries and healthy plants. Brambles are often pruned during the dormant season or after fruiting.

Shrubs Pruning a shrub usually involves thinning the bush by trimming stems off at ground level. Dense, twiggy growth prevents sunlight from reaching the center of the plant, which limits fruit production.

Grapes Extensive pruning and training is required to produce top-quality grape clusters. They are pruned after the leaves fall off in fall and before new growth emerges in spring.

Most raspberries spread by sending out underground shoots. Annual pruning prevents the plant from ranging out of its planting area.

Pruning lingo

Understanding pruning instructions is simple when you can talk the talk. Brush up on your pruning vocabulary with the help of these illustrations.

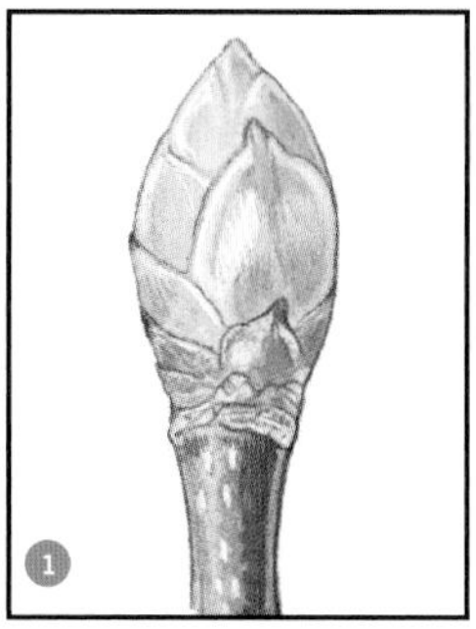

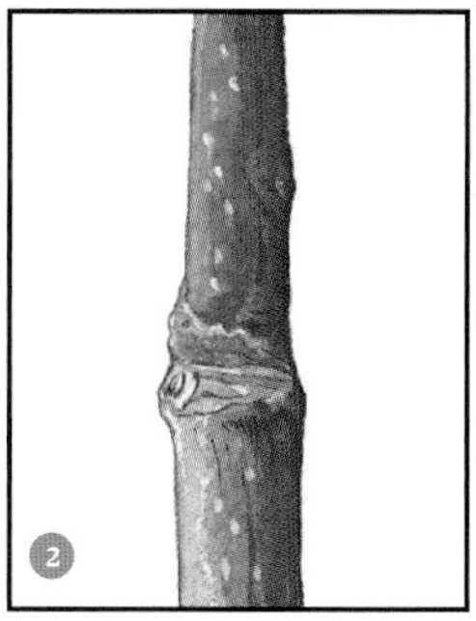

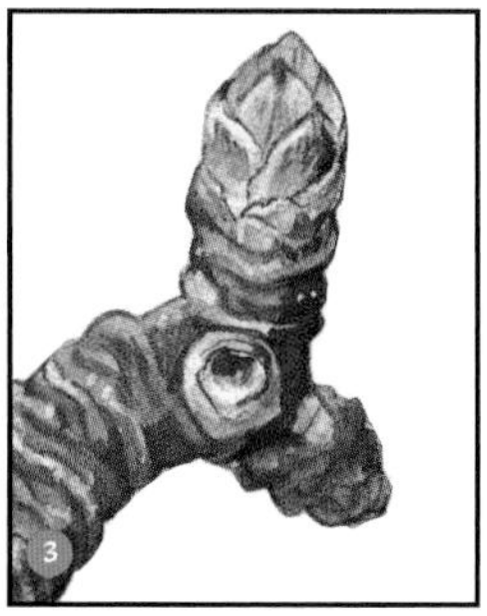

1 **TERMINAL BUD**
This large bud is on the tip of a branch. Terminal buds grow much faster than buds behind the tip. If the terminal bud is removed, several buds behind it will begin to grow.

2 **LATENT BUD**
Small latent buds are usually located above the scar left by last year's leaf. Latent buds begin to grow when the terminal bud is removed, creating shrubby, dense growth.

3 **FRUITING SPUR**
These short shoots produce the fat flowering buds that become fruit. Apples, apricots, pears, and plums have long-lived fruiting spurs.

4 **LEAF SHOOTS OR BUDS**
Small flat leaf shoots produce leaves and stems. Make a pruning cut just above a leaf shoot to force the branch's growth in the direction the bud points.

Pruning fruit trees

The branch collar is the optimal place to make a pruning cut. This swelled region where a branch attaches to the trunk of the tree has tissue that prevents decay.

Most fruit trees are pruned when they are leafless.

In freezing climates prune apples and pears in early spring just as the buds begin to swell, but prune stone fruits (such as peaches and cherries) after they bloom. Avoid pruning early in the dormant season, in November or December, in climates with severe weather. In moderate climates prune all but stone fruits anytime during the dormant period, which is between leaf fall and the beginning of bud swell in spring.

Don't leave stubs

When pruning limbs and small branches, make a pruning cut just beyond where the offending limb attaches to the larger branch or tree. This area is called the branch collar; it contains tissue that prevents decay. If disease does make its way into the branch through the wound, the chemicals in the branch collar will prevent it from infecting the rest of the tree.

When pruning branches more than 1½ inches in diameter, use a three-part cut. The first step is to saw an undercut from the bottom of the branch to about 6 to 12 inches out from the trunk and about one third of the way through the branch. Make a second cut about 3 inches beyond the undercut, cutting until the branch falls away. Cut the resulting stub back to the branch collar.

Types of pruning cuts

The two basic types of pruning cuts are heading and thinning cuts. Heading is the process of shortening a branch, not removing it entirely. It encourages buds on the remaining portion of the branch to sprout new growth.

Thinning removes a branch entirely and puts an end to growth. All thinning cuts are made to the base of the branch or watersprout (strongly upright growing shoot) so that there are no buds left to sprout new growth.

When you cut away part of a plant, you leave a wound that is susceptible to pests and diseases. To avoid trouble, always make wounds as small as possible. If a small, new sprout is growing in toward the center of the tree or toward the trunk or threatening to tangle with another branch when it grows longer, pinch it off now to prevent a more intense pruning cut later.

Always make cuts close to a node (point of leaf attachment or branching). Branches grow only at nodes, and if you leave too long a stub beyond the node, the stub will die and rot. Make cuts at a slight angle. A horizontal surface that holds water is more attractive to diseases and burrowing pests.

TEST GARDEN TIP

How to prune a fruit tree

Prune away dead, diseased, or damaged branches.

Remove branches that cross or rub against other branches. Rubbing branches cause wounds, making the tree susceptible to infection.

Thin dense growth in the top of the tree to allow sunlight to reach the center.

Reduce the height of excessively tall trees by cutting limbs out of the top, making cuts near the bark of a lower limb.

Remove all suckers—fast-growing shoots—that arise near the base of the tree.

Tools of the trade

Good pruning equipment ensures smooth cuts that are less likely to be invaded by insects. When you have these tools on hand, pruning will be a breeze.

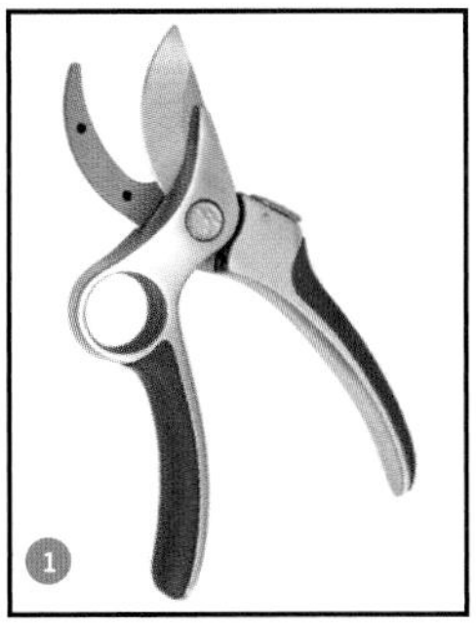
1

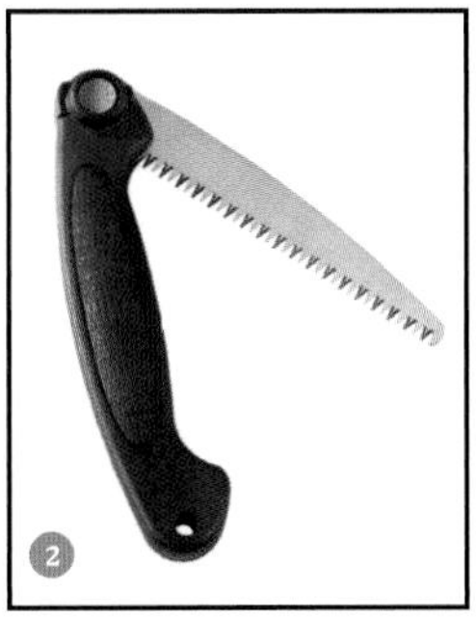
2

3

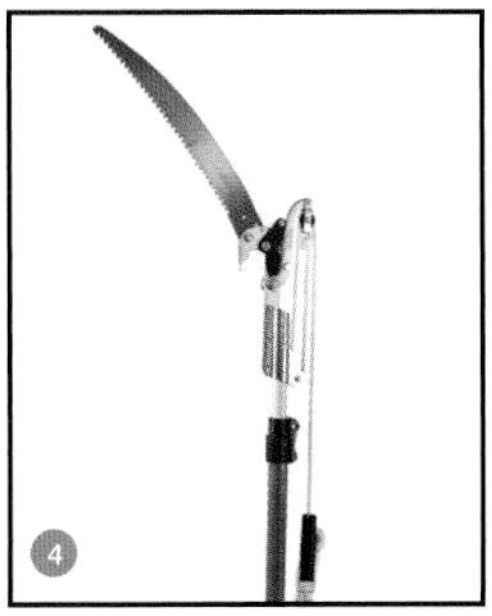
4

1 **HAND PRUNERS.** You'll use these more often than any other tool. Invest in a high-quality, ergonomically designed pair.

2 **FOLDING PRUNING SAW.** Small enough to tote around with ease but sharp enough to make quick work of cutting off limbs, a folding pruning saw is essential.

3 **LONG-HANDLED LOPPERS.** Thanks to the leverage provided by long-handed loppers, you can easily cut through 1-inch-thick branches. They are also indispensable for reaching into thorny brambles and dense shrubs.

4 **POLE PRUNERS.** Reach the top of a dwarf fruit tree from ground level with pole pruners. The handle can extend 10 to 15 feet high.

Training fruit trees

A mature tree that has been trained to an open center has several main branches that originate low on the trunk and radiate out evenly around the tree.

Fruit tree training involves a lot of careful pruning and a little bit of actual training— that is, tying or propping branches to create desired shapes. Training is not essential to good growth and fruiting, but it will keep the tree balanced in form and—more important—balanced in young and old fruit-producing wood.

There are three main training methods: open center, central leader, and modified central leader. Each method has its own advantages for the tree and the gardener.

Open center

Training to an open center creates a broad-spreading, vase-shape tree with sturdy, thick branches. This method is probably the most common shape for a fruit tree. It is used frequently for peaches and nectarines, which bear their fruits on one-year-old shoots. To train a young fruit tree into an open center form, begin by cutting it back at planting time to 2 feet above the ground for a dwarf and 3 feet for a standard tree. Cut just above a bud and then prune any side branches back to two buds.

After the tree has grown through the spring, summer, and fall and into its first winter dormancy, choose three or four branches attached to the trunk at wide angles. These branches are called scaffolds. Examining the tree from above, look for scaffold branches that radiate evenly around the trunk with almost equal distance between them. You should also try to maintain at least 6 inches of vertical distance between branches, with the lowest branch about 15 inches above the ground. If there are three such branches, cut off the vertical stem just above the top branch.

If there are fewer than three good branches, leave the vertical stem and choose the remaining scaffold branches during the next dormant season, cutting off the vertical stem just above the highest selected scaffold. The scaffolds you chose during the first dormant season will have grown side branches. Remove the weakest of these, leaving the main stem and laterals on each branch. Do not prune twiggy growth.

During the third dormant season, thin surplus shoots and branches. Select the strongest and best-placed terminal shoot near the tip of each scaffold branch as well as one or two other side shoots on each branch. Remove all other shoots on the branch. Leave the watersprouts that grow straight from the trunk to shade it and help produce food for the tree. Remove them the following year.

Central leader and modified central leader

Training to a central leader produces a tree with tiers of branches and a pyramidal outline, which allows all branches to intercept sunlight. Trees trained to a central leader have a strong central trunk. This method is especially good for species that produce weighty fruit, such as apples.

A modified central leader system produces both the strength of a central trunk and the sun-filled center of a vase shape. A single trunk is allowed to grow vertically with whorls of branches in the same manner as a central leader form. At the end of the third or fourth growing season, when the tree is 6 to 10 feet tall, cut off the main leader at about 3 or 4 feet. Then select main scaffold branches and prune to form a vase shape.

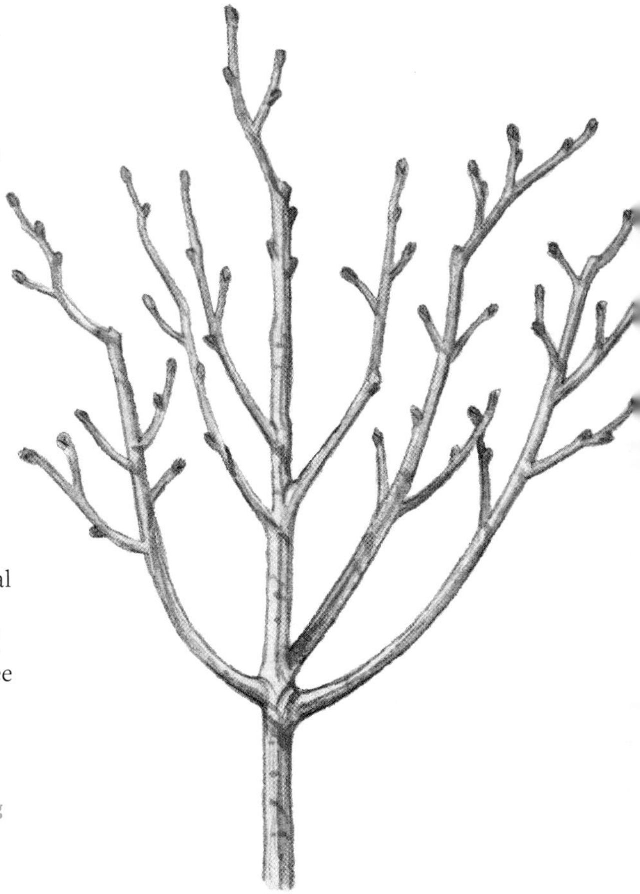

Training to a central leader creates a strong structure that is especially good for trees producing heavy fruit, such as apples.

Thinning fruits

Reducing the number of fruits on a tree is a form of pruning. Most common fruit trees require thinning in order to produce large, sweet, top-quality fruits. Thinning also moderates a tree's production, which encourages steadier production from year to year.

It is generally best to thin fruit before the natural fruit drop that occurs about three to six weeks after bloom. When fruits are about the size of a quarter, select the largest fruits and remove nearby fruit so there is a distance of twice the expected diameter of the mature fruit between all remaining fruits on the tree.

Pruning brambles

Red raspberries have a tendency to spread, creating a dense thicket if they are not kept in check with annual pruning. Snip off wayward canes at ground level.

Red, purple, and black raspberries

and other cane fruits in the *Rubus* genus of plants are collectively called brambles. Brambles produce fruit on biennial canes; the canes grow, produce fruit, and die within two years.

Pruning brings order to the bramble patch by removing second-year canes after fruiting and dead canes later in the season. Pruning is also a good way to control brambles' tendency to creep out of garden beds and become dense thickets.

While the pruning practices vary slightly among the specific types of brambles, there are a few basic tasks. Remove all dead, diseased, or damaged canes whenever you notice them in the garden. Prune the canes back to ground level.

Blackberries

When: late winter or early spring
First, remove injured and diseased canes as well as canes that fruited the previous year. Thin the remaining canes to two per linear foot of row. Shorten side branches to about 15 inches long. Trim the side branches of trailing types to about 18 inches long and thin them to six to eight canes per hill in northern regions, four to six in southern regions. Heaviest fruiting may occur at the stem tips, so avoid cutting canes back severely. When new canes reach about 36 inches, prune the shoot tips back by 3 or 4 inches to encourage side branch development.

Everbearing (fall-bearing) red and yellow raspberries

When: early spring and late summer, after harvesting summer crop
To prune for a summer crop and a fall crop: In spring remove any two-year-old canes along with any damaged, diseased, or dead canes. Then pinch the tips of canes where the previous fall crop was borne. The summer crop will fruit on the lower buds of these canes. Immediately after harvesting the summer crop, remove the two-year-old canes entirely.

To prune for one large late-summer crop: In early spring prune all canes back to ground level. This eliminates a summer crop, but the fall crop matures two weeks earlier—typically by late summer. Maintain the plants in a 1- to 2-foot-wide hedgerow, pruning wayward canes as necessary. No summer pruning is needed.

Summer-bearing red and yellow raspberries

When: early spring and late summer
Remove all weak, diseased, and damaged canes at ground level. Leave the most vigorous canes, those approximately ¼ inch in diameter when measured 30 inches from the ground. Cut as needed so remaining canes are spaced 6 inches apart. After the last harvest of summer, prune off the old fruiting canes at the soil surface.

Black and purple raspberries

When: early spring and early summer
Remove all the small, weak canes, leaving only four or five of the largest, most vigorous canes per clump or plant. Cut back the side branches to 12 inches long for black raspberries and 18 inches for purple raspberries.

Starting in late May or when the new growth reaches a height of 3 to 4 feet, cut the shoot tips back by about 3 or 4 inches. This pruning encourages side shoots, which will increase yield. Since all the new shoots will not reach the desired height at the same time, go over the planting about once a week until midsummer to remove shoot tips.

Above left: **Stem tips often produce the most blackberries. Avoid pruning them severely after early spring.**

Above middle: **Cutting back the tips of black and purple raspberries in early summer spurs plants to produce side branches and more fruit.**

Above right: **Everbearing and summer-bearing red raspberries are pruned differently. If you don't know what type of raspberries you are growing, it is simple to figure out. When does the fruit ripen? If all of your berries ripen over a couple of weeks in summer, your plants are summer bearing. If some fruit ripens in fall, the plants are everbearing.**

Pruning fruiting shrubs and grapes

Mature blueberry bushes produce the most fruit when they are pruned to contain 15 to 25 canes of varying ages. Annually remove the oldest canes at ground level.

Fruiting shrubs and grapes are some of the easiest

edibles to prune. They don't require a ladder and pruning doesn't involve working with long, thorny canes. Even though pruning blueberries, currants, and other shrubs is markedly easier than maintaining fruit trees and brambles, this annual chore is often neglected.

When riddled with leafy, excess growth and dead stems, fruiting shrubs and grapes produce a fraction of the fruit that they will when they are pruned annually. Grab a pair of sharp pruners and increase your plant's production with these pruning tips.

Fruiting shrubs

Blueberries, currants, gooseberries, and other small shrub fruits thrive when sunlight and air can easily reach the center of the shrub. Depending on the shrub's growth rate and age, annual pruning to create an open form will range from removing a few stems to snipping away what seems like half of the plant.

In early spring begin by cutting out all diseased, damaged, and crossing or rubbing stems. These troublesome stems are potential portals for pests. Next, examine the plant's form. If the center and top of the plant are dense with growth, remove two or three of the largest stems to encourage air and sunlight to reach the center of the shrub.

As a young fruiting shrub ages, annually remove one or two of the oldest stems to promote new, vigorous growth. In general, one-, two-, and three-year-old stems produce the most fruit.

Grapes

Grapevines produce fruit clusters on the previous season's growth. Canes that are two years or older will not produce fruit. If left unpruned, grapevines will quickly ramble out of control and fruit production will decrease due to overproduction of foliage.

Pruning grapes involves training the vines to grow on a trellis to maximize production. The most common trellis system for a home garden is the four-cane and six-cane Kniffin.

A four-cane Kniffin system consists of four fruiting canes, two on each side of the grape's trunk, trained onto two trellis wires. In addition, four short canes (called renewal spurs) are left on the vine. The renewal spurs will provide shoots and canes for next year's crop. A six-cane Kniffin system contains six fruiting canes on three trellis wires instead of four canes on two wires. In addition, six renewal spurs are left on the plant.

The best time to prune grapes is late in the dormant season, in late winter or early spring. Vines that are pruned after early spring are likely to bleed heavily, but the bleeding will not harm the vines. For step-by-step pruning instructions, see the guide below.

TEST GARDEN TIP

Thin grape clusters

Vigorous vines tend to overproduce; thinning fruit bunches helps the remaining grapes to grow large and sweet. Table grape clusters must be thinned to produce large grapes free from rot and insect damage. Thin clusters to one or two bunches per shoot by removing clusters when the grapes are no more than ⅛ inch in diameter.

Pruning grapes

1 **SELECT** the appropriate number of fruiting canes. These are the canes that will run along the wires on the training system. Select four canes for a four-cane Kniffin and so on. Tie a colorful piece of cloth to each cane you are saving to make it easy to identify when you are pruning off other canes.

2 **LEAVE** an equal number of renewal spurs or short canes; usually one renewal spur is left on each main cane. Remove all other canes.

3 **WEIGH** the pruned canes. The weight of the canes is used to determine the number of buds to leave on the grapevine.

4 **A SIMPLE FORMULA** called "30 plus 10" is a guide for how many buds to leave on the fruiting canes. For the first pound of canes removed, leave 30 buds. For each additional pound, leave an additional 10 buds. When counting the number of buds to be saved, include the buds on the fruiting canes and the renewal spurs.

5 **PRUNE** remaining canes and renewal spurs so the plant has the appropriate number of buds.

garden plans

Easy-to-follow planting plans make quick work of designing and planting your garden feast. You'll find planting plans for petite patios and large landscapes.

p. 136

CONTAINER GARDENS

Grow edibles anywhere with these self-contained pot gardens. Begin the season with fresh greens and then enjoy tomatoes, peppers, and onions in midsummer.

p. 140

INGROUND GARDENS

Whether you have a small plot near your patio or a more extensive backyard garden, these plans will produce tasty results.

p. 144

HERB GARDENS

Harvest handfuls of herbs with these herb garden planting plans. Productive and artful, herbs are an eyecatching part of the edible landscape.

ASK THE GARDEN DOCTOR

How can I have salad greens all summer?

ANSWER: Hot weather typically spells an end to cool-season greens. Plant varieties that are heat tolerant or slow to bolt (set seed). Move the container to a shadier, cooler location when temperatures warm.

Salad bowl

Toss together a big bowl of cool-season edibles including tender lettuce, violas, and pansies for garden-fresh spring salads. Sow lettuce seeds for a harvest in about 50 days, or go with nursery-started seedlings to enjoy your first harvest in half that time.

Essentials

container: 16-inch acid green glazed ceramic bowl

light: sun

water: keep soil moist

Ingredients

A. 3 pansy ('Ultima Baron Merlot')

B. 4 lettuce ('Esmeralda')

C. 3 ornamental cabbage ('Pigeon Red')

D. 3 viola ('Sorbet Primrose Babyface')

E. 3 viola ('Sorbet Yellow Delight')

F. 1 chives

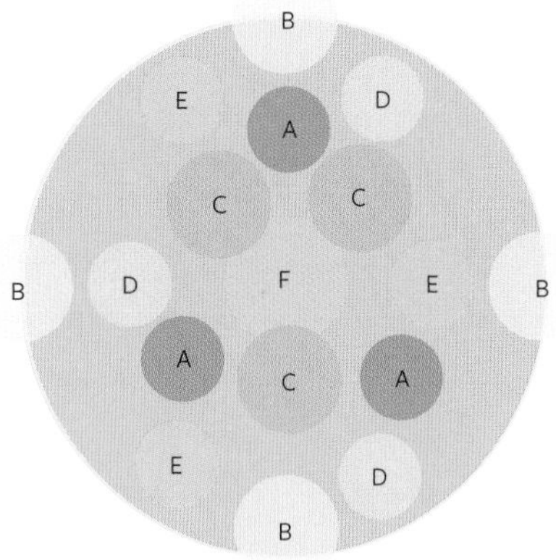

TEST GARDEN TIP

Snip flowers
Flower stalks on basil and parsley are signs that these plants are slowing production of their flavorful foliage. Snip away the flower stalks as soon as they appear to encourage plants to continue unfurling fresh new leaves that you can use to flavor your favorite dishes.

Small wonder

The best flavors of summer are contained in these four action-packed pots. Cultivar selection is key to the success of this patio-friendly container garden. If you cannot find the cultivars listed below, choose bush-form or dwarf varieties.

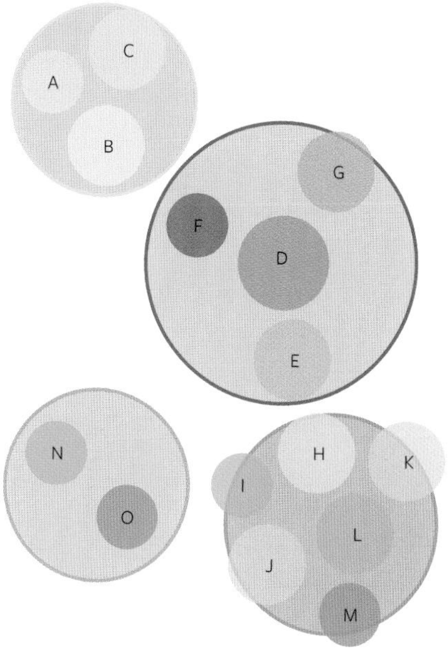

Essentials
container: 1 each, 12x12-, 15×24-, 20×32-, and 24×40-inch lightweight pots
light: sun
water: when soil begins to feel dry

Ingredients
15×24 lightweight pot
A. 1 nasturtium ('Jewel Mix')
B. 1 cantaloupe ('Sweet 'n Early')
C. 1 bush sweet potato ('Porto Rico')
24×40 lightweight pot
D. 1 tomato ('Health Kick')
E. 1 tomato ('Patio Princess')
F. 1 sweet pepper ('Red Delicious')
G. 1 hot pepper ('Mariachi')
20×32 lightweight pot
H. 1 kale ('Dwarf Blue Curled Vates')
I. 1 kale ('Red Winter')
J. 1 parsley Italian
K. 1 basil ('Summerlong')
L. 1 oregano
M. 1 marjoram
12x12-inch lightweight pot
N. 1 basil
O. 1 Italian parsley

ASK THE GARDEN DOCTOR

Can I grow any kind of tomato in a container?

ANSWER: You can, but tomatoes bred for growing in pots are easier to manage. Most tomatoes, including heirlooms, are tall and sprawling, making them tough to grow in a container. Go with a short, stocky container variety such as 'Patio', 'Tiny Tim', or 'Bush Big Boy'.

Taste of summer

Repurposed baskets are the perfect home for this collection of essential kitchen herbs and summer vegetables. Begin harvesting the herbs shortly after planting in late spring or early summer. The vegetables will begin ripening in midsummer and produce succulent fruits through early fall.

Essentials

container: repurposed wooden crates (produce or wine boxes); baskets. Line the crates or baskets with landscape fabric

light: sun

water: when soil begins to feel dry

Ingredients

Container #1
- A. 1 thyme
- B. 1 chives
- C. 1 pepper

Container #2
- D. 1 tomato ('Patio')
- E. 1 basil
- F. 1 parsley

Container #3
- G. 1 bush cucumber
- H. 5 onion

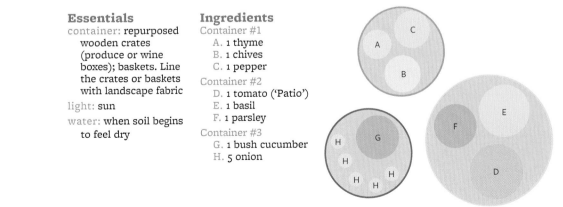

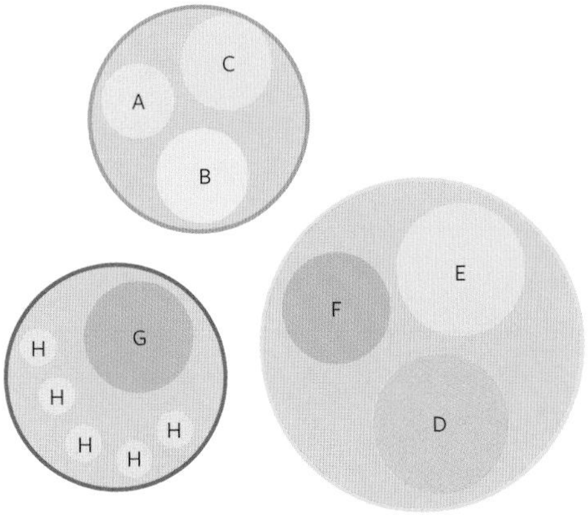

TEST GARDEN TIP

Stand tall

Many tomato, pepper, and eggplant cultivars need extra support when grown in containers. At planting time sink a sturdy stake into the container alongside the plant. Use strips of cloth or plant ties available at your garden center to loosely but sturdily tie the main stem to the stake.

Flowers and fruit

When this container combination is decked with glistening eggplant, you'll hesitate to harvest the meaty fruit. Rest assured that the more you pick, the more eggplant you'll get. Long-blooming annuals provide color from spring through fall.

Essentials

container: 20×24-inch lightweight pot

light: sun

water: when soil begins to feel dry

Ingredients

A. eggplant ('Little Fingers')

B. *Verbena bonariensis*

C. floss flower (*Ageratum*)

D. *Bacopa*

E. sage

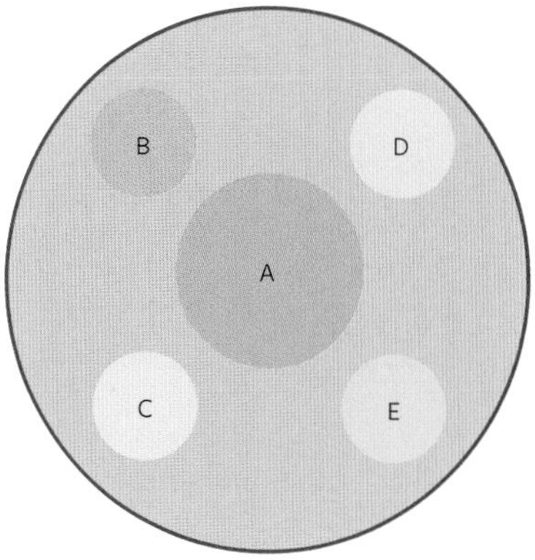

Seasonal harvest

Keep your pantry full with a succession garden where past-their-prime plants are regularly replaced with fresh varieties. This hardworking garden plan packs many vegetables in a tiny space, making it perfect for small yards, courtyards, or a community garden plot.

Essentials

plot: 8 feet long by 4 feet wide; build a raised bed using 2×6 lengths of untreated lumber if you like

light: full sun

water: water when the soil feels dry 1 inch below the surface

Ingredients

Spring

A. 7 kale
B. 4 chives
C. 12 lettuce
D. 6 sweet alyssum (*Lobularia maritima*)

Summer

E. 1 tomato
F. 2 pepper
G. 1 basil
H. 1 bush cucumber
I. 8 bean
J. 28 onion
K. 1 eggplant

Fall

L. 9 spinach
M. 8 cabbage
N. 20 lettuce
O. 2 broccoli

TEST GARDEN TIP

Compost annually

The soil supporting this long-season garden works overtime supplying valuable nutrients to plants. Replenish lost nutrients by annually blanketing the soil with a 2-inch-thick layer of compost in fall and mixing it into the top 6 to 8 inches of soil. If you forget to add compost in fall, spread a 2-inch-thick layer in spring.

SPRING

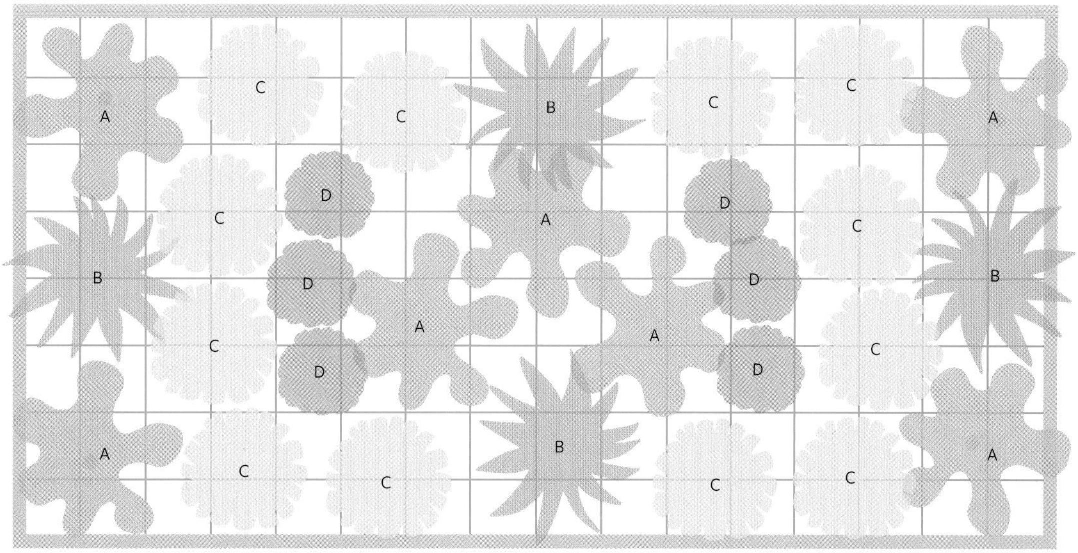

SUMMER

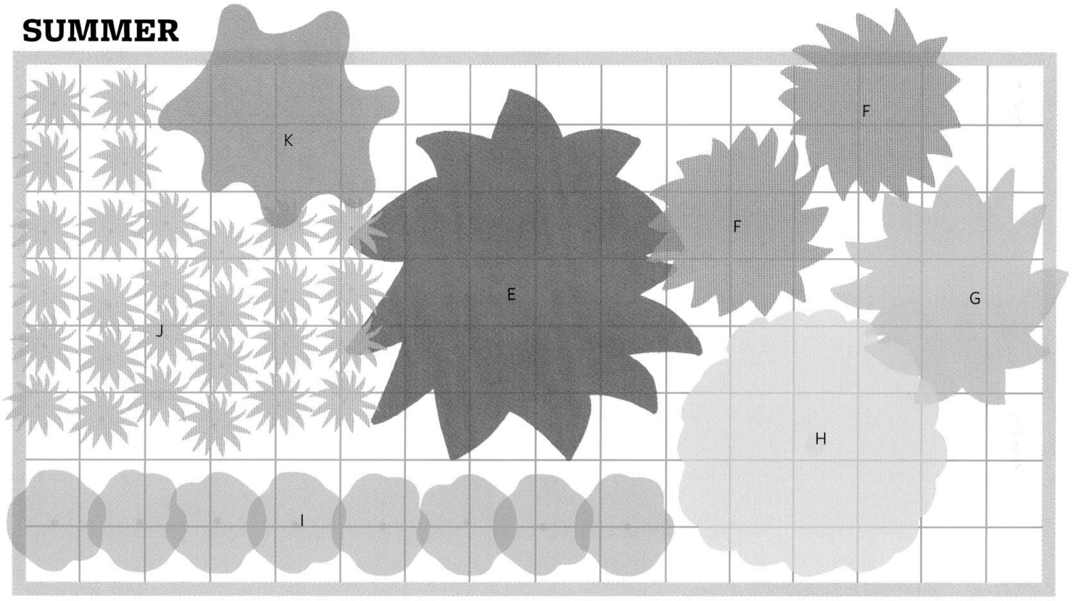

FALL

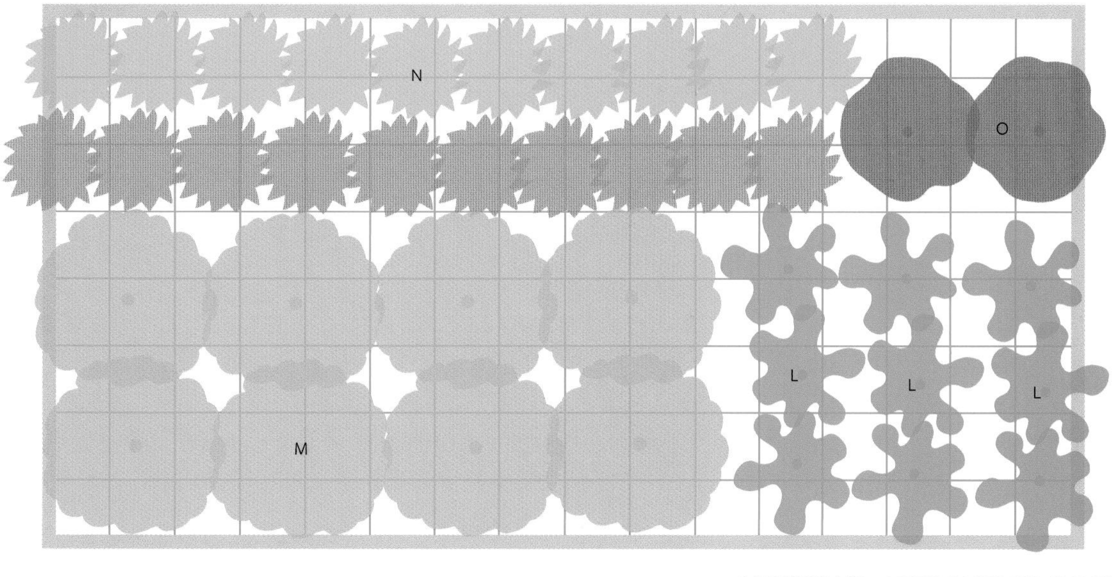

ASK THE GARDEN DOCTOR

Besides spinach and lettuce, what other vegetables grow in partial shade?

ANSWER: Vegetables that are grown for their foliage rather than for fruits or roots grow best in low-light areas, but there are a few exceptions. Try chard, cabbage, kale, leek, parsnip, pea, radish, and turnip. Most herbs will withstand a few hours of shade. Parsley, mint, and sage do well in partial shade.

Patio garden

Garden patioside with this bountiful plan that includes nutrient-rich spinach and broccoli and a host of tender lettuces. Enjoy the cool-season crops into summer by planting the garden on the east side of the house or in dappled shade to protect the plants from extreme heat.

Essentials

plot: 7×7 foot garden; 5×4 foot garden

light: part shade

water: keep soil moist

Ingredients

A. 7–10 romaine lettuce

B. 20–30 mesclun lettuce

C. 15 spinach

D. 15–30 carrot

E. 6 chives

F. 1 dwarf apple

G. 12 looseleaf lettuce

H. 7 broccoli

I. 5 pole bean

J. 1 cardoon

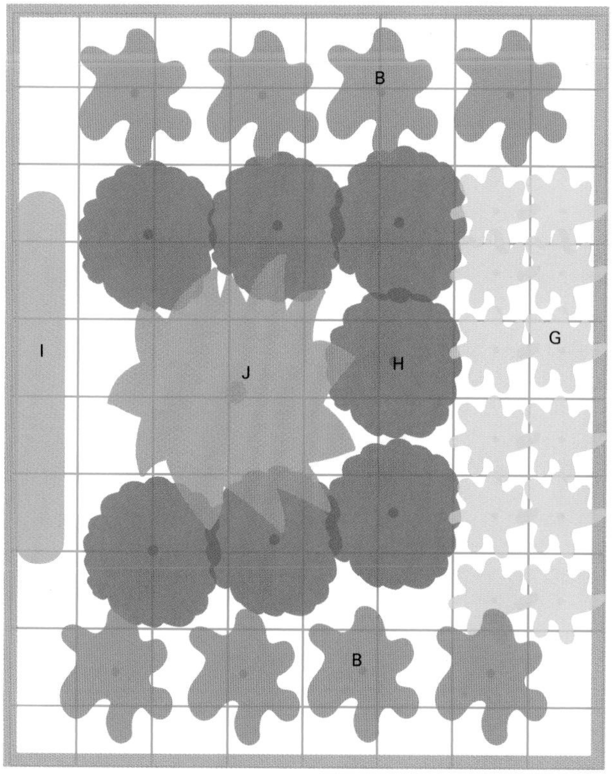

TEST GARDEN TIP

Dwarf trees

Petite versions of their standard-size cousins, dwarf fruit trees produce regular-size fruit on trees that stand 10 feet tall or less. Easy to grow and maintain in courtyards, patios, and other small spaces, dwarf fruit trees respond well to pruning and shaping and can even be pruned so they grow against a wall or fence. This intense method of training is called espalier.

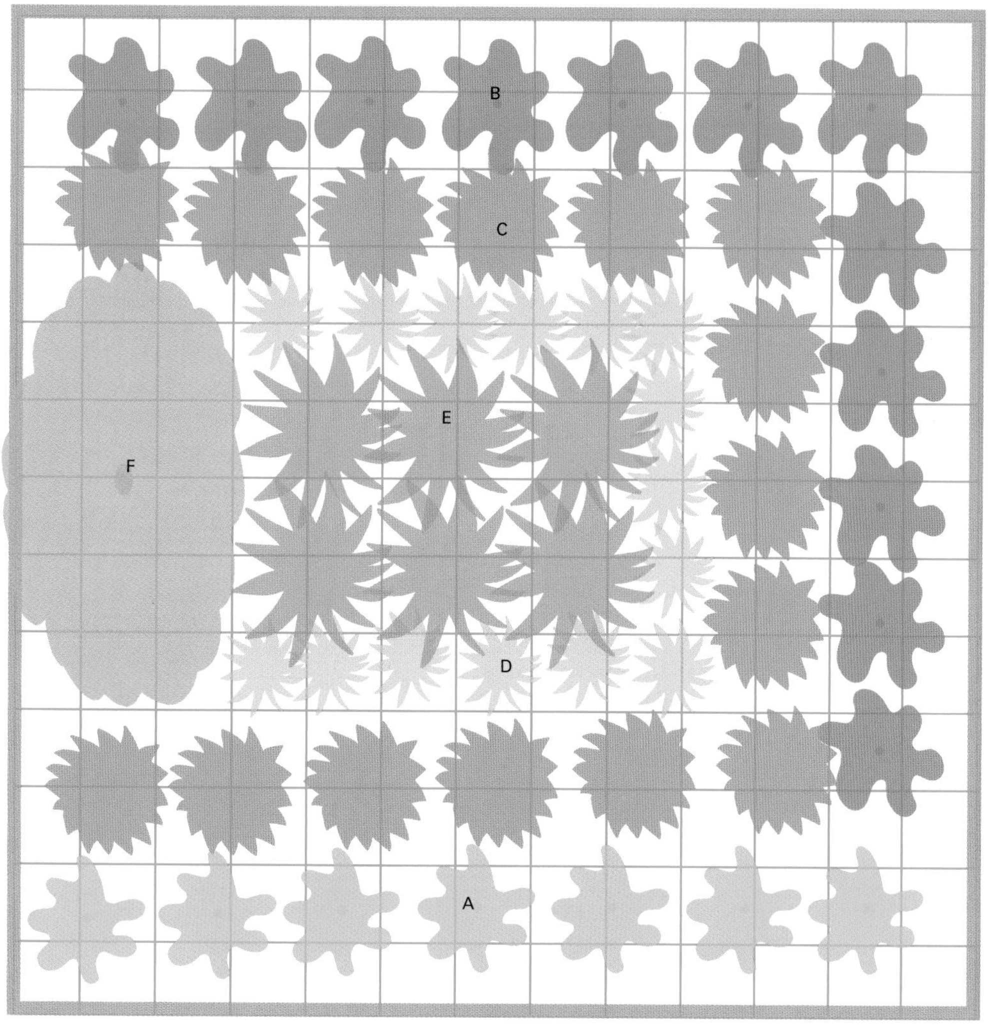

ASK THE GARDEN DOCTOR

Can I bring herbs inside in winter?

ANSWER: Yes, but don't expect lush growth. Indoor light is often not bright enough for sun-loving herbs. Place herbs in a bright, sunny window or grow them under a set of seed-starting lights. Water plants when the soil is dry 1 to 2 inches below the soil surface.

Fresh snips

With this container of fresh flavor right outside your door, grabbing a pinch of this or a sprig of that only takes a few seconds. Many herbs thrive in containers. Count on this compendium of versatile culinary herbs to offer leaves and stems from spring to fall.

Essentials

container: 24 inches diameter; at least 8 inches deep

light: sun or part shade

water: when soil begins to feel dry

Ingredients

A. 2 sage ('Icterina')
B. 2 sage ('Tricolor')
C. 2 oregano
D. 2 marjoram
E. 2 thyme ('Aureus')
F. 2 common thyme

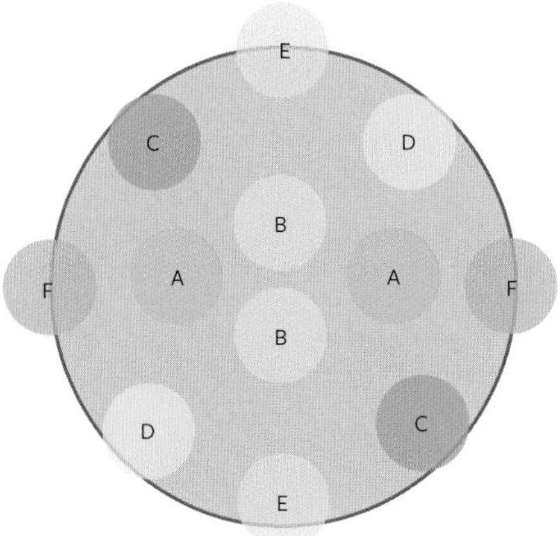

TEST GARDEN TIP

Time to divide

Most perennial herbs benefit from division every three to five years. Divide plants in spring by digging up the plant's entire root ball. Use a sharp spade to slice the root ball into two or three pieces, each with ample foliage and roots. Replant the divisions and water well until the plants are established.

Pretty herbs

Herbs are excellent landscape plants. They keep their good looks for most, if not all, of the growing season and often have a neat and tidy habit that requires little maintenance. An armillary sphere is used as a focal point in the center of this garden, but you could easily incorporate a pretty urn, piece of statuary, or dwarf tree instead—make the garden yours!

Essentials

container: 5×5 feet, edged with wood, brick, or stone

light: sun

water: When soil is dry 2 inches below the surface

Ingredients

A. armillary sphere
B. 2 winter savory
C. 2 lavender
D. 12 signet marigolds
E. 2 roses (Flower Carpet 'Yellow')
F. 2 golden oregano ('Aureum')

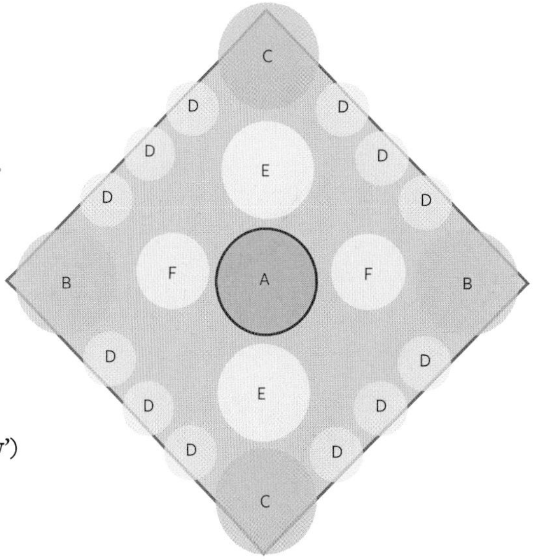

vegetable encyclopedia

Stock your garden with a variety of spring, summer, and fall vegetables and you'll enjoy months of garden-fresh flavor.

GROW YOUR FAVORITES

Grow the juiciest tomatoes, spiciest peppers, and most tender sweet corn with these easy-to-use growing guides for all your favorite vegetables.

TRY SOMETHING NEW

A small investment of a packet of seeds or a tiny transplant will introduce you to fresh new flavors.

KNOW ALL ABOUT IT

From when to plant to cues that indicate ultimate ripeness, each encyclopedia entry includes the nitty-gritty of growing tasty produce.

Artichoke

(Cynara scolymus)

This thistle-family member produces large attractive plants. If the edible flower buds are not harvested, they will unfurl to reveal fuzzy purple flowers. Bold leaves and a unique structure make artichoke a valuable member of the edible landscape as well as the vegetable garden.

YOU SHOULD KNOW

The edible part of an artichoke is the flower bud. Harvested while young and tender, the buds are wrapped with leaves, which are easy to pull away from the tender heart after steaming the bud in a saucepan of water for 30 to 45 minutes.

Best site

Plant in full sun and moist, well-drained soil. Artichoke requires ample, consistent moisture for best growth. It survives drought but will not produce well.

Planting

Start artichoke from root divisions or seeds. Root divisions are preferred because seeds often produce inferior plants. Plant root divisions after the last frost, 24 to 36 inches apart in rows that are about 36 inches apart. Amend the soil prior to planting by mixing in a 2-inch-thick layer of compost. Artichokes grow best in fertile, well-drained soil. If your soil doesn't fit that description, try planting on 6-inch-tall mounds or in raised beds.

varieties:

1. **GREEN GLOBE IMPROVED** is a widely grown variety that produces globe-shape, thick buds with a purple tinge on the leaf bracts.
2. **IMPERIAL STAR** is an excellent plant, producing fruit in midsummer.
3. **VIOLETTO** bears slightly elongated violet or green flower buds. It tolerates cold temperatures well and is a good choice for northern gardens.

Growing

A heavy feeder, artichoke benefits from fertilizing. Fertilize plants monthly with a high-nitrogen fertilizer. Keep the soil consistently moist by watering and mulching with organic mulch, such as straw.

When growing artichoke as a perennial, amend the soil around plants each spring with a 1- to 2-inch-thick layer of compost. In Zones 6 and 7, where artichokes are marginally hardy, cut back the plant in fall and cover with a 6-inch-thick layer of straw.

Harvest

Where artichoke is grown as a perennial, the main harvest is in spring. Plants continue producing throughout the growing season with a secondary peak in fall. Where artichoke is grown as an annual, harvest from midsummer through fall from a spring planting.

Harvest flower buds when the stalk has fully extended but the bud has not opened. Err on the side of early harvest rather than late harvest to avoid the delectable heart becoming woody. Harvest buds with a sharp knife, cutting 1 to 2 inches below the bud base. Some blackening of the outer leaves may occur if the buds are exposed to frost. After removing all the buds on a stalk, cut it back to the ground.

Store harvested artichokes in the refrigerator.

Pests and diseases

Slugs and snails feed on artichokes, making holes in leaves and deforming flower buds. Fungal diseases are most prevalent during rainy weather, resulting in damaged flower buds. Grow artichoke in raised beds and rotate crops to avoid these diseases.

Asparagus

(Asparagus officinalis)

Asparagus is one of the first vegetables to the table in early spring. The spears can be harvested for up to eight weeks. This hardy crop lasts for decades in the garden. Unharvested spears grow into tall fernlike stems that rejuvenate the roots for next year's crop.

Best site

Plant in full sun and moist, well-drained soil. Fertile soil is key. Mix a 2-inch-thick layer of compost into the planting site. Since asparagus is long lived, it is important to adequately prepare soil before planting.

Planting

Grow asparagus from rooted crowns. Find them at garden centers and through online sources. A month before the last frost in early spring, dig trenches 6 inches deep in clay soil or 8 to 10 inches deep in sandy soil. Space the trenches 36 inches apart.

Young asparagus plants benefit from phosphorus, so add a phosphate fertilizer to the planting trench according to package directions. Avoid fertilizers high in nitrogen.

varieties:

1. **UC 157** grows well in hot, dry climates.
2. **JERSEY SUPREME** has higher yields than others in the Jersey series, with good disease resistance.
3. **JERSEY GIANT** is the most widely available variety and features green spears with purple bracts. It has good disease resistance.

Set root crowns 12 inches apart in the trenches. Cover the crowns loosely with about 3 inches of soil. After the new plants grow for six weeks, add another 3 inches of compost-enriched soil. Finish filling the trench in fall.

Growing

Each spring spread a 2-inch-thick layer of compost over the planting bed. Weeding is critical to keep an asparagus bed productive. Hand weeding is the best option to avoid damaging roots. Water young asparagus plantings until established. Allow fernlike shoots to develop after the last spring harvest, but cut them back to the ground in fall after a hard freeze.

Harvest

Leave asparagus unharvested the year of planting. In the second year after planting crowns, harvest for only two weeks. In the third year, harvest for the usual five to eight weeks in midspring. Start harvesting when the spears are ½ inch in diameter. In the morning when it is still cool, cut or break off 7- to 9-inch-long spears with tightly closed tips. Harvest every day during warm weather and about every three days during cool weather.

To store, wrap asparagus in damp paper towels and place in a plastic bag in the refrigerator for up to one week.

Pests and diseases: Fusarium root rot fungal disease can attack crowns and eventually destroy them. Rust disease can disfigure and kill the ferny stalks and branches. To avoid these problems, select disease-resistant varieties.

YOU SHOULD KNOW

Tender asparagus spears are tastiest when eaten as soon as possible after harvest. Roasted or blanched, these flavor- and vitamin-packed vegetables need little more than a sprinkle of coarse salt to become a quick and easy side dish or healthy snack.

Bean (*Glycine, Phaseolus, Vicia, Vigna* species)

Beans are some of the easiest vegetables to grow. Perfect for a first-time gardener or a child's vegetable garden, beans quickly germinate and produce copious amounts of tasty treats. They are available in a variety of shapes, colors, and sizes; some plants produce colorful flowers, pods, and seeds. From snap beans to edamame—you can grow them all. No matter the name, expect a bountiful bean harvest.

Best site

Plant in full sun and moist, well-drained soil. Beans are adaptable to many soil types as long as the soil drains readily. They can also be grown in almost any climate.

Types of beans

Snap beans (*Phaseolus vulgaris*) are harvested when young, before the seeds mature. Plants may be bush or vining in form. Once called string beans, snap beans received a new name when plant breeders eliminated the fibrous seam along one side of the pod. This group includes green beans, wax, and purple-pod varieties.

Shelling beans are harvested after the seeds mature but the pods are still green.

Dried beans are harvested after the pod is dried and the seeds mature. While some beans can be harvested at any stage, most varieties are best at only one stage. If you would like to grow beans for drying, select a dried bean variety rather than allowing snap beans to remain on the bush until they are dry. Dried beans vary widely by color and size.

Pole beans are the vining form of snap beans, and often require a slightly longer growing season than snap beans. Grow them on a sturdy trellis that is at least 6 feet tall.

Lima beans (*Phaseolus lunatus*) develop flat pods with several seeds in each that may be harvested as shelling beans or as dried beans. The plants may be either bush or vining.

Asparagus beans (*Vigna unguiculata*) climb 8 to 12 feet tall and need support. They produce beans that are more than 10 inches long.

Fava beans (*Vicia faba*) grow into majestic 5-foot-tall plants. They grow best in cool climates or as a winter crop in warm climates.

Edamame (*Glycine max*), also called soybeans, grow on shrubby plants that are 2 to 3 feet tall.

Southern peas (*Vigna unguiculata*), also called cowpeas, come in bush and vining varieties.

Planting

Plant seeds in the garden after the danger of frost passes in spring. Daytime temperatures between 70° and 80°F are ideal. Before planting, mix a 1-inch-thick layer of compost into the soil. Sow snap bean seeds 1 inch deep and 2 to 3 inches apart in rows 24 inches apart. Thin seedlings to 4 to 6 inches apart after they form true leaves.

Plant pole and asparagus beans so they can climb 6- to 8-foot-tall poles arranged in a tepee. Plant three to five seeds 2 to 3 inches apart. Plant southern peas 6 to 12 inches apart in rows that are 24 to 36 inches apart.

For a continuous harvest, sow snap beans every two to three weeks until midsummer. Beans will ripen into fall.

Fava beans are the exception in the heat-loving bean family. They require cool temperatures to grow and produce best. Staking or trellising is also recommended. Plant favas in early spring, about two to four weeks before the last frost. In warm areas plant fava beans in fall for a winter harvest. Plants can survive temperatures down to 15°F. Space the seeds 4 to 6 inches apart in rows 24 to 36 inches apart. Thin seedlings to 12 inches apart.

YOU SHOULD KNOW
Whether you eat them steamed, stir-fried, or blanched and marinated in herb vinaigrette, fresh-picked snap beans have a sweet flavor and crispness that can't be beat.

bush snap bean varieties:

1 **DERBY** is a tender bean and exceptional producer. Good disease-resistance. 7 inches green. 57 days.
2 **ROC D'OR** has thin, yellow pods and is very productive. 6 inches yellow. 52 days.
3 **BLUE LAKE 274** is widely adapted and a reliable producer in all climates. 6 inches green. 58 days.
PROVIDER is known for fast growth. Expect beans to ripen about one week before other green varieties. 5 inches green. 50 days.
VENTURE is another quick grower that is a great choice if you would like to harvest beans over a couple of weeks. Harvest as many as you would like and leave others to ripen a bit longer; they'll remain tender for days. 5–6 inches green. 55 days.

Growing

Shallowly weed around the rows and poles, being careful not to disturb the tender bean roots. When the beans are 3 to 4 inches tall and the planting is free of weeds, mulch the area with a 2- to 3-inch-thick layer of straw, pine needles, chopped leaves, or grass clippings to conserve soil moisture and prevent weeds.

Keep beans evenly watered, especially during flowering and fruiting. Aim to provide about 1 inch of water per week. Apply fertilizer only if the soil is poor, in which case incorporating a 3-inch-thick layer of compost at planting time often provides all necessary nutrients. Beans can also be fertilized with a balanced liquid fertilizer during watering.

Harvest

Harvest snap bush beans 40 to 60 days after planting, when the pods are full and 5 to 8 inches long. Modern varieties are considered stringless, but pick beans before the seeds reach full size or the pods will become tough and chewy. Harvest filet beans, or flat pod beans, when they are very slender—about ¼ inch in diameter.

Snap bush beans tend to produce all at once, making them perfect for canning or freezing. After two or three pickings, bush beans are mostly finished producing and can be pulled out. Plant another bean crop, or if it is late in the season, a cool-season vegetable such as spinach where the beans were growing. To avoid a glut of bush beans, stagger your plantings, sowing short rows every two weeks.

Snap pole beans and asparagus beans begin producing around 60 to 80 days after planting and produce handfuls of 6- to 12-inch-long beans until frost.

Store freshly harvested beans unwashed in plastic bags in the refrigerator for several days.

pole snap bean varieties:

1 **ROMANO** is an Italian bean, known for its flat pod. It has a distinctive, full flavor and produces heavy yields. Expect it to produce tender, stringless beans until frost. 6 inches flat green. 70 days.

2 **KENTUCKY WONDER** is an old-fashioned, vigorous variety that is a favorite of many gardeners. This disease-resistant variety also comes in bush form. 8 inches green. 67 days.

edamame varieties:

1 **SAYAMUSUME** is one of the highest yielding edamame. Expect three or four light green beans per pod. 85 days.

ENVY is a very early-maturing edamame variety. Expect two or three flavorful beans per pod. 75 days.

Harvest shelling beans once the seeds have reached full size, about 80 days from seeding but before the pods dry. Harvest dried beans around 100 to 120 days after planting, when the pods have changed color and are fully mature. Because pods split and can drop beans when dry, set a wide pan beneath the plants when picking. In humid climates pull out the plants when the pods have matured and suspend plants upside down to dry in a shady, dry room with good air circulation. Store dried beans in an airtight jar in a cool, dry location.

Harvest lima beans, edamame, and fava beans 70 to 85 days after sowing the crop, when the seeds have reached full size and the pods are plump. Store shelled beans unwashed in plastic bags in the refrigerator for a few days.

Pests and diseases

The Mexican bean beetle is the main pest that attacks beans. This brown beetle has black spots and is sometimes confused with the beneficial ladybug beetle. The soft-bodied yellow Mexican bean beetle larvae eat bean foliage, reducing the bean harvest. To control this pest, crush eggs and larvae by hand and spray adults with a pest control product. Cutworms attack germinating bean seedlings, and Japanese beetles can also feed on bean foliage.

Rust is a serious disease of beans. This fungus causes orange spots on the leaves and bean pods. To avoid spreading the disease, don't weed after a rain or early in the morning when foliage is still wet from dew. Grow disease-resistant bean varieties to avoid the problem.

Animals, such as woodchucks, deer, and rabbits, can quickly decimate a crop. Fence or use animal repellents to deter these pests.

1

2

3

shelling and dried bean varieties:

1 **BLUE SPECKLED TEPARY** is a good choice for the Southwest, especially desert climates. It has brown seeds with red speckles. 90 days dried.

2 **CANNELLINI** is a white kidney-shape bean with mild flavor. Plants have a bush habit. 80 days shelled; 100 days dried.

3 **SCARLET RUNNER** produces lima-shape beans and is commonly grown for its showy red flowers. The seeds of this pole bean are red with black blotches. 70 days shelled; 115 days dried.

PINTO produces buff-color seeds that are speckled with brown. It has a bush habit. 90 days dried.

1

2

lima bean varieties:

1 **FORDHOOK 242** is an adaptable variety, tolerating cold, heat, and drought. It has a bush habit and produces three to five white beans per pod. 85 days.

2 **JACKSON WONDER** is a baby lima bean that is good for cool-summer areas. It has a bush habit and produces three to four light brown seeds per pod. 75 days.

Beet *(Beta vulgaris)*

Beets do double-duty in the kitchen. Both their roots and shoots are edible. The roots come in striped, yellow, pink, and red, and the greens sometimes have red stems. Colorful leaves and stems make beets a great choice for the edible landscape. Beets grow fast, making it possible to have multiple crops a year.

YOU SHOULD KNOW

Because beets contain more natural sugar than starch, they are particularly tasty roasted in a hot oven. Roasting concentrates the sugar rather than leaching it out into cooking water when the beets are boiled. Beets are done when they are easy to prick with a fork.

Best site

Plant in full sun or part shade and loose, well-drained soil. Beets tolerate low fertility, growing well in sandy loam soil, but they require consistent moisture.

Planting

Mix a 1- to 2-inch-thick layer of compost into the soil before planting. Beets need loose, stone-free soil. Remove any debris before planting and if your soil is poorly drained or heavy, build a raised bed for growing beets.

Sow seeds in the garden in spring two weeks before the average last frost. Sow seeds ½ inch deep and 1 inch apart in rows 15 inches apart. Keep the seedbed well watered to increase germination. The ideal temperature for growing beets is 60 to 65°F. In cool-summer areas sow every three weeks into the summer for a continual harvest. In warm-summer areas sow in spring and again in fall so that the roots mature during cool periods.

Beets are closely related to Swiss chard and spinach. Avoid planting in a site that hosted either of these crops during the previous year.

Growing

When beets are 4 inches tall, thin to 4 inches apart. Cut rather than pull plants when thinning, to avoid disturbing nearby roots. Save the thinnings for salads. Hand weed carefully until the beets are established in the bed. Mulch around plants with a 1- to 2-inch-thick layer of organic material to deter weeds and conserve soil moisture. Keep beets well watered so that sweet, blemish-free roots develop.

Harvesting

Collect beet greens when they are 4 to 6 inches tall. Beet roots can be eaten at any time during their development, but they are best harvested around 55 to 80 days after seeding or when they are 1 to 2 inches in diameter. When harvesting, leave 1 inch of foliage on the root to keep it from bleeding during cooking. Beets can be stored for three to four months if kept in conditions similar to a root cellar—temperatures near freezing with high humidity. Otherwise, store the roots in a refrigerator crisper at 40°F.

Pests and diseases

Aphids, leaf miners, and flea beetles can attack beet leaves, causing holes. Cover plantings with floating row covers to prevent this damage.

1

2

varieties:

1. **LUTZ GREEN LEAF/WINTERKEEPER** features green leaves, pink stems, and purplish red roots; its roots stay tender even when allowed to grow large. 80 days.
2. **GOLDEN** has green leaves with yellow stems and sweet golden roots. 55 days.

Broccoli

(*Beta oleracea* Italica group)

Easy to grow and packed with nutrients, broccoli is one of the first vegetables to mature in late spring. This cool-season crop grows best when daytime temperatures are around 60°F. Plant it in early spring and again in late summer for harvest in fall.

YOU SHOULD KNOW
A rich source of antioxidants, broccoli packs more nutrients than any other vegetable. Delicious raw or blanched for three or four minutes and dusted with fresh cracked black pepper, it is a quick and easy side dish.

Best site

Plant in full sun and rich, well-drained soil. Work a 2-inch-thick layer of compost into the soil before planting.

To help reduce diseases, do not plant broccoli or other cole crops, such as cabbage and Brussels sprouts, in the same location more than once every three years.

Planting

Direct-sow seeds in spring two weeks before your last frost date or start transplants indoors four weeks before setting them in the garden. Plant a fall crop in late summer or early fall. Where winters are mild, such as along the Pacific and Gulf coasts, grow overwintering varieties in fall to mature the following spring.

Sow seeds ½ inch deep and 3 inches apart in rows 36 inches apart. Thin seedlings to 18 inches apart when the second set of leaves appears.

Growing

Hand weed established plants, being careful not to disturb their shallow roots. Keep the soil evenly moist by applying 1 inch of water per week. Mulch the broccoli bed with a 2- to 4-inch layer of organic material to prevent weed growth, conserve soil moisture, and keep the soil cool.

Ten or more days with high temperatures reaching only about 40°F causes some cultivars to flower prematurely, producing small heads called buttons. Cover transplants with a floating row cover during periods of cool weather.

Harvest

Most varieties of broccoli produce one main head and then smaller side heads after the main head is cut. Sever heads with a sharp knife when they're tight and firm, keeping a 6-inch stem. Slice the stem at an angle to reduce the likelihood of the stem rotting. Heads with buds beginning to separate into yellow flowers indicate the broccoli is past its peak.

Harvest smaller side heads as they mature. The flavor is best right after harvest, but broccoli heads can be stored unwashed in open plastic bags in the refrigerator's crisper drawer.

Pests and diseases

Cabbageworm and cabbage looper are the primary insect pests of broccoli. The small green caterpillars eat holes in the leaves and are often found hiding, but dead, in harvested heads when cooked. Woodchucks and rabbits eat seedlings.

varieties:

1. **PACKMAN** bears a 9-inch-diameter main head and is ideal in the South because it produces early and tolerates heat. 52 days.
2. **GREEN GOLIATH** Widely adapted hybrid produces a tight, 8-inch-diameter main head that is good for freezing. 55 days.
3. **ARCADIA** is a disease-resistant variety for wet areas such as the Pacific Northwest. It produces an 8-inch-diameter main head. 69 days.

Brussels sprouts

(*Brassica oleracea* Gemmifera group)

Brussels sprouts look like tiny cabbages clustered on a stalk. This cool-season plant is often planted in summer for a late fall harvest because sprouts take on a pleasing, sweet flavor when they are exposed to a few light frosts.

YOU SHOULD KNOW

A surprisingly high source of protein, Brussels sprouts have a deliciously delicate flavor and crisp texture when they're cooked to perfection. Avoid mushy, overcooked sprouts by cutting the heads in half and steaming or boiling them. Remove them from the water the second the bright green color begins to fade.

Best site

Plant in full sun or light shade and moist, well-drained soil. Work a 2-inch-thick layer of compost into the soil before planting.

To help reduce diseases, do not plant Brussels sprouts or related crops, such as collards, cauliflower, and broccoli, in the same location more than once every three years.

Planting

Plant transplants or sow seeds in the garden in early summer, at least 100 days before the first average fall frost. Brussels sprouts that mature in cool fall weather have a flavor that is much sweeter than those that mature in the summer. Avoid bitterness by delaying planting until early to midsummer. Space plants 18 inches apart in rows 24 inches apart.

varieties:

1. **DIABLO HYBRID** is a late-maturing variety with sprouts that keep well on the plant once they've matured. 110 days.
2. **JADE CROSS E** produces uniform sprouts all the way up the stalk. 90 days.
3. **RED RUBINE** is an heirloom variety with purplish red sprouts that hold their pretty color even after cooking. 95 days.

Growing

Plants do best when they receive about 1 inch of water a week. Hand weed these shallow-rooted plants to avoid damaging their delicate surface roots, then mulch around plants with a 2- to 4-inch-thick layer of organic material, such as straw, pine straw, or grass clippings. Stake mature plants to prevent them from blowing over during storms.

Harvest

Brussels sprouts' flavor sweetens with a touch of frost. After a few light frosts and the sprouts are 1 to $1\frac{1}{2}$ inches in diameter, harvest them with a sharp knife. First remove the leaf under the sprout, then the sprout. To hasten maturity, remove the growing tip (top of the stalk) when the bottom sprouts measure $\frac{1}{2}$ inch in diameter; sprouts should be ready about two weeks later.

The fresher the sprouts, the better the flavor, so do not let refrigerator storage exceed one or two days. To store, remove damaged outer leaves and store unwashed sprouts in a plastic bag in the refrigerator's crisper.

Pests and diseases

Cabbageworm and cabbage looper are the two primary insect pests of Brussels sprouts. The small green caterpillars riddle the leaves with holes and may be found hiding in harvested sprouts. Aphids and cutworms also attack seedlings. Woodchucks and rabbits munch on young seedlings.

Cabbage

(Brassica oleracea Capitata group)

Cool weather and cabbage plants partner to create dense, vitamin-packed green or red cabbage heads in early summer and late fall. Plant in early spring so the crop matures before the heat of summer, or plant in midsummer to take advantage of cool fall temperatures.

1

Best site

Plant in full sun or light shade and moist, well-drained soil. Cabbage is an exceptionally heavy feeder; work a 2-inch-thick layer of compost into the soil before planting.

To help reduce diseases, do not plant cabbage or related crops, such as Brussels sprouts and broccoli, in the same location more than once every three years.

Planting

Start from transplants or seeds. For a spring crop, plant frost-tolerant transplants outside as soon as the soil can be worked. Or start from seeds planted ½ inch deep and thinned to 12 to 24 inches apart in rows about 32 inches apart. Plant small-headed varieties closer together.

For a fall crop, set out transplants or sow seeds in midsummer. If possible, select a site where young plants will have some shade from the intense summer sun.

Growing

Cabbage needs ample water to thrive. Provide about 1 inch of water a week. Carefully weed around shallow-rooted cabbage plants. Spread a 2- to 4-inch-thick layer of mulch around plants to prevent weeds and conserve soil moisture. Apply high-nitrogen fertilizer about four weeks after transplanting. Avoid fertilizing during head formation; fertilizing at this time causes fast growth, which can lead to cracked heads.

Harvest

Harvest cabbage anytime after heads form. For greatest yield, cut heads when they feel solid. Harvest by cutting heads at their base with a sharp knife. After cabbage heads mature, a sudden heavy rain may cause them to split.

After the first head is harvested, small cabbage heads or sprouts may form at the plant base. Allow them to grow and form 2- to 4-inch-diameter baby cabbages.

Unwashed smooth-leaf cabbage can be stored for as long as two months in the refrigerator. Store savoy (crinkled-leaf) varieties for only a few days.

Pests and diseases

Cabbageworm and cabbage looper are the two primary insect pests of cabbage. The small green caterpillars eat holes in the leaves. Aphids and cutworms also attack seedlings. Woodchucks and rabbits munch small seedlings.

2

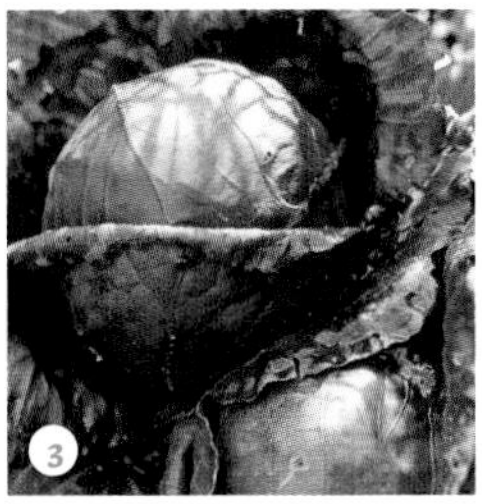
3

varieties:

1 **DANISH BALL HEAD** is a green cabbage that is best for late-season planting. This heirloom stores well in winter. 100 days.

2 **SAVOY QUEEN** produces deep green crinkled leaves and has great heat tolerance. 88 days.

3 **RED METEOR** is a red cabbage with a large firm head. It is a good choice for both spring and fall. 75 days.

YOU SHOULD KNOW

The top half of a head of cabbage is more tender than the bottom half. If practical, slice the head horizontally and use the top raw in salads and slaw, and the bottom half in cooked recipes.

Carrot (*Daucus carota sativus*)

Add crunch to your garden-fresh meal with carrots. Whether you eat them raw, sautéed, or cooked, homegrown carrots have a distinct, sweet flavor that will make you want to plant an extra row next year. This easy-to-grow root crop produces the best roots in loose, stone-free soil. If your soil is heavy clay or full of rocks, plant carrots in a raised bed.

Best site

Plant in full sun and moist, well-drained soil. Deep, loose soil is a must. Roots can become twisted or forked in heavy or stony soil.

Types of carrots

Baby carrots are just 1 to 4 inches long, making them a good choice for heavy soils and containers. They are quick to mature.
Chantenay carrots grow up to 5 inches long. This type of carrot is wide at the top and tapers to a slender point.
Danvers carrots are known for their strong flavor. They grow up to 7 inches long.
Imperator carrots are long and slender, usually reaching about 10 inches long.
Nantes carrots are more cylindrical than tapered. They are often considered to have the best flavor and grow to about 7 inches long.

Planting

Before planting, rake the soil smooth and remove any rocks. Sow seeds in the garden two to four weeks before the last frost date, or in warm climates, in late summer and autumn for winter or spring crops. Carrots taste best when grown at temperatures between 60 and 70°F. Sow seeds ¼ inch deep, ½ inch apart, in rows 12 to 24 inches apart. Or broadcast seeds in a wide bed.

Growing

Carrots are slow to germinate. They often germinate sporadically over a one- to three-week period. To speed germination, water lightly daily if the soil is dry. To mark a row of carrots, sow radishes in the same row. They germinate quickly and mark the row.

Thinning seedlings is critical to producing long, uniform carrots. Thin to 1- to 4-inch spacing (depending on the variety and size of root desired) before the plants are 2 inches tall.

Carrots are not drought tolerant. Seeds need constant moisture while germinating. After the seedlings appear, water deeply every few days as needed. Carrots don't compete well with weeds so hand weed, especially early in the season, to give the roots room to expand. After weeding, apply an organic mulch such as straw around rows to conserve soil moisture and prevent weed growth. As the carrots mature, cut back on water or the roots may crack.

If the tops of carrot roots show aboveground, cover them with mulch or soil. Exposed carrot roots turn green and bitter.

Harvest carrots into fall in cool climates by making additional sowings every three weeks until midsummer.

Harvest

Begin pulling carrots as soon as they're at full color. This is also a good way to thin rows to give the remaining carrots a chance to grow larger. Small roots tend to be juicier and more tender. If the tops break off when you pull them, use a garden fork to gently pry the roots loose. In northern areas wait until after a heavy frost before digging the rest of the carrots; the cold will increase their sweetness.

Carrots can be overwintered in the ground. In fall cut the foliage to about 1 inch tall and mulch the plants with a 6- to 8-inch-thick layer of straw.

Carrots will keep for several months in the refrigerator in perforated plastic bags. The roots store better when the leaves are removed.

Pests and diseases

Carrot roots can be damaged due to several causes. Too much nitrogen in the soil causes hairy roots. Forked or deformed roots may be caused by overwatering, rocks or debris in the soil, or insect damage.

YOU SHOULD KNOW
Loaded with beta carotene, a powerful antioxidant, carrots are tasty and good for you. Grow a rainbow of orange, purple, yellow, and white carrots to create an eyecatching appetizer plate.

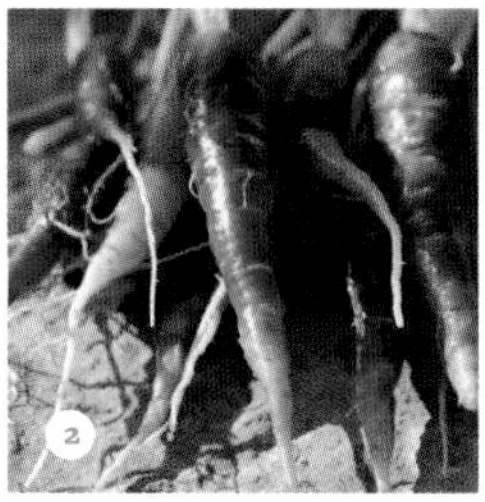

varieties:

1 **ROYAL CHANTENAY** has strong tops, making for easy pulling. Great for juice or storage, this variety is bright orange. 5–6 inches long. 70 days.

2 **PURPLE HAZE** has purple skin, an orange core, and sweet tender flesh. Its color fades when cooked. 10–12 inches long. 70 days.

3 **DANVERS HALF LONG** is a very easy-to-grow variety with sweet flavor and tender flesh. It produces notably uniform roots. It's a good choice for all soils. 6–8 inches long. 78 days.

4 **BOLERO HYBRID** is a disease-resistant Nantes variety that is great for growing in fall and stores exceptionally well. 7–8 inches long. 75 days.

5 **THUMBELINA** is a small, almost round baby carrot about the size of a silver dollar. It's a good variety for baking. 2 inches long. 65 days.

Cauliflower (*Brassica oleracea,* Botrytis group)

Growing cauliflower requires a little planning and some luck. Unlike its easy-to-grow cousin broccoli, cauliflower has exacting growing requirements. It thrives in moist soil and consistently cool weather that does not rise above 70°F or dip below freezing.

YOU SHOULD KNOW
Available in purple, chartreuse, and orange in addition to the typical white, cauliflower is an eyecatching addition to the table and the garden.

Best site

Plant in full sun and well-drained fertile soil. Before planting, mix a 2-inch-thick layer of compost into the soil.

To help reduce diseases, do not plant cauliflower or other cole crops, such as cabbage and broccoli, in the same location more than once every three years.

Planting

Start cauliflower from transplants in early spring or fall. In spring set out transplants no earlier than two to three weeks before the last frost. Cauliflower is sensitive to cold temperatures. Start cauliflower early enough so that it matures before the heat of summer but not so early that it is injured by cold. Plant fall crops 90 days before your first fall frost date.

Cauliflower needs plenty of room to grow. Space plants 18 to 24 inches apart in rows 36 inches apart. Fertilize with a complete fertilizer such as 5-5-5 at planting time and water frequently to keep soil consistently moist.

varieties:

1. **SNOW CROWN HYBRID** is a large, white variety that is heat and cold tolerant and matures quickly. 60 days.
2. **GRAFFITI** is a purple variety that turns smoky purple when cooked. 80 days.
3. **CHEDDAR HYBRID** produces orange heads that remain orange after cooking. 68 days.

Growing

Cauliflower produces the best heads when it grows vigorously from seedling stage until harvest. After fertilizing at planting, fertilize again one month later with a high-nitrogen fertilizer such as 15-5-5.

When the head begins to form (the plant shows 2 to 3 inches of white curd at the growing point) it is ready to blanch. Blanching ensures a bright white head and a mild flavor. To blanch, wrap the long outer leaves over the head and hold them together with twine, clothespins, or rubber bands. Many modern varieties naturally wrap leaves over their heads and don't need any help. Color varieties don't need blanching.

Harvest

Pick a head when it is 6 to 8 inches in diameter, about 10 days after blanching. Harvest before the curds separate and develop a ricelike appearance. Use a sharp knife to cut the head below the inner leaves. Store cauliflower in the refrigerator.

Pests and diseases

Cabbageworm and cabbage looper are the two primary insect pests of cauliflower. The small green caterpillars damage plants by eating holes in the leaves; you might find them hiding in harvested heads. Aphids, cutworms, woodchucks, and rabbits also attack seedlings.

Celery

(Apium graveolens dulce)

Celery is the plant to grow if you're looking for a challenge. It's difficult to start from seed, requires very specific temperatures for good growth, and demands consistently moist soil. Celery grows best in areas with moderate summer and winter temperatures.

YOU SHOULD KNOW
Consisting mostly of water, celery is a low-calorie treat. Lend your favorite greens a bit of crunch by topping them with chopped celery.

Best site
Plant in full sun and moist, well-drained soil. Celery will tolerate slightly wet soils. Enrich the planting area by incorporating a 2-inch-thick layer of compost before planting.

Planting
Start celery from seeds indoors 10 to 12 weeks before your last spring frost date. Soak seeds overnight to speed germination. Sow several seeds per pot and cover them lightly with soil because celery seeds require light to germinate. After the last chance of frost has passed, transplant seedlings into the garden, spacing them 12 inches apart in rows 18 inches apart. Do not plant outside too early; 10 or more days with temperatures below 55°F will cause celery plants to bolt.

varieties:

1. **GIANT RED RESELECTION** has good red color and hardiness. 120 days.
2. **VENTURA** is a widely grown variety that's disease resistant and adaptable. 100 days.

CONQUISTADOR is an early-maturing variety that grows well under drought and heat stress. 80 days.

GOLDEN SELF-BLANCHING is a unique pale yellow variety with a mild flavor. 110 days.

Growing
Keep the soil evenly moist by applying 1 inch or more of water per week. Lack of water will produce bitter stalks. Cover the soil with a 2- to 4-inch-thick layer of organic mulch to conserve moisture and suppress weeds around the shallow-rooted plants.

Fertilize celery monthly with a balanced fertilizer such as 5-5-5.

Blanching the stalks gives them a mild flavor. Wrap the mature stems with any convenient light-blocking cylinder. Then mound 6 inches of soil around the base of the plant. Stalks are usually ready for harvest two to three weeks later. Be sure the cyclinder does not block water from reaching the roots; consistent moisture is the key to good flavor.

Harvest
Start harvesting individual stalks when they reach about 10 inches tall, cutting them at the base of the plant with a sharp knife. You can also harvest the entire plant at one time. Store celery in a refrigerator for up to two weeks.

Pests and diseases
Aphids and slugs may feed on transplants and stunt their growth. Leaf blights and root rot can attack plants, especially during wet periods.

Chard, Swiss chard

(Beta vulgaris cicla)

Popular in the landscape and on the table, chard is packed with color, texture, and vitamin A. The leaves and stalks are edible and tasty. Grow chard, with its red, yellow, white, or orange stalks, in landscape beds for a summer-long punch of color.

YOU SHOULD KNOW

Chard can be used in place of spinach in any recipe, but it must be cooked a bit longer. Unlike spinach, chard does not bolt in hot weather, making it an excellent summer green.

Best site

Plant in full sun and moist, well-drained soil. Chard tolerates some shade, especially in summer. It grows best in fertile soil. Incorporate a 2-inch-thick layer of compost into the soil before planting. Chard's strong, upright stalks are perfect for growing in container gardens. Combine chard with additional greens for a patioside salad garden.

Planting

Start chard from seeds or transplants planted directly in the garden after the danger of frost has passed. Soak seeds overnight to hasten germination. Sow seeds ½ inch deep and 2 inches apart in rows 24 inches apart. Thin seedlings to 12 inches apart after they develop four leaves.

varieties:

1 **BRIGHT LIGHTS** produces stem and leaf veins of many colors, including gold, pink, orange, purple, red, and white, with slightly ruffled, mild-tasting leaves. It's slightly less frost tolerant than other chard varieties. 55 days.

2 **BRIGHT YELLOW** bears yellow stems and veins on deep green leaves. 57 days.

3 **RHUBARB** produces dark green, red-veined leaves on deep red stems. 59 days.

Growing

Keep the soil evenly moist and weed free by mulching with an organic material such as straw or grass clippings. Chard produces best when given ample nutrients. Sidedress plants with a 2-inch-thick layer of compost one month after planting or fertilize with a liquid high-nitrogen fertilizer.

As plants age, the older leaves become tough. In midsummer, after harvesting several stems, cut plants back to 3 to 5 inches tall to encourage a flush of new, tender growth.

Harvest

Chard can be harvested throughout the summer. Start picking outer leaves when plants are about 5 inches tall. Removing the outer leaves encourages the development of tender inner leaves. Cut the whole plant at ground level before a hard freeze.

Store unwashed leaves and stalks in plastic bags in the refrigerator crisper for just two to three days.

Pests and diseases

Aphids, flea beetles, and leaf miners attack young chard leaves, causing holes and lowering yields. Remove and destroy damaged leaves.

Collards (*Brassica oleracea* Acephala group)

Collards are cabbages that don't form heads. Instead they produce clusters of stalks and leaves that are loaded with vitamins A and C. Plants grow best in warm climates, but they are frost tolerant and many varieties thrive in northern regions.

Best site

Plant in full sun and moist, well-drained soil. Collards tolerate some shade in summer. They grow best in fertile soil. Mix a 2-inch-thick layer of compost into the soil before planting.

To help reduce diseases do not plant collards or other cabbage family crops such as cabbage, broccoli, and cauliflower in the same location more than once every three years.

Planting

For a summer crop, sow seeds in the garden four weeks before the last frost date. For a fall crop, sow seeds three months before the first fall frost. Plant seeds ½ inch deep and 1 inch apart or transplant seedlings 6 to 8 inches apart. Grow collards in rows 24 to 36 inches apart.

varieties:

1. **CHAMPION** is a popular, compact Vates-type variety that's slow to bolt. 60 days.
2. **FLASH HYBRID** is known for high yields of smooth leaves and is also slow to bolt. 78 days.
3. **GEORGIA** produces sweet ruffled leaves over a long growing season. 60 days.

Growing

Although collards tolerate drought, they grow best in moist soil, so be sure they receive at least 1 inch of water per week. Mulch with an organic material such as straw or grass clippings to conserve soil moisture, keep the soil cool, and prevent weed growth.

Harvest

Pick leaves as needed, harvesting outer leaves of the plant first. The top bud is a delicacy, but don't pick it if you want the plant to continue making leaves. You can also harvest the whole plant at once, 50 to 70 days after seeding.

As with other cole crops, collards' flavor improves with frost in fall. Many varieties are so cold hardy that harvest can continue through snow in early winter. Collards store better than most greens. Wrap unwashed leaves in moist paper towls and place in a sealed plastic bag for as long as one week.

Pests and diseases

Cabbageworm and cabbage looper are the two primary insect pests of collards. The small green caterpillars damage plants by eating holes in the leaves; you might find them hiding in harvested heads. The most effective control of these pests is prevention. Placing row covers over plants in late spring and early summer will prevent many insect problems.

Aphids, cutworms, woodchucks, and rabbits also attack seedlings. In general, collards are usually less susceptible to pests than other crops in the cabbage family.

YOU SHOULD KNOW

Collards have enjoyed grand popularity in southern states and recently they have become a favorite green all across the nation. These fibrous, mild-flavored greens require a longer cooking time than other greens.

Corn *(Zea mays)*

Fresh corn is the best corn, and by growing a few rows of sweet corn outside your back door you'll have the best corn on the block. Sow successive crops every two weeks through early July for a harvest that will last from midsummer until frost. For years the key to delicious corn on the cob was cooking the ears immediately after harvesting. With the advent of new varieties that hold their sweetness after harvest, the pressure is off.

Best site

Plant in full sun and moist, well-drained soil. Corn thrives in fertile ground. Incorporate a 2-inch-thick layer of compost into the soil before planting in spring.

Types of corn

There are three main types of sweet corn based on their genetic background, plus specialty corns such as popcorn and decorative corn.

Standard sweet corn varieties (Su varieties) are best suited for being picked, husked, and eaten within a very short time.

Sugary enhanced hybrids (Se varieties) contain significantly more sugar than Su varieties while maintaining superior taste and texture that is synonymous with great sweet corn. Se varieties hold their taste longer than Su varieties and are the gourmet corns of choice for gardeners.

Supersweet hybrids (Sh2 varieties) are exceptionally sweet but they tend to have a tough-skinned texture that is not readily apparent when eaten fresh, but becomes more pronounced when the corn is frozen or canned.

Specialty corn includes varieties grown for popping, those grown for their colorful ears used in fall decorations, and baby corn, which is used in Asian cuisine.

Planting

Sow corn seeds directly in the garden after the last average frost date. Corn requires warm soil for germination; do not plant it until the soil is at least 55°F. Plant seeds 1 inch deep and 4 to 6 inches apart in rows that are 30 to 36 inches apart. To ensure good pollination, plant in blocks of at least four short rows, as opposed to fewer, longer rows.

Cross-pollination can be a problem with corn, especially supersweet varieties that cross with standard varieties and become starchy. Avoid problems either by planting varieties that mature at different times or by planting supersweet varieties at least 250 feet away from other types of corn.

For a sequential harvest, plant another block of corn two weeks after the first planting. Choose a midseason variety if possible. Continue planting blocks of corn until early July.

If you grow corn in a heavy clay soil in a cool area, presprout seeds to hasten germination. Soak them overnight in warm water, drain, and place them in a partially open clear plastic bag in a warm location. Rinse the seeds daily. In four to five days the corn will start to sprout. Carefully plant the sprouted seeds in a 4-inch-deep furrow; cover them with 1 inch of soil. Gradually fill in the furrow as the seedlings grow.

Growing

Weed carefully around shallow-rooted corn. Keep corn blocks weeded by hilling the soil around the base of each plant when it is 8 inches tall. Hilling not only kills weeds, but also it helps hold the corn plants upright during windstorms.

Corn is a heavy feeder. Fertilize plants with a high-nitrogen fertilizer when they are knee-high and again when the silks form.

Keep the soil evenly moist by applying 1 to 2 inches of water per week. To prevent diseases, water in the morning so the leaves dry before evening. Water to a depth of at least 6 inches; light sprinklings only encourage shallow-rooted plants that are more likely to blow over. Thin and curled corn leaves are signs of water stress. The most critical periods for watering are during pollination and ear filling.

If suckers or sprouts form at the base of a plant, leave them. Removing suckers won't increase ear size or quality.

YOU SHOULD KNOW
For a new flavor, instead of smothering a ear of corn with butter, squeeze on fresh lemon or lime juice or brush it with olive oil and sprinkle with your favorite dried herb blend.

standard hybrids (Su) and heirloom varieties:

1 **SUGAR AND GOLD** has bicolor kernels and is excellent for fresh eating or freezing. Easy to grow, this hybrid does especially well in cooler-season areas. 8-inch ears. 75 days.
2 **SILVER QUEEN HYBRID** has white kernels and is considered one of the best-tasting corn varieties. 7-8-inch ears. 92 days.
GOLDEN BANTAM is an heirloom with yellow kernels. It is a good cultivar for small gardens. 5–7-inch ears. 85 days.

Harvest

Most corn varieties yield one or two good-size ears per stalk, and some heirlooms produce two or three per stalk. Sweet corn is ready to harvest roughly 20 days after the first silks appear, about 60 to 95 days after planting.

Perfect harvest time is referred to as the "milk stage." Kernels are smooth and plump but not mature and tough. Puncture a kernel with your thumbnail and a milky sap will squirt out. Sweet corn remains in the milk stage for less than one week. As harvest time approaches, check kernels frequently so they do not become too mature.

Other signs that the corn is ready for harvest are drying and browning of the silks and fullness of the tip kernels and firmness of the unhusked ear. A nighttime raid by raccoons almost always indicates that the corn is ripe.

Harvest by pulling the ear downward sharply and twisting to break the shank or stem below the ear without breaking the parent stalk. If a plant produces more than one ear, often both ears are ready for harvest at the same time.

Unhusked corn can be stored in the refrigerator for about one week. Freezing is the best preservation method.

Baby corn, popular in many Asian dishes, is easy to grow at home. Grow it much like sweet corn except harvest the ears one or two days after silks emerge, when the cobs are only 2 to 4 inches long.

Harvest popcorn and ornamental corn once the stalks and husks are brown and dry. In rainy regions cut the stalks when the corn is mature, and hang them to dry in a well-ventilated place away from rain and animals.

sugary enhanced (Se) varieties:

1 **PEACHES AND CREAM** is a popular bicolor kernel variety that has great flavor and stores well. It is a vigorous grower. 8-inch ears. 83 days.

2 **BODACIOUS** is a yellow kernel variety with excellent flavor. It stores well and is disease resistant. 8-inch ears. 75 days.

DIVINITY has snow white kernels and a sweet flavor. 8-inch ears. 78 days.

Pests and diseases

Many insects and pests attack corn. The best line of defense against most pests is to select disease- and pest-resistant varieties.

Corn earworm adults lay eggs on corn silks; the eggs hatch and the young caterpillars tunnel into the ears, producing wormy, rotted tips. Corn borer larvae tunnel into cornstalks, causing them to snap. Japanese beetles feed on corn foliage and the pollen on the tassels, resulting in weakened plants and poor pollination. Corn rootworm larvae feed on the roots of corn plants, weakening and stunting them; rotate crops to avoid this pest.

Birds and raccoons are two of the most notorious animal pests of corn. Birds pull up young corn sprouts to eat the seeds. They also sit on the maturing ears and peck away at the tender kernels. Cover young seedlings with a floating row cover to prevent bird damage. Cover a small block planting with bird netting to prevent birds from eating the ears.

Raccoons have the uncanny ability to know just when the corn is ready to pick. Invariably they attack your garden the night before you're going to harvest your first crop. Raccoons are messy eaters, often taking small bites from many ears of corn, ruining them all. An electric fence can keep them away. In small plantings consider covering individual ears with paper bags after pollination to thwart this animal.

Diseases such as bacterial wilt, leaf blight, and mosaic virus can infect corn plantings. Plant disease-resistant varieties.

1

2

3

5

4

supersweet (Sh2) hybrids and specialty varieties:

1. **ILLINI XTRA SWEET** is a variety with yellow kernels that freezes well. The plant grows 8 feet tall. 8-inch ears. 85 days.
2. **HOW SWEET IT IS** is a cold-sensitive variety with white kernels. It holds its quality well on the stalk and after harvest. 8-inch ears. 85 days.
3. **HONEY 'N PEARL** has tender bicolor kernels. It matures about 10 days before other varieties. 9-inch ears. 76 days.
4. **MIRAI HYBRID** is a sweet but not too sugary variety that stores well for up to six weeks in the refrigerator. 7–8-inch ears. 71 days.
5. **BONUS** is a baby corn. 2–4-inch ears. 32 days.

Cucumber *(Cucumis sativus)*

A couple cucumber plants will easily produce enough fruit for a family of four—you might even have some extra bounty to share with friends and neighbors. Easy to grow and productive, cucumbers thrive in the heat of summer. Their trailing vines can sprawl across the garden or they can be trained onto a sturdy trellis. Bush types are excellent for small-space gardens and containers.

Best site

Plant in full sun and moist, well-drained soil. Heavy feeders, cucumbers require fertile ground. Add nutrients before planting by incorporating a 2- to 3-inch-thick layer of compost into the soil.

Types of cucumber

Picklers are short with pronounced spines or bumps on their skin, and are most often used preserved but can be eaten fresh too.

Slicers are long and thin with dark green, thick skin. They are best eaten fresh in salads and cold soups and on sandwiches.

Burpless types usually develop long, thin, deep green fruits. Many can form fruits without pollination. They are called burpless because they are less likely to cause digestive problems.

Asian cucumbers are extra-long types.

Planting

Cucumbers are best started from seeds planted directly into the garden. Seeds require warm soil to germinate. Don't rush to plant cucumbers too early; wait until after the chance of frost has passed. For an earlier crop start seeds indoors.

Sow seeds ½ inch deep and 2 inches apart in rows 4 feet apart. Thin plants to 12 inches apart. Or sow four to six seeds per hill and thin to three plants per hill after the true leaves emerge.

Growing

Young cucumber plants are susceptible to cold winds. In cool areas protect seedlings with a floating row cover until the weather has warmed. Row covers not only shield the tender plants from low temperatures, but also they provide some defense against insects. Remove the row covers before the cucumbers flower so that bees can reach and pollinate the blossoms.

Cover cucumber beds with a 2- to 4-inch-thick layer of organic mulch to suppress weeds and conserve soil moisture. Cucumbers need a steady supply of water. Dry conditions cause bitter flavor. Provide at least 1 inch of water per week.

Make the most of your garden space by growing trailing cucumbers—which can trail up to 5 feet—onto a trellis. Place posts 5 to 10 feet apart and string wire tightly between them. Fruits supported on a trellis are less susceptible to pests and diseases and have fewer blemishes. Since a cucumber plant cannot easily climb a trellis on its own, you'll need to train it on the support. Attach the main stem loosely to the trellis and guide it until it reaches over the top. For higher yields cut off the first four to six side runners near the bottom of the plant. Allow higher runners to stay on the plant.

Harvest

Once cucumber fruits form, they grow quickly, especially during periods of warm, humid weather. Check plants every few days to keep up with the harvest. The more you harvest, the more the plants will produce.

Start harvesting slicing, burpless, and Asian cucumbers when the fruits are 6 to 9 inches long. Harvest pickling cucumbers when the fruits are less than 2 inches in diameter and about 2 to 4 inches long. Store cucumbers in the refrigerator.

Pests and diseases

Striped or spotted cucumber beetles are the most troublesome insect pests of cucumbers. They can transmit diseases such as bacterial wilt from plant to plant, ruining an entire crop.

Aphids and flea beetles can be problems early in the season as the seedlings emerge, and they transmit cucumber mosaic virus.

YOU SHOULD KNOW
Grocery store cucumbers are coated with an edible wax to prevent moisture loss. The wax gives them an unnatural sheen. Your garden-fresh cucumbers will be dull green, but count on them to add a crisp crunch to salads and sandwiches.

varieties:

1 **COUNTY FAIR** is an excellent pickling cucumber with notable bacterial wilt resistance. It matures quickly. 3 inches. 50 days.

2 **MARKETMORE 76** is a popular slicer that produces uniform fruit. Plants have good disease resistance. 8–9 inches. 63 days.

3 **STRAIGHT 8** is a slicer grown for its evenly dark green fruit and excellent flavor throughout the growing season. 8 inches. 58 days.

4 **TASTY JADE** is an Asian cucumber that produces high yields on vigorous vines. 12 inches. 54 days.

5 **SWEET SUCCESS** is a burpless cucumber that is disease resistant. 14 inches. 54 days.

SALAD BUSH is a bush cultivar that is good for growing in containers. 8 inches. 57 days.

Eggplant *(Solanum melongena)*

Glossy purple, white, orange, green, or bicolor fruits and bold foliage make eggplant a pretty plant for the edible landscape. Eggplant thrives in warm-summer areas. A relative of tomato and pepper, it is usually planted one or two weeks after the last average frost date. For an ample harvest plant three to six plants. Many small varieties are perfect for planting in containers.

Best site

Plant in full sun and well-drained, fertile soil. Eggplant is a heavy feeder. Boost the nutrient content of soil before planting by mixing in a 2- to 4-inch-thick layer of compost. Reduce diseases by not planting eggplant or any other tomato-family crops, such as peppers and potatoes in the same ground for three years.

Types of eggplant

Large, oval-fruited types grow 3 to 4 feet tall and produce 8 to 10 fruits that reach 6 to 10 inches long and 3 to 6 inches in diameter. Varieties may be purple, white, or streaked purple and white.

Cylindrical-fruited plants grow 24 to 36 inches tall and bear 12 to 15 thin fruits 6 to 12 inches long and 1 to 2 inches in diameter. Fruits may be purple, white, or striped.

Small, round-fruited plants grow 12 to 24 inches tall and typically produce 20 to 25 fruits 2 to 4 inches in diameter.

Planting

Eggplant is easiest to grow from purchased transplants. Wait until the soil has adequately warmed—about two weeks after the last average frost date—to set plants out in the garden. Cool conditions can weaken plants, and frost will kill them. Space plants 18 to 24 inches apart in rows that are 30 to 36 inches apart. Apply a starter fertilizer at planting.

You can start eggplant from seeds planted indoors six to eight weeks before the last spring frost. Plant seeds ¼ inch deep and maintain a soil temperature of about 80°F.

Growing

In cool areas protect young transplants with a floating row cover if necessary. Keep the area around plants weed free by spreading a 2-inch-thick layer of organic mulch, such as straw or grass clippings over the soil. Provide plants with 1 to 2 inches of water per week.

Eggplants are heavy feeders. Fertilize them monthly with a balanced fertilizer such as 5-5-5. Avoid high-nitrogen fertilizers, which promote excess leaf growth at the expense of fruit.

Stake individual plants or use small tomato cages to keep the plants upright and long fruits straight and off the ground.

Harvest

Pick eggplant 60 to 90 days after transplanting outside. Ripe fruits are shiny and firm to the touch. An eggplant is ripe if the skin bounces back when you press it with your finger. If it is still hard, the eggplant is not ripe. If your finger indents the skin, the fruit is overripe and should be composted. The more you pick, the more fruits will continue to develop. Use a knife or shears to cut the fruit from the plant stem.

Eggplant bruises easily; handle with care. It does not store well and should be eaten soon after harvest. If you must store eggplant, keep it in the refrigerator.

Pests and diseases

Eggplant suffers from many of the same pests that attack potatoes and tomatoes. Colorado potato beetles prefer eggplant to potatoes. The orange-red larvae can quickly defoliate a plant. Check the undersides of leaves for the orange eggs and crush them to reduce the population. Flea beetles attack young eggplant seedlings creating "shotgun" holes in the leaves.

Verticillium wilt causes stunting and wilting of plants. To keep plants from succumbing to wilt, rotate crops.

YOU SHOULD KNOW
Eggplant contains a lot of water. Coax most of the water out of sliced eggplant before cooking by sprinkling it with salt and allowing water to drain for 30 minutes. Rinse the eggplant slices and pat dry.

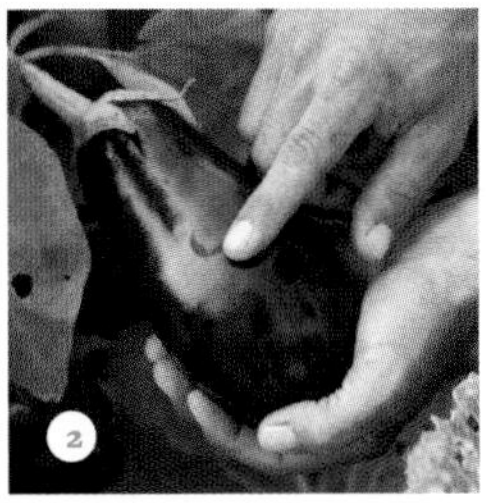

varieties:

1 **BLACK BEAUTY** is a long-time favorite that produces large, oval fruit with purple-black skin. It is ideal for cooking. 6–7 inches. 80 days.

2 **DUSKY** is a large, oval-fruited cultivar that matures early. It is a compact plant and good for containers. 6–7 inches. 60 days.

3 **PURPLE BLUSH** is another large, oval cultivar. The very sweet fruit has white skin tinged with purple. 6 inches. 62 days.

4 **CRESCENT MOON** is a very productive cylindrical cultivar with creamy white skin. 6–7 inches. 62 days.

5 **LITTLE FINGERS** produces clusters of purple, cylindrical fruits. 6–8 inches. 68 days.

6 **EASTER EGG** is a favorite ornamental edible with egg-shape white fruit. 2 inches. 52 days.

7 **TWINKLE** yields many small, round fruits and is a great choice for containers. It has white and violet-streaked skin. 4–5 inches. 60 days.

Garlic (*Allium sativum*)

Garlic is exceptionally prolific. One pound of cloves can produce 7 to 10 pounds of garlic the following year. The trick to growing garlic is remembering to plant it in fall. It forms deep roots in fall and then matures the following summer. Grow all three types and choose your favorite.

YOU SHOULD KNOW

For an exceptionally large garlic harvest, fertilize plants with a high-nitrogen fertilizer in spring. Begin fertilizing once three leaves have formed and continue monthly until bulbs begin to develop.

Best site

Plant in full sun and well-drained soil. Garlic thrives in slightly dry sites. Incorporate a 2-inch-thick layer of compost into the soil.

Types of garlic

Softneck garlic packs the strongest garlic flavor and stores well for up to nine months.
Hardneck garlic varieties have a good, mild flavor and store for only about six months.
Elephant garlic is a leek that is similar to garlic in flavor but is intermediate between garlic and onion in pungency. It stores for six months.

Planting

Plant garlic around the first frost date in fall. In mild-winter areas you can plant until January. Purchase garlic bulbs or sets from a nursery or mail-order source. Do not plant garlic purchased at the grocery store; it is often not hardy and has been treated to prevent sprouting.

Garlic grows best during cool weather and stops growing at temperatures above 90°F. You can also plant garlic in the early spring, but plants will yield smaller bulbs.

Plant by setting individual cloves pointy side up, 6 inches apart and 2 to 3 inches deep in rows 12 to 24 inches apart. Plant elephant garlic 8 inches apart and 6 inches deep.

Growing

Water garlic well in the fall to promote root growth. In cold-winter areas, mulch after a few hard freezes with a 4- to 6-inch-thick layer of straw to prevent the bulbs from heaving out of the ground. Garlic competes poorly with weeds; hand weed regularly to encourage the plant to produce large bulbs.

Harvest

When about half of the garlic leaves begin to yellow and wilt, stop watering and knock over the tops. Let the garlic cure for one week in the garden. Harvest the bulbs, knock off any extra soil, and hang the garlic to dry in a cool, shady location with good air circulation. After the tops are dry, trim them off to ½ inch above the bulb and trim the roots at the base of the bulb. Store the garlic in mesh bags in a cool room.

Pests and diseases

The same pests that attack onions can cause similar damage to garlic bulbs. Rotate crops and keep beds weed free to reduce troublesome insect populations.

varieties:

1. **INCHELIUM RED** is a softneck that produces hard-to-peel cloves that are white with purple skin. However, it's one of the best softneck varieties for cold climates.
2. **PERSIAN STAR** is a hardneck that produces 8 to 10 purple-skin cloves per bulb and is a good warm-climate variety.
3. **RUSSIAN RED** is a hardneck that has purple stripes, six to nine large cloves per bulb, and good winter hardiness.

Kale (*Brassica oleracea* Acephala group)

Becoming incredibly popular with dieticians, chefs, and foodies, kale is one of the most nutrient-dense vegetables available. Colorful leaves in a variety of shapes and colors make kale a great plant for the edible landscape too.

YOU SHOULD KNOW
Kale is a great plant for containers. Combine it with edible flowers for a colorful edible container garden or simply mix it with your favorite annuals and enjoy the plant's unique texture and color.

Best site
Plant in full sun and moist, well-drained soil. Kale tolerates partial shade, especially during the heat of summer. It grows best in soil that is high in organic matter. Incorporate a 2-inch-thick layer of compost in the growing location before planting.

To help reduce diseases, do not plant kale or other cabbage family crops such as cabbage, broccoli, and cauliflower in the same location more than once every three years.

Planting
Plant seeds or transplants four weeks before your last frost date in spring for a summer harvest and again six weeks before your first frost date in fall for autumn and early winter harvest. In warm climates plant kale in winter for an early spring harvest. Sow seeds ½ inch deep and 1 inch apart. Thin to 18 inches apart. Plant transplants 18 inches apart in rows 24 to 36 inches apart.

Growing
When seedlings are 4 inches tall, fertilize with a liquid high-nitrogen plant food. Mulch with a 2- to 3-inch-thick layer of organic material, such as straw, to conserve moisture, keep the soil cool, and prevent weed growth.

Harvest
Pick baby greens 20 to 30 days after seeding, and mature leaves 50 to 75 days after seeding. Wait until frost or cold weather has turned the leaves sweeter. To keep a plant producing, pick the big outer leaves and let the center continue to grow. The tender, young, center leaves are fine in salads. The chewier, larger, older leaves are best steamed, sautéed, or cooked like cabbage. Store fresh greens for up to one week in the refrigerator.

Pests and diseases
Kale has similar pest problems as cabbage and broccoli, but in general it is relatively pest free.

Cabbageworm and cabbage looper are the two primary insect pests of kale. The small green caterpillars damage plants by eating holes in the leaves; you might find them hiding in harvested heads. The most effective control of these pests is prevention. Placing row covers over plants in late spring and early summer will prevent many insect problems. Aphids and cutworms also attack seedlings.

varieties:

1. **TOSCANO** is a kale with long, thin, puckered dark green leaves that tolerate heat and cold. 65 days.
2. **REDBOR** hybrid features highly attractive frilly burgundy red leaves that darken in cold weather. 55 days.
3. **RED RUSSIAN** has purple stems and purple-veined, flat leaves that are more tender than those of other frilly kale varieties. 50 days.

Kohlrabi (*Brassica oleracea* Gongylodes group)

With an appearance similar to a creature out of a Dr. Seuss book, kohlrabi is a unique member of the cabbage family. Like broccoli and cauliflower, it thrives in cool weather. Take advantage of kohlrabi's shape by using it as a focal point in an edible landscape.

YOU SHOULD KNOW
Kohlrabi has the best flavor when it is between the size of a golf ball and a baseball. Harvest it as soon as it reaches this stage because it will grow large quickly. Enjoy its mild, sweet turnip taste fresh with your favorite herb dip.

1

Best site
Plant in full sun and moist, well-drained soil. Kohlrabi thrives in soil that is high in organic matter. Incorporate a 2-inch-thick layer of compost into the garden site before planting.

To avoid diseases, rotate crops; do not plant a cabbage-family crop in the same ground for three years.

Planting
Direct-sow seeds four to six weeks before your last average frost date. Or set out transplants two to three weeks before your last average frost date. Sow again for a fall crop about 10 weeks before your first fall frost date.

Plant seeds ½ inch deep and 1 inch apart in rows 18 inches apart. Transplant seedlings and thin direct-sown seeds to 8 inches apart.

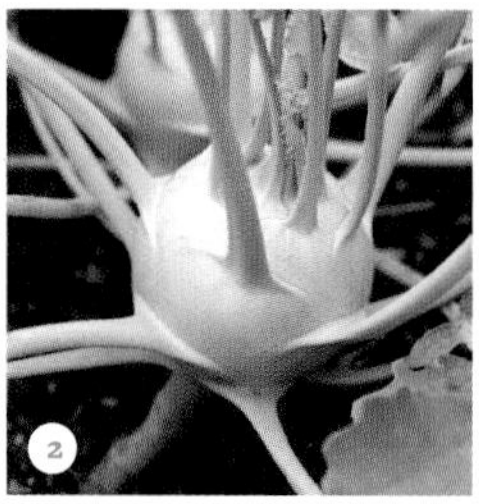
2

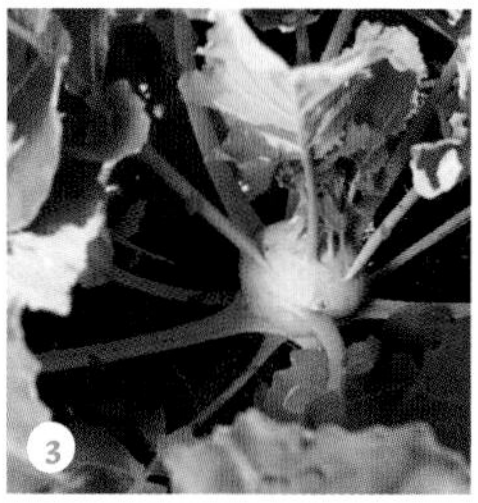
3

varieties:

1. **KOLIBRI** is a purple-skinned variety with fiberless white flesh. 50 days.
2. **EARLY WHITE VIENNA** has smooth light green skin and mild-flavored, tender, white flesh. 55 days.
3. **KOSSACK HYBRID** produces an 8- to 10-inch-diameter stem with green skin and white flesh; it isn't woody despite its size. 75 days.

Growing
Kohlrabi is the least hardy of the cabbage-family crops. Temperatures below 45°F will force the plant to bolt. Conversely, hot weather causes the stems to become tough and woody.

Three weeks after transplanting kohlrabi, side-dress it with a balanced fertilizer such as 5-5-5. Keep the soil moist by watering as needed, providing at least 1 inch per week. Hand weed carefully around plants to avoid disturbing the shallow roots. Mulch with a 2-inch-thick layer of organic material, such as straw or grass clippings, to conserve soil moisture, keep the soil cool, and prevent weed growth.

Harvest
For best quality, begin harvesting 45 to 65 days after transplanting, when the stems are 1 inch in diameter. Continue to harvest until stems reach 3 inches in diameter. On most varieties any stems larger than 3 inches will be tough and woody.

Kohlrabi lasts for three weeks or longer in a refrigerator crisper drawer. The stems also freeze well when peeled, diced, and blanched. Young leaves may be steamed and eaten like greens.

Pests and diseases
Cabbageworm and cabbage looper are the two primary insect pests of kohlrabi. The small green caterpillars damage plants by eating holes in the leaves; you might find them hiding in harvested heads. The most effective control of these pests is prevention. Placing row covers over plants in late spring and early summer will prevent many insect problems. Aphids and cutworms also attack seedlings.

Leek *(Allium porrum)*

Considered a gourmet vegetable by many people, leek is very easy to grow. This cool-season vegetable requires a long growing season, but as long as you give plants an early start, rich soil, and ample moisture, they'll produce brilliant white, elongated onionlike bulbs in four or five months.

YOU SHOULD KNOW

Choose leeks when you are looking for a sweet onion flavor in salads, soups, and stir-fries. In areas with mild winters, mulch leeks and enjoy garden-fresh flavor in the depths of winter.

Best site

Plant in full sun or part shade and moist, well-drained, fertile soil. Good drainage is essential in growing leeks. In clay or heavy soils, plant them in a raised bed. Leeks thrive in soil that is enriched with organic matter. Incorporate a 2-inch-thick layer of compost into the garden before planting.

Leeks have striking blue-green foliage that is a bold addition to the landscape. Plant a few rows of this showy vegetable alongside perennials, shrubs, and other traditional landscape plants.

Planting

Direct-sow leeks in the garden four weeks before your last frost date. They grow to a larger size if started as seedlings indoors. Start transplants eight weeks before the last frost date in your area. Set out transplants on or just after the last frost date.

Direct-sow seeds ½ inch deep and 1 inch apart in rows 18 inches apart. Thin seedlings to 6 inches apart. Set transplants about 6 inches apart and 4 inches deep in 8-inch-deep trenches spaced 18 inches apart.

Growing

To blanch stems, slowly fill in the trenches as the plants grow or mound about 6 inches of soil around the stems. Keep the soil evenly moist by applying 1 inch of water weekly or as needed. Hand weed frequently to keep the soil around the growing leeks free of weeds, which otherwise will reduce the quality of the leeks.

Harvest

Leeks take 90 to 120 days to mature, and they taste sweeter after a frost. Harvest when the stem is at least ½ inch in diameter. The best leeks will have a white stem or shank at least 3 inches long. Although leek leaves are edible, trim the tops to a manageable size for cooking.

In mild climates, overwinter leeks and harvest in early spring. In cold areas mulch leeks with a 4- to 6-inch thick layer of straw to protect the plants when overwintering them in the garden. Keep leeks in a refrigerator for up to one week.

Pests and diseases

Leeks have no significant pest problems.

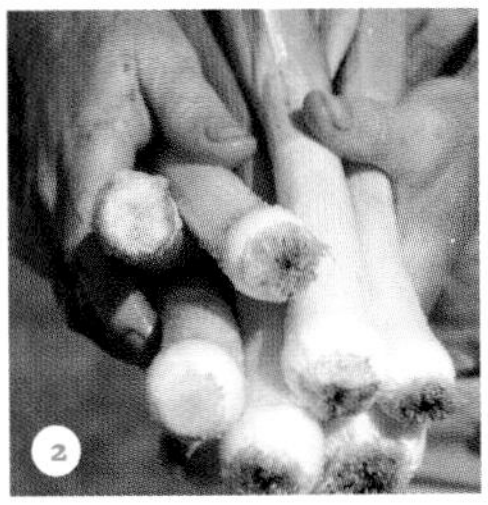

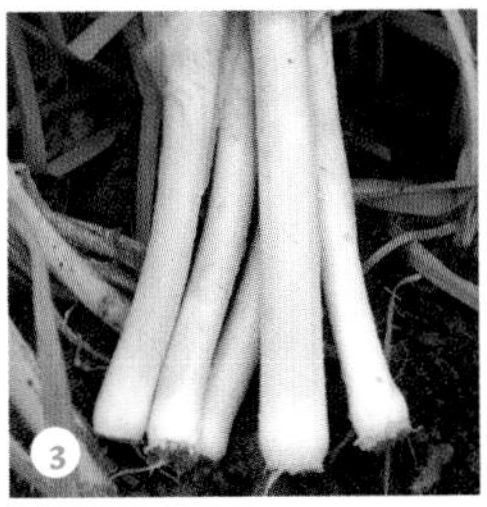

varieties:

1. **GIANT MUSSELBURGH** is a Scottish heirloom that produces 2- to 3-inch-thick stems and is very cold tolerant. 105 days.
2. **LANCELOT HYBRID** is a cold-tolerant variety with bold blue-green leaves. 100 days.
3. **KING RICHARD** is a tall, thin variety with medium-size green leaves. 75 days. This fast-growing variety can be harvested early for baby leeks.

Lettuce *(Lactuca sativa)*

Lettuce usually leads the charge from garden to table. This fast-growing crop can be planted as soon as the soil can be scuffled with a hoe in early spring. It thrives in cool weather and is easy to grow in containers and small spaces. A plant for the edible landscape, lettuce creates a frilly chartreuse, pinkish red, or deep green border along a planting bed and adds early-season interest to any garden.

Best site

Plant in full sun or part shade and moist, well-drained soil. Lettuce yields best in full sun during cool weather, but also does especially well in part shade when temperatures rise above 75°F. It is easy to grow in a container.

Types of lettuce

Looseleaf varieties are the easiest to grow. They have an open growth pattern and do not form a head. Looseleaf lettuce is available in a variety of colors and textures.

Crisphead lettuce forms a tight, firm head of crisp leaves. This true head lettuce is similar to the iceberg lettuce in the grocery store and requires exacting growing conditions. It is challenging to grow.

Butterhead lettuce produces a small, soft head of loosely folded medium green leaves.

Romaine, or cos, lettuce forms upright, cylindrical heads of tightly folded leaves. Romaine lettuce is consider the sweetest of the lettuce types and is used in Caesar salads. Enjoy baby romaine by harvesting it before it forms a dense head.

Planting

Sow looseleaf, butterhead, and romaine types in early spring as soon as you can work the soil. Gardeners in northern regions often scatter seeds on top of the snow in later winter for an exceptionally early spring harvest. Sow small beds every three weeks until late spring. Start sowing again in late summer for a fall or winter harvest. Lettuce can become bitter and bolt in summer heat. Sow seeds ¼ inch deep and 1 inch apart in rows about 18 inches apart.

Start crisphead lettuce varieties indoors four to six weeks before the last frost date in your area to transplant three to four weeks later.

Growing

After three or four leaves form, thin looseleaf varieties to 4 to 6 inches apart, butterhead and romaine types to 6 to 10 inches apart, and crisphead to 10 to 12 inches apart in the row.

Lettuce has a shallow root system. Pull weeds by hand or hoe lightly to avoid damaging roots. Keep the soil consistently moist but not waterlogged. Mulch the rows with a 2- to 3-inch layer of organic mulch to keep the soil moist, cool, and weed free.

Harvest

Pick the outer leaves of butterhead, looseleaf, and romaine varieties when the leaves are 2 inches long, about 40 to 50 days after seeding. When the leaves reach 4 to 6 inches long, cut the whole plant to within 1 inch of the ground with a sharp knife. If lettuce is harvested in spring, new leaves will emerge to be harvested later before the hot weather. If harvesting lettuce in late spring or fall, pull up the whole plant. Pick crisphead lettuce when the center is firm, about 60 to 80 days after seeding.

To store lettuce, wash, pat dry, and place in a plastic bag in the refrigerator. Lettuce keeps for about one week.

Pests and diseases

Aphids and slugs are two of the main pests of lettuce. Rabbits and woodchucks love tender lettuce greens.

Damping off fungal disease affects young seedlings, causing them to wilt and die. To prevent this disease, grow lettuce in a raised bed and don't overwater. Keep plants adequately thinned to prevent other rot diseases such as botrytis and mildew. Grow disease-resistant varieties to avoid tip or leaf burn.

YOU SHOULD KNOW
Extend your harvest by planting a combination of lettuce types. In cool-summer areas you can grow lettuce all summer and into fall. In areas where winters are mild you can grow lettuce into winter.

varieties:

1 **SALAD BOWL** is a looseleaf lettuce with a pleasing mix of red- and green-leaf varieties. It's good in hot areas. Green and red. 45 days.
2 **BLACK SEEDED SIMPSON** is an easy-to-grow looseleaf variety with large, crinkly leaves. Light green. 46 days.
3 **ROYAL OAK LEAF** is a looseleaf variety with a unique leaf shape. It has good heat tolerance. Dark green. 50 days.
4 **RED SAILS** is a looseleaf lettuce with eyecatching red-fringed leaves, it stays mild without bitterness and is good for warm regions. Burgundy red. 55 days.
5 **LITTLE GEM** is a very early-maturing crisphead. Small 4-inch heads. Green. 55 days.
6 **BUTTERCRUNCH** has a yellow blanched heart in the center of tightly bunched leaves. This butterhead has a crisp and sweet flavor. Dark green. 46 days.
7 **PARRIS ISLAND COS** is an old-time favorite romaine with a white blanched heart. It is disease-resistant and slow to bolt. Green. 68 days.

Melon *(Cucumis melo)*

Sweet garden treasures, heat-loving melons hide under rambling vines and leafy foliage. Harvesting them is like going on a treasure hunt. Melon vines require much garden space for good production and are not suited to small gardens, but if you have room, these plants are productive. Two plants will yield enough melons for a family of four with enough to share with friends and neighbors.

Best site

Plant in full sun and well-drained soil. Melons grow best in soil that is high in organic matter. Incorporate a 2-inch-thick layer of compost into the soil before planting.

Types of melons

SUMMER MELONS

Muskmelons (also called cantaloupes) are the most widely grown melons. They produce 2- to 5-pound fruits with a netted tan rind and sweet orange to salmon-color flesh.

Charentais melons look like muskmelons but have a smooth gray-green rind and honey-flavor orange flesh.

WINTER MELONS

Honeydews require a longer, warmer growing season than muskmelons. Honeydew melons typically weigh 5 to 6 pounds and have a smooth creamy white rind and sweet light green or orange flesh. **Casaba melons**, which weigh 7 to 8 pounds, feature a grooved yellow to greenish yellow rind and spicy-sweet white flesh. Shaped like a long acorn, **crenshaw melons** weigh 7 to 10 pounds and have a rough rind and sweet pinkish orange flesh.

Planting

Melons need heat to germinate. Wait until two weeks after your last frost date to sow seeds. Or start seeds indoors four weeks before your last frost date. Melon seedlings are sensitive to root disturbance so plant seeds in individual peat pots that can be planted directly in the garden without disturbing the roots.

In the garden, sow seeds in hills 4 to 6 feet apart, with six seeds per hill. Set transplants 12 to 18 inches apart in rows 36 inches apart.

Growing

Melons need ample space, nutrients, and water to grow best. Thin direct-seeded plants to three seedlings per hill after the first set of true leaves appears. Keep plants well watered, applying at least 1 inch per week and more during hot, dry, windy periods. The most critical watering periods are when the vines are flowering and fruiting. Spread a 2-inch-layer of mulch around plants to help conserve soil moisture.

To prevent rot and insect damage on ripening fruits, place melons on cardboard, upside-down pots, or pieces of wood. Hasten ripening of fruits by removing vine tips and new flowers when nights grow cool. To speed ripening of existing fruits, place aluminum-covered cardboard under immature fruits to intensify the heat of the day.

Harvest

Harvest muskmelon when the vine easily separates, or slips, from the melon's stem. This "slip stage" signifies the time when the fruit has absorbed the maximum amount of sugar. The rind, too, will darken to a tan or yellow when the fruit is fully ripe.

Harvest honeydew, casaba, and crenshaw melons when the green rind turns pale yellow and the blossom end of the fruit is slightly soft. You can harvest them a few days before full maturity to continue ripening off the vine at room temperature.

Store melons in the refrigerator.

Pests and diseases

The main insect pests of melons are cucumber beetles, squash bugs, and aphids. Select disease-resistant varieties, rotate crops, clean up plant debris in fall, and control insects that transmit diseases to avoid problems.

1

YOU SHOULD KNOW
Harvest melons at just the right time—when the stem easily separates from the vine or, in the case of honeydew, casaba, and crenshaw, melons, when they turn completely yellow—to ensure maximum sugar content.

2

3

4

5

6

7

varieties:

1 **HALE'S BEST** is an heirloom muskmelon with sweet, fragrant, salmon-color flesh. It is very productive. 3–4 pounds. 80 days.

2 **SUPERSTAR** lives up to its name by producing many large muskmelons with orange flesh. 6–8 pounds. 86 days.

3 **PASSPORT** is a specialty tropical melon with mint green flesh and a pleasing tropical fruit flavor. 5–6 pounds. 73 days.

4 **CHARENTAIS** is a French heirloom with sweet, orange flesh and a bold melon fragrance when it is ripe. 2–3 pounds. 80 days.

5 **EARLY CRENSHAW** produces large, oblong fruits with pink, creamy flesh. 14 pounds. 90 days.

6 **VENUS** is a honeydew with a golden rind and juicy, fragrant, white flesh. 3–4 pounds. 88 days.

7 **SUPER DEW** is a very productive honeydew melon. It has fragrant, white flesh with green edges. 6 pounds. 80 days.

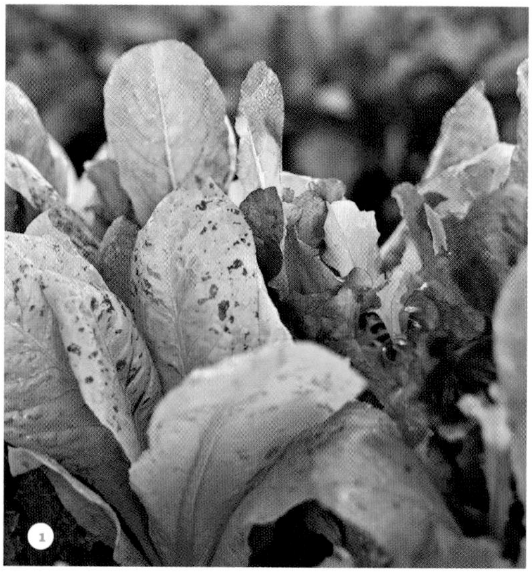

Mesclun mix

The word "mesclun" is French and originally referred to a mixture of tender salad greens that were wild-harvested in early spring. Today mesclun is cultivated in gardens and containers to make harvesting perfectly tender baby looseleaf lettuce as easy as stepping out the back door.

YOU SHOULD KNOW
A mesclun salad mix is all about diversity. A delicious compendium of tastes, textures, and colors unites to create a salad that needs nothing more than a dash of light vinaigrette.

Best site
Plant in full sun or part shade and moist, well-drained soil. Mesclun mixes thrive in soil that is high in organic matter. Mix a 2-inch-thick layer of compost into the garden before planting.

Mesclun, like lettuce, is easy to grow in a container. Plant it with pansies, an edible early spring flower, for a cheerful burst of color.

Planting
Sow seeds in the garden two to four weeks before the last frost date and every two to three weeks in spring until early summer. Start sowing again in late summer for a fall harvest. In mild climates, sow seeds in fall for a winter harvest.

Sow seeds ¼ inch deep and ½ inch apart in 24- to 36-inch wide rows. Cover the seeds with fine soil, potting soil, or sand.

varieties:

1. **ROCKY TOP MIX** is a colorful mix of 'Rouge d'Hiver', 'Trout Back', 'Red Salad Bowl', 'Rave', and 'Parris Island Green' romaine lettuces. 40 days.
2. **SALAD MIX** is specially made by combining red mustard greens and arugula. 40 days.
3. **PROVENÇAL WINTER MIX** is a mildly spicy mix of arugula, chervil, endive, French lettuces, Italian parsley, mache, and radicchio. 32 days.

The exact greens used to create a mesclun mix lend it a unique flavor. There are mixes that include mustard greens and have a spicy tang. Others include greens that are a hallmark of Asian cuisine or Italian cooking. If you have space, grow a few rows of mesclun and enjoy the many flavors of leaf lettuce.

Growing
Keep the planting moist until the seeds germinate. In cool areas cover the bed with a floating row cover to warm the soil in spring, prevent insects from attacking, and keep the bed moist. Hand weed as needed, though a thickly sown planting rarely requires weeding.

Harvest
Begin harvesting baby greens 14 to 30 days after sowing, when the leaves become 4 to 6 inches long. Handpick individual leaves or cut whole plants to 1 inch above the ground. If cut in spring, the plant can regrow for a second harvest. After cutting, water well.

Mesclun mix leaves do not store well and should be eaten soon after harvest. Gently wash and dry the leaves and store them in a plastic bag in the refrigerator crisper for a few days.

Pests and diseases
The primary pests of mesclun mixes are aphids and flea beetles. Control these pests with a jet spray of water or by applying insecticidal soap. Rabbits and woodchucks love to munch on the tender young greens.

Okra

(Abelmoschus esculentus)

This tall-growing vegetable is in the hollyhock and hibiscus family. Like its cousins, it has showy flowers and reaches impressive heights. Plant breeders have also developed shorter plants that are perfect for growing in containers. Okra is a standout in the edible landscape.

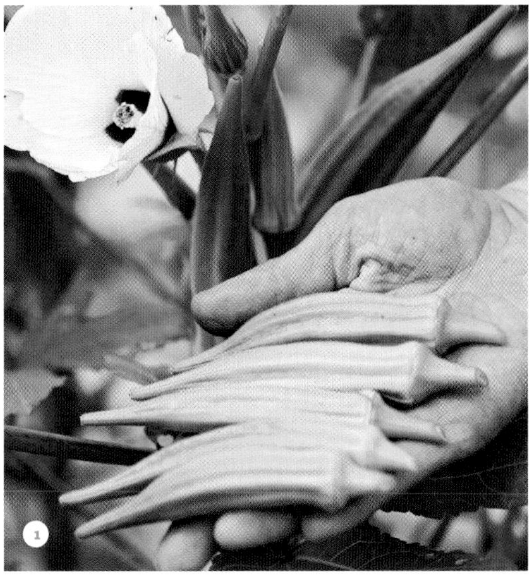

YOU SHOULD KNOW

Okra is a powerhouse of valuable nutrients and fiber. Its flavor is similar to that of eggplant. An integral ingredient in gumbo, it also complements tomatoes, onions, corn, and shellfish.

Best site

Plant okra in full sun and well-drained soil. It is drought tolerant but will not tolerate constantly moist sites. If your soil is poorly drained, plant okra in raised beds or in a container.

Okra thrives in soil that is high in organic matter. Incorporate a 2-inch-thick layer of compost into the soil before planting.

Planting

Plant transplants or sow seeds two weeks after all danger of frost has passed and the soil temperature is at least 60°F. In cool-summer areas, start seedlings indoors six to eight weeks before your last frost date.

Prior to sowing seeds, soak them in water for one hour to soften their seedcoats. Okra seedlings don't like to be disturbed, so plant seeds in individual peat pots when growing seedlings indoors to prevent damage to the roots while transplanting.

Plant okra seeds ½ inch deep or place transplants 12 to 24 inches apart in rows 24 inches apart.

Growing

Water plants deeply every 7 to 10 days, allowing the soil to dry out between waterings. Deep irrigation is particularly important during flowering and pod development.

Harvest

Pick okra pods when they are 2 to 4 inches long, about five or six days after flowering. Use scissors to snip the tough stems from the plant. Harvest frequently, especially during hot weather, because pods become tough quickly. If you overlook some pods when harvesting and they become large and tough, pick them and toss them in the compost pile. These old, mature pods sap nutrients from the plant that could go into making new, young pods.

Store pods in the refrigerator for five to seven days or blanch and freeze them for longer storage.

Pests and diseases

Okra plants can be attacked by aphids, stinkbugs, or cabbageworms. Dislodge pests with a strong spray of water from a garden hose. Rotate crops or grow okra in well-drained soil, raised beds, or containers to prevent pest and disease problems.

varieties:

1. **ANNIE OAKLEY II** is a good variety for northern regions, producing pods on 3- to 4-foot-tall plants. 55 days.
2. **BURGUNDY** has colorful red stems and pods on 7-foot-tall plants; the pods turn deep purple when cooked. 75 days.
3. **LITTLE LUCY** grows only 24 inches tall and produces 4-inch-long burgundy pods. It's a great cultivar for containers. 55 days.

Onion *(Allium cepa)*

A key to success with onions is choosing the right variety for your region. They produce bulbs according to the number of hours of daylight they receive. For that reason, if you live north of an imaginary line from Bakersfield, California, through Memphis, Tennessee, to Charlotte, North Carolina, grow long-day onions transplanted in spring. If you live south of the imaginary line, grow short-day onions planted in fall or winter.

Best site

Plant in full sun and moist, well-drained soil. Onions thrive in fertile soil. Mix a 2-inch-thick layer of compost into the soil before planting. Onions don't grow well in waterlogged soil. Plant in raised beds or containers if your soil is excessively moist.

Types of onions

Sweet onions are flavorful, mild tasting, and great raw in salads or cooked, but they don't last long in storage.
Storage onions have a more pungent taste and are best cooked.
Shallots, an onion relative, are known for their small bulbs and mild flavor.
Multiplier onions are bulbs that reproduce like shallots and are planted in fall for a spring harvest. They keep for months in storage.

Planting

Start onions from seeds, transplants, or sets. Sets and transplants are easiest. They are hassle-free methods that allow plants to establish quickly and become vigorous and strong. Choose sets if you want green onions. Sets also produce good dry onions for slicing and storage. Transplants regularly produce large onions for slicing. Use seeds to grow scallions.

Plant onions as soon as the soil can be tilled in spring in the North or early fall in the Deep South. Plant sets or transplants 4 to 6 inches apart. Place the onion sets about 2 inches deep in the soil so the pointed end is just showing aboveground. Sow seeds ½ inch deep and 3 inches apart. If you plan to harvest the tops for scallions, space the seeds 2 inches apart and thin the seedlings to the proper spacing.

Growing

Plentiful moisture—about 1 inch per week—is especially important when bulbs begin to increase in size. To keep onion plants moist and weed free, mulch between the onion beds with a 1- to 2-inch-thick layer of organic material such as straw. Remove flower stems if they form. Side-dress plants with a balanced (5-5-5) fertilizer every three to four weeks.

Harvest

Pick scallions when they are 6 to 8 inches tall, usually eight weeks after planting. Harvest green onions anytime after the bulb begins to form.

Storage onions take three to five months to mature in the North. In mild climates fall-planted onions mature in early summer. Once the tops start yellowing, stop watering. When half of the stems have collapsed, bend the rest down. After one more week you can pull up the bulbs. Lay them in a warm dry place. When the skin is dry and papery, cut off the foliage, leaving a 1-inch-long stub above the bulb. Store the onions in mesh bags in a cool, dark place.

Sweet onions can be stored for only a few weeks, while more pungent storage varieties will last as long as four months.

Harvest shallots about 90 days after planting, after the side bulbs have formed and the tops have begun to dry. Remove the entire plant, separate the side bulbs, and store them as you would onions. Bulbs left in the ground will regrow next year.

Pests and diseases

Because of their pungency, onions are relatively pest free. Onion thrips and onion maggots can attack the leaves and bulbs. Cover the transplants with a floating row cover to prevent thrips damage, or spray with insecticidal soap. Spread diatomaceous earth around the plants to control onion maggots. Rotate crops and grow onions in well-drained soils to avoid diseases.

1

YOU SHOULD KNOW
Plant an onion crop in early spring and harvest a portion in early summer for use as scallions. Pull up larger onions as the season wears on; harvest mature onions in late summer or fall for months-long storage.

2

3

4

5

6

7

varieties:

1 **GIANT RED HAMBURGER** is a short-day onion with sweet white flesh. It matures earlier than many other large onions. Dark red. 95 days.
2 **AMBITION** is a shallot that can be grown in all regions. It has reddish copper skin and white flesh. Grow it from seed. Red. 100 days.
3 **SUPER STAR** is adapted to growing in all regions and regularly produces 1-pound bulbs with a mild, sweet taste. White. 109 days.
4 **CANDY** has a welcome mild flavor and can be grown anywhere. It grows very large in the South. This onion stores fairly well. Yellow. 110 days.
5 **REDWING** is a long-day onion with pungent red flesh. It stores very well. Red. 110 days.
6 **COPRA** has firm, sweet flesh and is an early-maturing, long-day storage onion. Yellow. 104 days.
7 **WALLA WALLA** is a classic long-day onion with a sweet, juicy flavor. In mild-winter areas, plant it in fall. Yellow. 125 days.

Parsnip
(*Pastinaca sativa*)

Parsnip is one of the hardiest vegetables. In fact, the root does not develop its sweet flavor until after soil temperatures hover around freezing for two to four weeks in fall. A good keeper, parsnip will store for weeks after harvest.

YOU SHOULD KNOW
Parsnip's sweet nutty flavor is especially tasty when the roots are mashed like potatoes, chopped in soups and stews, or sliced and glazed with butter and brown sugar, for a side dish.

Best site
Plant in full sun and well-drained soil. Parsnip tolerates some shade but yields better in full sun. Loose, rock-free soil is essential for growing this root vegetable. It does not grow well in clay. If your soil is clay or poorly drained, grow parsnip in raised beds that are at least 12 inches tall and filled with loose, fertile soil.

Planting
Parsnip requires a long growing season. Sow seeds directly in the garden about two weeks before your last frost date. Plant seeds ½ inch deep and ½ inch apart in rows 18 inches apart. The seeds take about three weeks to germinate when they receive consistent moisture. Because parsnip is slow to germinate, mark the spot by planting radishes in the same row.

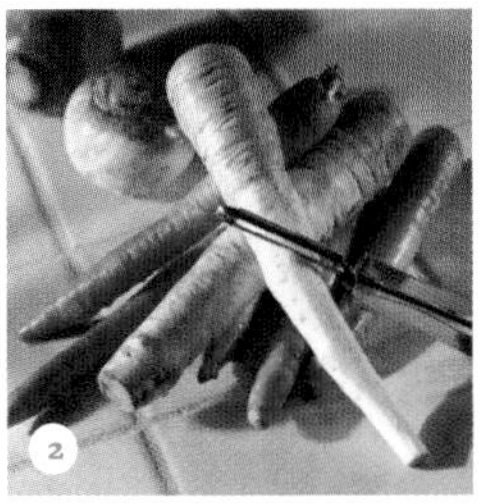

varieties:

1. **ANDOVER** has long, slender disease-resistant roots. 120 days.
2. **GLADIATOR** is a fast-maturing variety with silky smooth white skin and good disease resistance. 105 days.
3. **COBHAM IMPROVED MARROW** is a disease-resistant variety that stays smooth when grown in heavy soils. 120 days.

Growing
Thin seedlings to 4 inches apart after true leaves emerge. Weed by hand to protect their roots. After the plants are established, mulch between rows with a 2- to 3-inch-thick layer of organic material, such as straw or grass clippings, to keep the soil cool and moist and to prevent further weed growth.

Harvest
Parsnip tastes best when exposed to two to four weeks of low temperatures during which the starch in the roots is converted into sugars. In warm areas you can harvest roots all winter.

In northern areas mulch the parsnip bed with a 2- to 4-inch-thick layer of straw in late fall to protect the plants from freezing weather. In late winter or early spring, remove the mulch and harvest the roots before they start to grow again. A spading fork is handy for dislodging the large roots. They can be stored in the refrigerator for up to two months.

Pests and diseases
Parsnips are relatively pest free. To avoid disease rotate crops. Young parsnip seedlings may be attacked by leafhoppers. A severe attack may reduce the size of the roots. Cover the beds with floating row covers to stop leafhoppers from reaching the plants. A row cover will also keep carrot rust flies, which may attack parsnip roots, from laying eggs on the plants.

Peanut (*Arachis hypogaea*)

Depending on the variety, a peanut plant will either vine or bunch. After the flowers fade, short stems called pegs form; in approximately 10 days the pegs push their way underground, where shells and nuts develop. The whole process from planting to harvest can take up to 120 days.

Best site
Plant in full sun and well-drained soil. Peanuts do not grow well in clay or poorly drained soil.

Planting
Sow seeds or set out transplants two weeks after your last frost date. Peanuts require warm soil for germination. In cold-winter areas start seedlings indoors four weeks before your last frost date. Plant seeds 2 inches deep and 4 inches apart in rows 24 inches apart for bunching types and 36 inches apart for vining types.

Growing
Thin bush-type seedlings to 6 to 8 inches apart and vining seedlings to 12 to 15 inches apart once true leaves form. Shallowly hoe around peanut plants, mounding the soil to remove weeds and to allow the pegs to easily make their way underground. Once the pegs enter the soil, stop weeding. That's also the time to mulch with a 1- to 2-inch-thick layer of organic material such as straw. After the flowers fade, side-dress the peanuts with a low-nitrogen fertilizer. Keep the beds well watered, especially when the pegs are forming; deliver at least 1 inch of water a week during dry periods.

Harvest
Harvest peanut plants after the leaves have yellowed and the plants have begun to dry, usually three to four months after seeding. Pull or carefully dig up individual plants with a spading fork and shake off the loose soil. Mature peanuts will have ridged shells and filled pods. Dry the plants and pods for one week in a warm, well-ventilated location indoors. Separate the pods from the plants and continue to dry the shells for another week. Peanuts stored in the shell in a cool, well-ventilated location can last for months. Shell and roast the peanuts as needed. Roast at 325°F for 20 minutes.

Pests and diseases
Wireworms, nematodes, and animals such as mice and voles can attack developing peanuts underground. Aphids and leafhoppers may feed on leaves, reducing yields. Fence out rabbits and other animals, and rotate crops to control wireworms and nematodes.

Peanuts grown in heavy, wet soils are susceptible to rot diseases. Leaf spot can cause leaves to yellow and drop prematurely, especially in hot humid areas. Grow peanuts in well-drained soil or raised beds to prevent diseases.

varieties:

1. **VIRGINIA JUMBO** is a vining type that bears two or three large nuts per shell and up to 50 shells per plant. 120 days.
2. **EARLY SPANISH** is a bush type that matures quickly, producing two or three papery, red-skin nuts per shell. 100 days.
3. **TENNESSEE RED VALENCIA** is a bush type that makes two to five red-skin nuts per shell. 110 days.

YOU SHOULD KNOW
Peanuts are actually seeds that grow in pods underground, hence their alternative names groundnut and ground pea. A traditional Southern crop, peanuts grow well throughout warm-summer regions.

Pea *(Pisum sativum)*

Garden-fresh peas are the ultimate springtime treat. This cool-season crop thrives in cool, moist weather and can be planted in early spring as soon as the soil can be worked. Best eaten fresh, some peas convert as much as 40 percent of their sugar to starch in just a few hours in the refrigerator. This fact alone practically guarantees your garden peas will far surpass any you can purchase at the supermarket or farmer's market.

Best site

Plant in full sun and well-drained soil. Peas will grow in part shade, but they yield best in full sun. Peas don't grow well in poorly drained soil. If you garden in heavy clay soil, plant peas in raised beds. Incorporate a 2-inch-thick layer of compost into the soil before planting.

Types of peas

Edible pod peas are eaten whole. **Snow peas** and **snap peas** fall into the edible pod group. Edible pod peas are harvested while the peas inside the pods are still small.

Garden peas, also called **English peas**, are varieties grown for their plump, juicy peas inside nonedible shells. There are smooth and wrinkled-seed varieties. The wrinkled-seed selections are generally sweeter and best for the home garden.

Planting

Sow peas in the garden in early spring as soon as the soil reaches 45°F and can be worked. Sow seeds 1 inch deep and 2 inches apart in rows 8 to 12 inches apart. In hot, dry areas dig a trench 2 inches wide and 4 inches deep, moisten the soil, and plant the seeds; cover them with 2 inches of soil. Rainwater will collect in the trench, aiding pea germination and early growth. Slowly fill in the trench as the peas grow.

Peas thrive in cool weather and are hardy to 25°F. Temperatures above 80°F, on the other hand, cause flowers to drop.

Growing

Keep the beds weed free, especially for the first six weeks that peas are growing. Maintain even soil moisture, applying 1 inch of water per week. Mulch established plants with a 2-inch-thick layer of organic material such as straw to keep the soil cool, prevent weed growth, and conserve soil moisture.

Harvest

Harvest snap peas when the pods first start to fatten but aren't completely full. Don't shell them; instead, eat the whole pod. Overmature pods become stringy or fibrous. Snap pea vines continue to grow and produce pods as long as the weather is cool and the plants are healthy.

Harvest snow peas when the pods are still flat and the seeds inside small and undeveloped, usually five to seven days after flowering. If you miss a few pods, let the peas inside mature and harvest them like garden peas. Keep the pods picked every few days and snow peas will continue to produce. Store snap peas and snow peas in the pod in the refrigerator.

Pick garden peas when the pods are full and rounded. Pick a few pods every day or two near harvest time to determine when the peas are at the perfect stage for eating. Garden peas are best when they are fully expanded but immature, before they become starchy. The peas lower on the vine mature first; pick them daily. Pea plants usually finish producing one to two weeks after the first pea is picked. Peas are best when consumed shortly after harvest but you can store shelled garden peas in the refrigerator for up to one week.

Pests and diseases

Peas are susceptible to a variety of diseases such as blight, root rot, fusarium wilt, powdery mildew, botrytis, and damping off. Plant in well-drained soil, choose varieties bred for resistance to diseases common in your area, and rotate crops to avoid these diseases.

The pests most prevalent on peas include slugs, aphids, and leafhoppers when the plants are young. Rabbits and woodchucks love young pea vines. Use fencing to protect the plants.

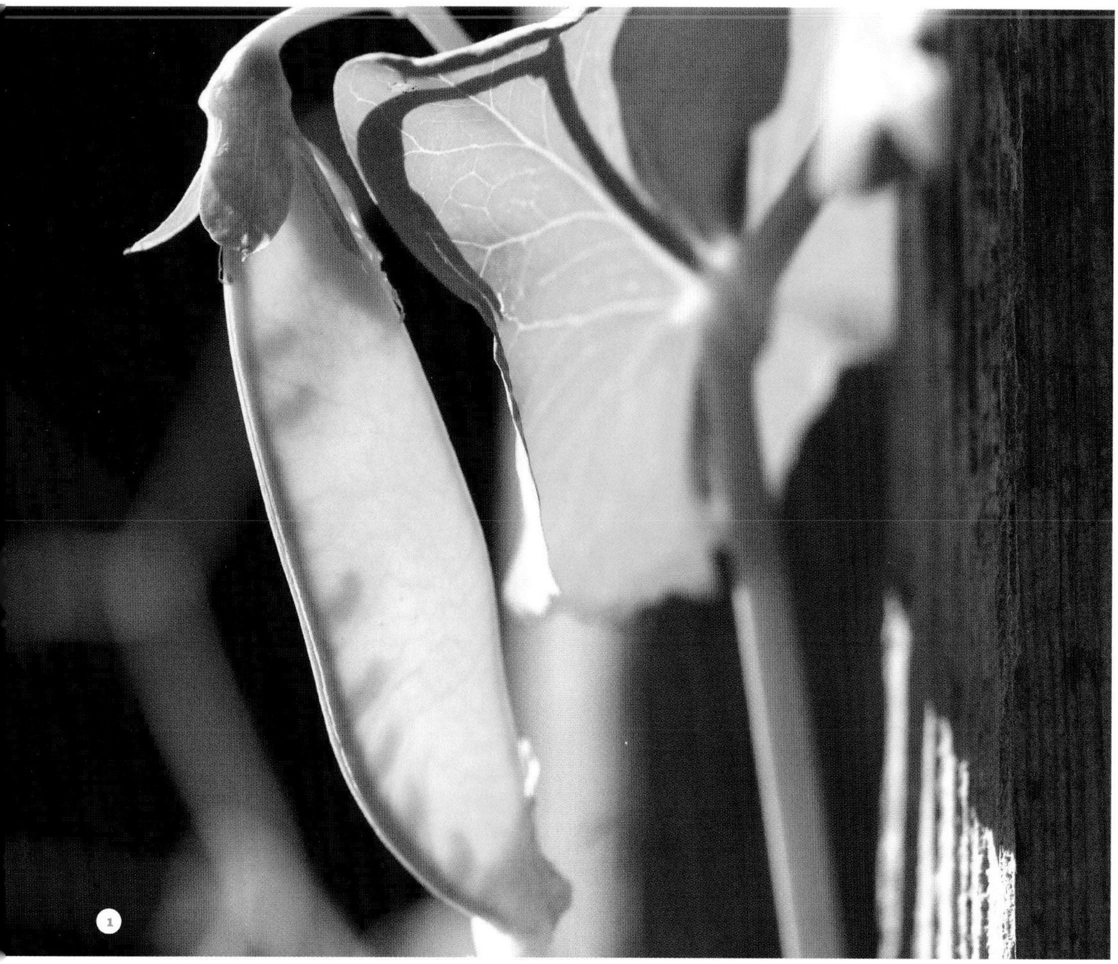

1

YOU SHOULD KNOW
If you don't have time to shell peas, grow edible pod peas such as snow peas or snap peas. Delicious in salads, sautés and many other dishes, these vitamin-rich vegetables require little preparation.

2

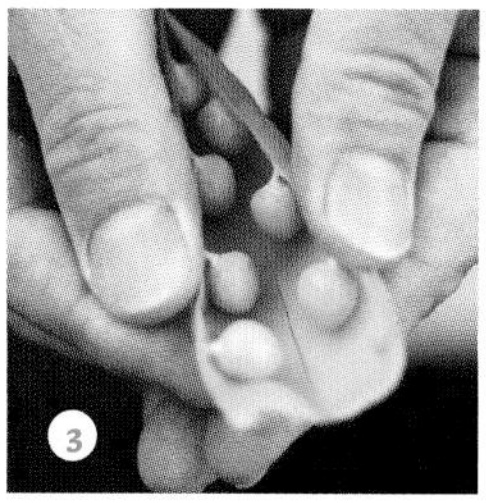

3

4

5

6

7

varieties:

1 **DWARF GREY SUGAR** is a 36-inch-tall, vining snow pea with sweet pods. It is a good source of pea shoots. 66 days.

2 **ALDERMAN TALL TELEPHONE** is a vigorous garden pea that produces 6- to 8-foot-tall vines. This popular heirloom has large pods. 74 days.

3 **WANDO** has good heat tolerance, making it a good choice for mid- to late-spring plantings. It is an heirloom garden pea with 24- to 36-inch-tall vines. 68 days.

4 **ECLIPSE** peas are known for keeping their sweet taste long after harvest. This garden pea produces 36-inch-tall vines. 63 days.

5 **SUGAR ANN** is an easy-to-grow snap pea. The 24-inch-tall bush plants support themselves and don't require staking. 52 days.

6 **SUGAR SNAP** has extra sweet pods and peas on 6-foot-tall vines. 65 days.

7 **SUPER SUGAR SNAP** is similar to 'Sugar Snap' except it has improved disease resistance and 4- to 5-foot-tall vines. 64 days.

Pepper *(Capsicum annuum)*

Peppers are just as useful in the landscape as they are in the kitchen. This essential ingredient in salsa, key component of many ethnic cuisines, and vitamin-packed snack is also eyecatching in the garden and easy to grow in a container. Plant peppers alongside lettuce and spinach. When greens succumb to hot temperatures, peppers will provide interest as their fruits ripen from green to orange, yellow, red, purple, or brown.

Best site

Plant in full sun and well-drained soil. At least eight hours of direct sunlight a day are essential for good plant growth and pepper formation. Peppers thrive in soil that is high in organic matter. Prior to planting, mix a 2-inch-thick layer of compost into the planting site.

Peppers are easy to grow in containers. Choose a large, sturdy pot to support the plants, which become heavy with fruit at harvest.

Types of peppers

Sweet peppers may be bell-shape, small and round, or shaped like a horn. **Bell peppers** are the most popular garden variety of sweet peppers. Left to ripen, they turn red, purple, orange, or yellow and contain various amounts of sugar depending on the variety. Green bell peppers are the most common.

Paler green and yellow elongated pepper sweet pepper varieties often have a more intense flavor. All sweet peppers are crisp and refreshing raw and pleasantly assertive when cooked to tenderness. Because peppers require a long, hot growing season, in cool regions or areas with short growing seasons they may never develop their ripe color.

Chili, or hot, peppers are famous throughout the world, from the spicy cuisines of Mexico, India, Thailand, and Africa, to the subtle flavor they impart on the most delicate dishes. The hot varieties can be picked at any color stage but are hottest if they are allowed to fully ripen.

Chili peppers include Anaheims, anchos, jalapeños, serranos, hot wax, tabasco, cayenne, and habanero peppers that ripen through a wide range of colors from yellow, orange, purple, and even brown. Some chili peppers turn bright red, which is more often an indication of ripeness than hotness. The burning sensation associated with fiery chilies is attributed to chemical compounds in the walls surrounding the seeds. The pepper flesh is usually not as hot as the scorching seeds.

Peppers are ranked on a scale called the Scoville Heat Scale according to their hotness or the amount of a chemical compound called capsaicin in their fruit and seeds. The scale starts with bell pepper at 0 and goes up to hot peppers, such as habanero, rated at more than 500,000 at the hottest. Some peppers are so hot that handling them can burn your hands.

The measurement is imprecise due to differences in varieties and individual tastes. However, the rating is useful for knowing which types of peppers are hotter than others.

Planting

Peppers are easiest to grow from transplants. Set out transplants when the soil temperature is at least 60°F, about two weeks after the average last frost date.

Peppers are sensitive to frost. If a late frost is predicted, protect peppers by covering them with cloth, an empty pot, or a 5-gallon bucket. Peppers require a long growing season and in most regions must be started from transplants or seeds planted indoors six to eight weeks before the last frost date.

The increasing popularity of unique pepper varieties has made many more available as transplants, nearly eliminating the need to start plants from seeds.

If you decide to start plants from seeds, sow seeds ¼ inch deep and maintain soil temperatures of at least 80°F for best germination. Be sure to place seedlings in a bright, sunny location. Lack of light will produce leggy, unproductive transplants.

YOU SHOULD KNOW
Try roasting peppers under a broiler, over an open flame, or on the grill until the skin is black. While the peppers are still hot, place them in a paper bag or cover them with foil and allow steam to quickly loosen the charred skin.

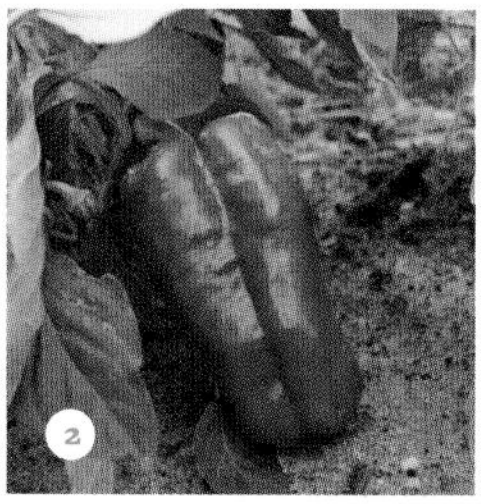

sweet bell varieties:

1 **CALIFORNIA WONDER** has thick walls and is good for stuffing. The green bells are produced on leafy plants that protect fruit from sunburn. The fruits ripen green to red. 4 inches. 65 days.
2 **CHINESE GIANT** is known for its huge fruits. It ripens green to red. 6 inches. 75 days.
3 **PURPLE BEAUTY** is an heirloom with purple fruits on a short, bushy plant. Purple fruits mature to red. 4 inches. 75 days.

Growing

Peppers grow best when temperatures are between 70° and 80°F. Temperatures below 60°F or above 90°F cause pepper flowers to drop. Protect the plants under a floating row cover to keep them warm or under a shade cloth so they remain cool.

Apply supplemental fertilizer after the first flush of peppers is set. A balanced fertilizer (such as 5-5-5) is a good choice; avoid high-nitrogen fertilizers, which promote lush foliage growth but few flower and fruits.

The fastest way to deliver fertilizer to pepper plants is with a liquid fertilizer product. Following package directions, mix the fertilizer with water in a watering can. Convenient hose-end canisters of fertilizer make mixing water and nutrients as simple as attaching the canister to your garden hose and watering the plants as you normally do. Look for these products at your local garden center.

Keep plants well weeded and watered. Apply a 2- to 3-inch-thick layer of organic mulch, such as straw or grass clippings, after the soil has warmed to prevent further weed growth and conserve soil moisture.

Apply at least 1 inch of water per week, being careful not to get the foliage wet when possible. Water early in the day so foliage has time to dry before night. Wet leaves at night will foster diseases. Watering is especially important at bloom time or blossoms may drop without setting fruit.

Plants with exceptionally large fruits occasionally need staking. Sink a sturdy stake into the ground alongside the plant and use twine or cloth to gently anchor the plant's main stem to the stake. Continue anchoring the stem to the stake as the plants grow.

1

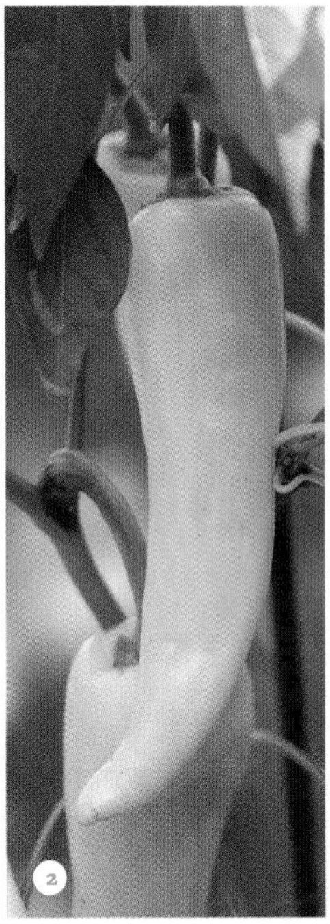

2

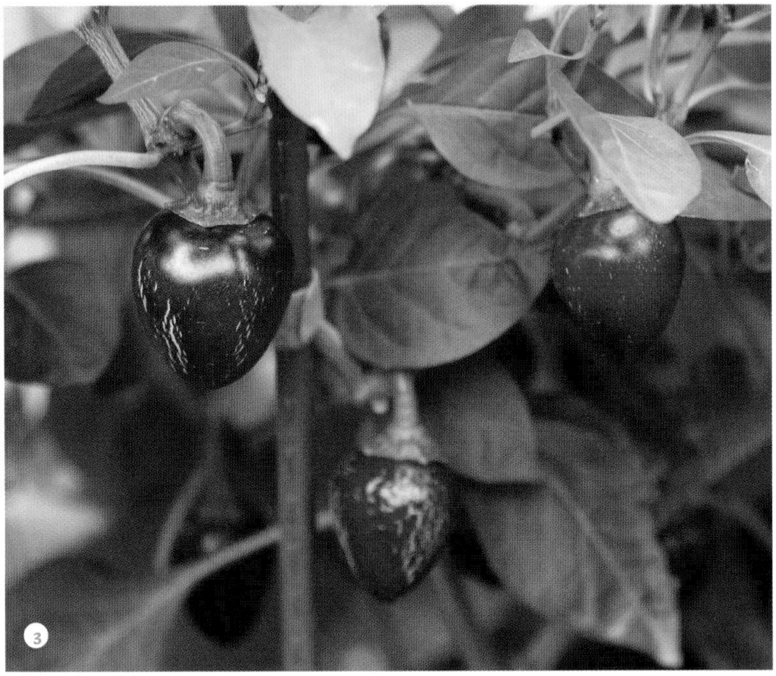

3

sweet elongated or round pepper varieties:

1 **CORNO DI TORO** is an Italian heirloom with long, curved fruits. It is very productive. 8–10 inches. 68 days.

2 **SWEET BANANA** starts yellow and matures to red. This sweet, mild-tasting pepper is easy to grow. 4 inches. 68 days.

3 **RED SWEET CHERRY** has round, sweet, slightly tapered fruits. It is a favorite addition to salads, and the plants grow well in containers. 1–2 inches. 78 days.

Harvest

Green bell varieties are usually picked when they are fully grown and mature—3 to 4 inches long, firm, and green. When the fruits are mature, they break easily from the plant. Less damage is done to the plants, however, if the fruits are cut rather than pulled off.

Red, yellow, orange, and brown bell pepper fruits may be left on the plant to develop full flavor and ripen to their mature color or they may be harvested at any color stage.

Harvest hot peppers in the green or red stage. Watch them carefully; they are quicker to turn red than sweet peppers.

Hot peppers vary in hotness depending on weather and stress. Plants suffering from water or nutrient stress produce fewer but hotter peppers. Cool, cloudy weather makes peppers less hot. Wear gloves when harvesting and handling hot peppers to protect your hands and face from capsaicin, the chemical compound that makes peppers hot.

If kept harvested, all types of peppers will develop fruit until frost.

Pests and diseases

Aphids, cutworms, corn earworms, and occasionally pepper maggots attack pepper plants and fruits. Remove aphids with a strong spray of water or by applying insecticidal soap. Protect young seedlings from cutworms by placing a paper collar around each seedling, setting the collar 1 inch below the soil and at least 2 inches aboveground. Protect your fruits from maggots by covering the plants with a floating row cover when the fruits are forming.

To avoid soilborne diseases rotate crops and do not plant a tomato-family crop (tomato, tomatillo, potato, or eggplant) in the same place for three years. Blossom-end rot is a physiological condition that causes the base of pepper fruits to rot. Mulch and keep plants evenly watered and fertilized to prevent it.

1

2

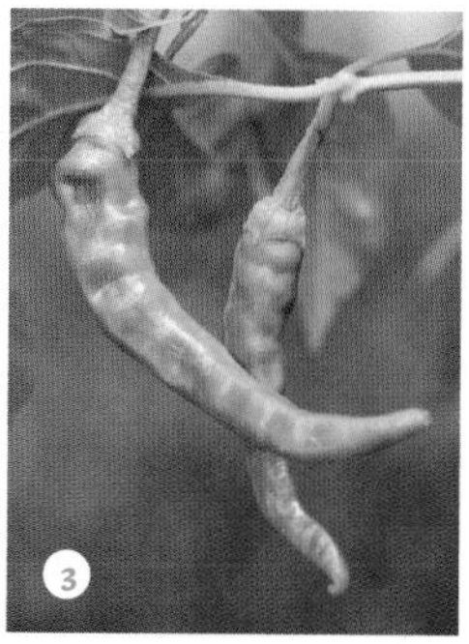
3

4

5

hot pepper varieties:

1 **ANCHO 211** has mildly hot, heart-shape fruits. They are good for stuffing, making chili rellenos, and drying. 4 inches. 80 days.

2 **EARLY JALAPEÑO** produces thick-walled fruits about 20 days before similar hot peppers. They have a full jalapeño flavor. 2 inches. 60 days.

3 **KUNG PAO** has very hot, slender fruits that mature to red. 4–5 inches. 85 days.

4 **HABANERO** produces golden orange, wrinkled fruits that are blisteringly hot at maturity. 1–2 inches. 110 days.

5 **BLACK PEARL** is a dwarf plant with black leaves, stems, and immature fruits. The fruits turn red at maturity. This plant is good in pots. ¾ inch. 60 days.

Potato *(Solanum tuberosum)*

While the potato that most people are familiar with is the white-flesh Irish potato, there are many other varieties of this native South American plant. And many of these unique varieties with red, blue, yellow, or bicolor flesh have a richer flavor than Irish potatoes. Plant three or four different varieties and explore different colors, shapes, and flavors.

Best site

Plant in full sun and well-drained soil. Potatoes will rot in poorly drained soil or heavy clay. They grow best in soil that is rich in organic matter. Incorporate a 2-inch-thick layer of compost into the garden prior to planting.

Prevent disease by planting potatoes and tomato-family members including tomatoes, peppers, and eggplant in the same ground only once every three years.

Types of potatoes

Early potatoes mature in 65 days.
Midseason potatoes are ready to harvest 75 to 80 days after planting.
Late potato varieties require 90-plus days to reach maturity.
Fingerling potatoes produce long, thin tubers that resemble fingers. They may fall into any of the maturity groupings.

Planting

Plant potatoes two to four weeks before your last frost date. In warm regions plant them in the fall or winter. Potatoes are easiest to start from certified disease-free seed potatoes. These small, sprouted pieces of potato readily send out roots and shoots and produce a large crop of spuds.

Presprouted seed potatoes develop faster than those without sprouts. To form sprouts, set uncut seed potatoes in a sunny place for one to three days before planting. Sprouting happens when the buds swell and expand. Small seed potatoes—those less than 2 inches across—can be planted directly in the ground, but cut the larger ones into pieces. Use a sharp knife to cut 1-inch fleshy chunks, each with two or more eyes. Dry the pieces overnight to form a callus layer on the cut ends and to help protect them from rot.

Plant pieces, as well as whole seed potatoes, eyes up in trenches dug 4 inches deep in heavy soil and 6 inches deep in light soil. Space the tubers 12 to 15 inches apart in rows 24 inches apart. Cover potatoes with 2 to 4 inches of soil.

Growing

Keep the soil evenly moist until sprouts emerge, usually about one week after planting. When sprouts are about 6 to 8 inches tall, hill the soil around them, creating a mounded ridge. Hill the potato rows again two to three weeks later.

Hilling creates an area of loose soil where tubers can easily form and shades the potato tubers from the sun.

Harvest

Harvest small, 1- to 2-inch diameter new potatoes six to eight weeks after planting, usually when the plants are flowering. Use a small digging fork to loosen the soil and lift the small tubers by hand, then replace the soil. Select a few potatoes from each plant so as not to significantly decrease the later harvest. Once the potato plant tops start dying back, dig and lift the entire plant with a garden fork and harvest the tubers.

Sort tubers after harvest. Separate the damaged tubers into a pile for eating first. Gently remove loose soil from the tubers. Cure them unwashed in a dark, humid place at 65 to 70°F for two weeks. Move the potatoes to a cool, dark, humid cellar, shed, or garage to store at 40 to 50°F for up to nine months, depending on the potato variety.

Pests and diseases

Rotate crops to prevent many potato pests and diseases. Grow certified disease-free tubers, clean up plant debris in fall to prevent potato scab, blight, and other potato diseases.

YOU SHOULD KNOW
Potatoes form below the soil surface, but they are not roots. They are specialized underground storage stems called tubers. Potatoes form best at soil temperatures between 60° and 70°F.

TEST GARDEN TIP

Healthy rotation

Growing a pest- and disease-free potato crop is often as simple as practicing crop rotation. By planting potatoes and their close relatives—tomatoes, peppers, and eggplant—in a new area each year, you'll thwart perennial pests by moving their crop of choice out of the immediate area. Combine crop rotation with growing certified disease-free tubers and cleaning up all the plant debris in fall for a hefty harvest of spuds.

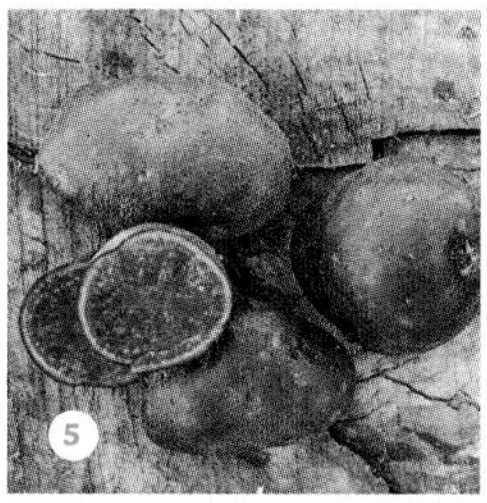

varieties:

1 **DARK RED NORLAND** produces oblong tubers with red skin and white flesh. Tasty harvested as new potatoes, the variety is resistant to scab and foliar diseases. Early.

2 **YUKON GOLD** has yellow skin and moist yellow flesh; the plant is drought tolerant and very productive. Early.

3 **CARIBE** is grown for its blue-purple skin and pure white flesh. This variety is good harvested as a new potato. Early.

4 **RED CLOUD** has crimson skin and dry white flesh. It stores well. Midseason.

5 **ALL BLUE** is an heirloom with unique blue skin and moist purple flesh. It is excellent for purple mashed potatoes. Late.

6 **RUSSIAN BANANA** is a fingerling type with a banana shape and yellow skin and flesh. The tuber's waxy texture makes it a good boiling potato. Late.

7 **BUTTE** is a classic Idaho baking potato with russet skin and white flesh. Butte has 20 percent more protein and 58 percent more vitamin C than other varieties. Late.

Pumpkin (*Cucurbita* species)

Lots of space and a long growing season are essential for growing pumpkins. Most types are vining and need 50 to 100 square feet per hill. From tiny white pumpkins to massive jack-o'-lanterns, pumpkins come in all shapes, sizes, and flavors. If you grow pumpkins for cooking and baking, be sure to choose a variety bred for good flavor. Most pumpkins will store well—lasting two to three months.

Best site

Plant in full sun and well-drained soil. Good drainage is very important when growing pumpkins. Plants languish in poorly drained soil and fruits are more likely to rot when they rest in wet or boggy soil.

Pumpkins grow best in soil that is high in organic matter. Incorporate a 2-inch-thick layer of compost into the soil prior to planting.

Planting

Sow seeds in the garden when the daytime air temperature consistently reaches 70°F. Do not rush to plant seeds outdoors because pumpkins do not germinate well in cool soil and even a light frost will damage them. In cool-summer areas start seeds indoors four weeks before your last frost date and transplant the seedlings after the danger of frost has passed. Starting seeds indoors is especially helpful for ensuring winter squash has adequate time to mature in cool-summer areas.

Sow seeds 2 to 4 feet apart in rows 5 to 8 feet apart. Or plant five to seven seeds in hills spaced 4 feet apart, thinning to three plants per hill after true leaves form.

Growing

Pumpkins, especially the large varieties, require a constant supply of moisture to grow and size up properly. Apply 1 to 2 inches of water per week, increasing frequency during dry periods. Keep beds weeded by lightly cultivating around plants with a hoe. Mulch plants with an organic mulch, such as straw or grass clippings, after the soil has warmed.

If desired, fertilize at planting time using a balanced product such as 5-5-5. Once pumpkin vines start running, fertilize plants with a high-nitrogen fertilizer. In cool-summer areas pinch off blossoms and small fruits that form late in the season. These won't have time to mature before frost and will take energy away from the existing maturing fruits.

Let pumpkins run across a lawn, or trellis small-fruited varieties on a fence or other sturdy structure.

Harvest

Leave pumpkins on the vine until they reach a mature size and turn the appropriate skin color for their variety. The rind will feel hard when you press it with your thumbnail. Harvest fruits before a hard frost. Use a clean, sharp knife to cut the stems 2 inches above the fruits. Place pumpkins in an 80° to 85°F, humid room for two weeks to cure. Store them in a dark location at 50° to 55°F. Most pumpkins can be stored for two to three months.

Pests and diseases

Pumpkins are vulnerable to squash bugs, which gather under the leaves. They feed on the foliage and flowers, reducing the vigor of the plant. When you see the first brown nymphs, kill them with a spray of neem oil before they can reach adulthood. Set a sheet of cardboard under the plants and collect and destroy squash bugs hiding underneath. Rotate crops and clean crop debris in fall to eliminate squash bug overwintering spots and to fend off diseases.

Cucumber beetles harm pumpkins, feeding on young plants and flowers. They also spread diseases. See page 111 for more about controlling this pest. Watch for aphids feeding on young plants in spring. Remove them with forceful sprays of water or insecticidal soap.

Provide proper spacing, keep the pumpkin patch weed free, and select disease-resistant varieties to control fusarium wilt and powdery mildew diseases.

YOU SHOULD KNOW
Pumpkins' bright orange color is an indication that it is full of beta-carotene, an important antioxidant. Research indicates that beta-carotene may reduce the risk of developing certain types of cancer.

pumpkin varieties:

1 **HOWDEN** is a classic big pumpkin with defined ribs that is good for carving. Two or three fruits, each 20–30 pounds. Deep orange. 115 days.

2 **BABY BEAR** is a mini pumpkin with flesh good enough for pies. The seeds are good for roasting. 8 to 10 fruits, each 1–2 pounds. Deep orange. 105 days.

3 **BABY BOO** is a decorative mini pumpkin that is 2–3 inches in diameter. Harvest before the skin turns yellow. 8 to 10 fruits. White. 90 days.

4 **DILL'S ATLANTIC GIANT** produces the largest pumpkins, some more than 1,000 pounds. It requires a lot of space. Pink-orange. 120 days.

5 **LONG ISLAND CHEESE** is a flattened, ribbed pumpkin that resembles a cheese wheel. It has deep orange flesh and is good for pies. Two fruits, each 6–10 pounds. Tan. 108 days.

6 **LUMINA** is creamy white with smooth skin and orange flesh. Three to four fruits, each 10 pounds. White. 85 days.

7 **SMALL SUGAR** is an heirloom favored for pies and canning. Three to four fruits, each 5–8 pounds. Orange. 100 days.

Radish (*Raphanus sativus*)

Ready to harvest 25 to 30 days after planting, radishes are a fun crop to grow in early spring. They require just a few inches of growing space, perfect for small-space gardens and container plantings. Although the small red radishes with spicy flavor are most familiar, there are many more varieties.

YOU SHOULD KNOW
Radish foliage is edible and lends a slight peppery flavor to salads. Save thinned seedlings and the tops of mature radishes to spice up a bowl of greens.

Best site
For best yields plant in full sun and well-drained soil. Radishes will tolerate some shade. Incorporate a 2-inch-thick layer of compost into the soil before planting. Rake the soil smooth, removing any rocks or debris, to promote good radish formation.

Types of radishes
Spring radishes mature quickly and grow best during cool conditions. **Round red radishes** with crunchy texture and hot, spicy flavor are most familiar. **French radishes**, cylindrical types that mature earlier than round radishes, have white skin or red skin tipped in white. **Winter radishes** grow into large round or elongated roots. Slower to develop than spring radishes, they remain crisp longer, are more pungent, and can hold in the ground or store longer than spring varieties.

Planting
Sow seeds in the garden three to four weeks before the last average frost in spring and six weeks before the first frost in fall. Make successive sowings every week or two in spring to extend the harvest. Many winter radishes are best sown in midsummer for fall harvest.

Sow seeds ½ inch deep and 1 inch apart in rows 10 inches apart. Interplant carrots, beans, and cucumbers with radishes to maximize your planting space.

Growing
Thin small-rooted regular spring radishes to 2 inches apart when they are 1 inch tall. Thin larger-rooted winter radishes to 4 to 6 inches apart. Grow spring radishes quickly to maturity by maintaining a weed-free bed, hand pulling any weeds that emerge, and keeping the soil consistently moist.

Harvest
Harvest spring radishes as soon as the roots are large enough to eat. Radishes left in the ground too long can crack, become woody, develop a seed stalk, and have a hot flavor. Harvest winter radishes when they reach full size. Store both types of radishes in the refrigerator.

Pests and diseases
Avoid radish diseases such as club root by rotating radish crops every five to seven years. Flea beetles and aphids attack radish plants. Keep them in check with jet sprays of water or sprays of insecticidal soap.

varieties:

1. **CHERRY BELL** is an exceptionally fast-growing spring variety that produces round, red radishes. 22 days.
2. **FRENCH BREAKFAST** is a spring radish that has oblong red roots with white tips; it tolerates warm temperatures well. 23 days.
3. **APRIL CROSS** is a 12- to 16-inch-long white winter radish that is best planted in fall for spring to early summer harvest. 55 days.

Rhubarb

(Rheum rhabarbarum)

Exceptionally hardy, rhubarb is a bold, long-lasting plant in the edible landscape. Its large leaves remain dark green through mid- to late summer. The pies, tarts, and jams produced from fresh rhubarb make this easy-to-grow plant all the more desirable.

YOU SHOULD KNOW
Rhubarb is most flavorful and tender in early spring, but it can be harvested in summer too. In general, deep red stalks have the most intense flavor.

Best site

Plant rhubarb in full sun and moist, well-drained soil. Be sure to plant it where it will not be disturbed because it can be productive for many years. A perennial bed or shrub bed makes a fine planting place for rhubarb.

Planting

Plant crowns in early spring as soon as the ground can be worked. Plant so the central bud is 2 inches below the soil line. Space the crowns 6 feet apart.

Growing

Spread a 2-inch-thick layer of compost around new plants when the air temperature rises above 80°F. Keep the soil evenly moist and weed free. Cut off any flower stalks that develop down to the base of the plant. Rhubarb thrives with adequate soil nutrients. Apply a complete plant fertilizer annually in spring. After harvest, spread a 2-inch-layer of compost around plants.

When the leafstalks become thin (usually after six to eight years), dig and divide the plant in spring or fall. Divide the crown so the new plant has some buds and a generous amount of roots, then replant. Keep divided plants well watered the first year.

Harvest

Rhubarb leafstalks develop the best color and flavor when harvested during cool weather. Leave first-year plants unharvested. During the second year, harvest with a sharp knife or break stalks off by holding them close to the base and pulling down and to one side. Remove the leaves. Harvest for one week. In the third year, harvest all stalks larger than 1 inch wide for eight weeks.

Compost the leaves; although the leafstalks are completely edible, rhubarb leaves contain oxalic acid and are poisonous.

Store unwashed leafstalks in a plastic bag in the refrigerator for up to two weeks.

Pests and diseases

Few pests and diseases seriously affect rhubarb. Remove any Japanese beetles, rhubarb curculio beetles, or caterpillars by hand. Avoid verticillium wilt by planting rhubarb in well-drained soil.

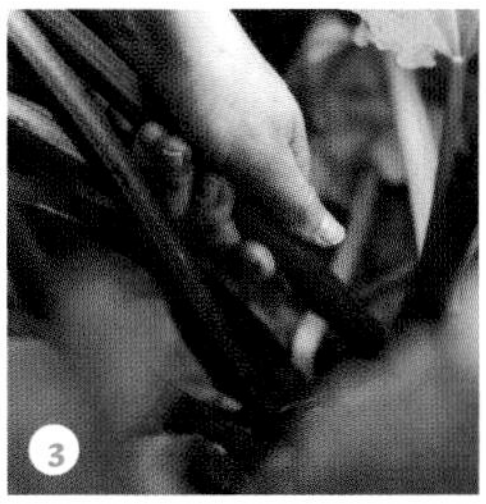

varieties:

1. **VALENTINE** has deep red stalks; it grows faster than other red varieties and can be harvested sooner.
2. **MACDONALD** is a high-yielding variety with green stems that have red overtones; it grows well in heavy clay soils.
3. **CANADA RED** is a popular variety with long, thick stalks that are extra sweet.

Rutabaga, Swede turnip

(Brassica napus)

A cross between a cabbage and a turnip, rutabaga produces large roots and bitter leaves. The roots, with white or yellow flesh, have a sweet nutty flavor when they mature in a long stretch of cool weather.

YOU SHOULD KNOW
Rutabagas are used much like potatoes in cooking. Peel and dice the roots and add them to soups and stews; mash or steam them for a side dish.

Best site

Plant in full sun or part shade and loose, well-drained soil. Rutabagas don't require rich soil and will readily adapt to a variety of growing conditions including containers. Choose a pot that is at least 12 inches deep. Before planting remove rocks and debris from the soil to promote smooth, round rutabagas.

Planting

Sow seeds in the garden four weeks before the last frost date in spring for an early summer crop or 90 to 100 days before the first fall frost for an autumn crop. In warm-summer areas, rutabaga produces larger roots and tastes sweeter when sown in midsummer for harvest in fall. Sow seeds ½ inch deep and 2 inches apart in rows about 24 inches apart.

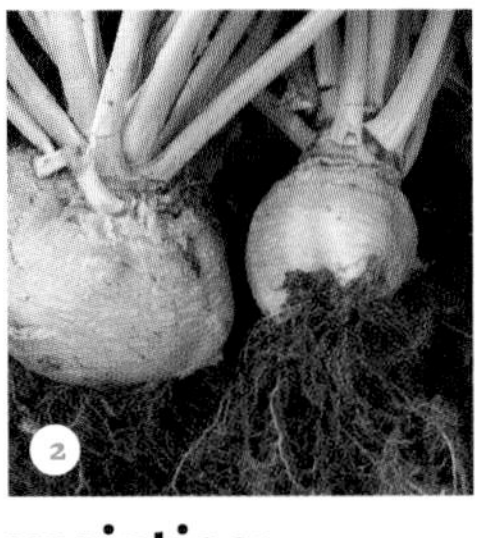

varieties:

1. **PURPLE TOP** features huge yellow roots with fine-grained flesh that turns orange when cooked. 90 days.
2. **MARIAN**, which has pale purple shoulders, keeps well and is disease resistant. 90 days.
3. **LAURENTIAN** roots have dark purple shoulders with pale yellow skin below and sweet, mild flesh. 95 days.

Growing

Thin seedlings to 8 inches apart once true leaves form. Hand weed the bed. Mulch with a 2- to 3-inch-thick layer of organic material such as straw after weeding to maintain soil moisture and to keep the soil cool. Provide plants with 1 to 2 inches of water per week, especially during periods of hot, dry weather.

Harvest

Pull rutabaga roots when they are 3 to 5 inches in diameter, about 90 days after seeding. Fall-grown roots taste sweeter if exposed to a few frosts before harvest. Since rutabaga can withstand frost, pick only what you need that day and leave the rest in the garden.

To store rutabaga, trim off the foliage with a sharp knife to within 1 inch of the crown. The roots can be stored for two to four months at 35°F and high humidity. You can also store rutabaga in the garden during winter by mulching the bed with a 6- to 8-inch-thick layer of straw in fall.

Pests and diseases

Aphids and flea beetles attack the greens, and root maggots can damage the roots. Keep aphids and flea beetles in check with jet sprays of water or sprays of insecticidal soap. Control maggots with floating row cover or diatomaceous earth.

Spinach

(Spinacia oleracea)

Scrumptious in a fresh salad and lovely in the garden, spinach is a plant for the edible landscape. Plant ribbons of spinach through a perennial border or use it as a tiny, tidy hedge around a plot of early-season vegetables. Plant a late summer crop for harvest in fall.

1

Best site

Plant in full sun or part shade and moist, well-drained soil. It grows well in containers. Spinach grows best in soil that has generous amounts of organic matter. Mix a 2-inch-thick layer of compost into the soil before planting.

Types of spinach

Smooth-leaf spinach produces relatively flat leaves that are easy to wash and clean after harvesting.

Crinkle-leaf or savoy spinach has highly textured leaves with more body than smooth-leaf types.

Planting

Begin sowing seeds in the garden four to six weeks before your last spring frost date. Spinach seeds can germinate in soils as cool as 35°F. If the soil was prepared in fall, seeds can be scattered over frozen ground or snow cover in late winter and they will germinate as the soil thaws. In warm areas plant seeds in fall to harvest during winter.

To speed germination, soak seeds in warm water overnight. Sow seeds ¼ inch deep and 1 inch apart in rows 12 inches apart or scatter seeds in a raised bed. If you are planting a fall crop, chill the seeds in the refrigerator for one to two weeks before planting.

2

3

varieties:

1 **BLOOMSDALE LONG STANDING** is a classic crinkle-leaf variety that's quick growing and slow to bolt. 42 days.

2 **OLYMPIA** is a smooth-leaf variety that is slow to bolt, disease resistant, and productive. 45 days.

3 **ORIENTAL GIANT** produces large, smooth 12- to 15-inch-long leaves and yields up to three times more foliage than other varieties. 40 days.

Growing

Thin seedlings to 6 inches apart when they're 3 inches tall. Maintain cool, moist soil by watering regularly and mulching with a 2- to 3-inch-thick layer of an organic material such as straw. It's best to water in the morning so the leaves can dry before evening.

Harvest

Begin harvesting individual leaves 20 to 30 days after sowing, when there are five or six leaves on the plant. Harvest whole plants in 35 to 50 days. Continue harvesting leaves until hot weather causes seed stalks to form, then pull and compost the plants. To store spinach leaves, wash, pat dry, and place them in a plastic bag in the refrigerator, where they will keep for about one week.

Pests and diseases

Use floating row covers to protect young plants from leaf miners. Choose disease-resistant varieties for blight and virus control, especially when growing spinach in humid, wet areas.

YOU SHOULD KNOW

Create your own gourmet greens blend by mixing baby spinach leaves with mesclun or other leaf lettuce. Homegrown spinach is especially tender and tasty when harvested shortly after leaves emerge in early spring.

Squash (*Cucurbita* species)

Squash plants are some of the most productive vegetables in the garden. Count on them to produce several pounds of fruit and edible flowers. These warm-weather lovers are easy to grow in well-drained soil. Some types have sprawling habits, sending vines out 20 feet or more from the center of the plant. There are many good options for small-space gardens; summer squash is a favorite for containers.

Best site

Plant in full sun and well-drained soil. Good drainage is very important when growing squash. Not only do plants languish in poorly drained soil, but fruits are more likely to rot when they rest on wet or boggy ground. If your garden soil is slow draining, plant squash in raised beds or choose varieties that can be grown in pots.

Squash grows best in soil that is high in organic matter. Incorporate a 2-inch-thick layer of compost into the soil prior to planting.

Types of squash

SUMMER SQUASH ripens in mid- to late summer, and includes **zucchini, yellow straightneck squash, yellow crookneck squash, scallop squash, and others.** These tender vegetables are best harvested when they are small, before they become seedy and tough. Summer squash is usually eaten fresh and produces copious amount of fruit when harvested every other day or so during the height of the season. Summer squashvines grow just 2 to 4 feet wide and are well suited to small spaces and containers.

WINTER SQUASH differs from summer squash in that it has a thick rind that makes it possible to store this late-season crop for months. **Butternut, acorn, buttercup, delicata, vegetable spaghetti, and hubbard** are all types of winter squash. There are several other unique heirloom varieties with interesting shapes, colors, and flavors. If your growing season is short, avoid varieties that require more than 100 days to mature.

Planting

Sow seeds in the garden when the daytime air temperature consistently reaches 70°F. Do not rush to plant seeds outdoors as plants do not germinate well in cool soil and even a light frost will damage them. In cool-summer areas start seeds indoors four weeks before your last frost date and transplant the seedlings after the danger of frost has passed. Starting seeds indoors is especially helpful for ensuring winter squash has adequate time to mature in cool-summer areas.

Plant seeds of bush varieties of summer and winter squash 1 to 2 inches deep and 2 to 3 feet apart in rows spaced 3 to 5 feet apart. For vining varieties, sow seeds 2 to 4 feet apart in rows 5 to 8 feet apart. Or plant five to seven seeds in hills spaced 4 feet apart, thinning to the three strongest plants per hill after true leaves form.

Growing

Squash requires a constant supply of moisture to grow and size up properly. Apply 1 to 2 inches of water per week; increase the frequency during dry periods. Keep beds weeded by lightly cultivating around the plants with a hoe. Mulch with an organic mulch such as straw or grass clippings after the soil has warmed.

Once squash vines start running, fertilize plants with a high-nitrogen fertilizer. In cool-summer areas pinch off winter squash blossoms and small fruits that form late in the season. These won't have time to mature before frost and will take energy away from the existing maturing fruits, slowing their development.

Let large-fruited winter squash run across a lawn or garden. Vining small-fruited winter squash can be trained onto a trellis. Avoid trellising large-fruited varieties as the weight of the fruit will stress the trellis and the vine. Train a vine to grow up a sturdy trellis by weaving the growing tips gently between the openings every few days. 'Cream of the Crop' and 'Delicata' winter squash are two small-fruited winter squash varietes that grow well on trellises.

YOU SHOULD KNOW
Generally, summer squash types can be used interchangeably in recipes. Choose your favorite zucchini, crookneck, or scallop squash and stir-fry it with onions, tomatoes, and okra for a rich vegetable medley.

summer squash varieties:

1. **YELLOW STRAIGHTNECK** is a bush straightneck type. Creamy yellow. 50 days.
2. **BLACK BEAUTY** is a zucchini type with excellent smooth, straight fruits. Dark green. 60 days.
3. **SUNBURST** produces pattypan-type fruit that is very tender. The vigorous plant is easy to grow and productive. Deep yellow. 52 days.
4. **EARLY SUMMER CROOKNECK** is a striking heirloom with bumpy skin. It produces many fruits over a long season. Yellow. 53 days.
5. **GOLD RUSH HYBRID** is a zucchini type with uniform straight fruits. Deep yellow. 50 days.

Harvest

SUMMER SQUASH

Zucchini, crooknecks, and straightnecks taste best when picked small, about 6 inches long. Pattypan, or scallop, squash is best harvested when the fruit is 3 inches across. Check plants daily because a fruit can reach edible size overnight. In hot weather, fruit are often ready for harvest four to eight days after flowering.

Use a clean, sharp knife to cut the stems of summer squash about 1 inch above the fruits. Store the squash for up to two weeks in the refrigerator. If a few fruits escape your detection, harvest them as soon as you see them. The more you pick, the more fruits will be produced.

WINTER SQUASH

Leave these long-season plants on the vine until they reach a mature size and turn the appropriate skin color for that variety. The rind will feel hard when you press it with your thumbnail. Harvest fruits before a hard frost. Use a clean, sharp knife to cut the stems 2 inches above the fruits.

Place winter squash in an 80° to 85°F, humid room for two weeks to cure. Store them in a dark location at 50° to 55°F. Most winter squash can be stored for two to three months under these conditions. Some, such as hubbard squash, can last up to six months.

FLOWERS

The bright yellow flowers of squash are edible. Stuff them with cream cheese or a cooked meat mixture or enjoy them raw or sauté some in your next stir-fry or vegetable medley.

Harvest only male blossoms for eating unless you are trying to reduce plant production. If that is the case, harvest both male and female blossoms. Male blossoms are easy to distinguish from female blossoms. The stem of the male blossom is thin and the stem of the female blossom very thick. At the base of the female flower below the petals is a small bulge, which is the developing squash. When harvesting, always leave a few male blossoms on the vine for pollination.

Use pruning shears or a sharp knife to cut squash blossoms at midday when the petals are open, leaving 1 inch of stem. Gently rinse them in a pan of cool water and store in ice water in the refrigerator until ready to use.

Pests and diseases

Squash, particularly winter types, are vulnerable to squash bugs, which gather under the leaves. They feed on the foliage and flowers, reducing the vigor of the plant. When you see the first brown nymphs, kill them with a spray of neem oil before they can reach adulthood. Set a sheet of cardboard under the plants and collect and destroy squash bugs hiding underneath. Rotate crops and clean crop debris in fall to eliminate squash bug overwintering spots and fend off diseases.

Cucumber beetles harm squash, feeding on young plants and flowers. They also spread diseases. See page 111 for more about controlling this pest. Watch for aphids feeding on young plants in spring. Remove them with forceful sprays of water or insecticidal soap.

Squash vine borers especially attack buttercup winter squash varieties. Larvae tunnel into the vines, opening them to disease and rotting. Before young plants flower, cover them with a floating row cover to prevent the adult flies from laying eggs in spring. Make vertical cuts with a sharp knife in the stems of wilted plants and remove larvae. Cover the wounded stem with soil.

Provide proper spacing, keep the squash patch weed free, and select disease-resistant varieties to control fusarium wilt and powdery mildew diseases.

winter squash varieties:

1 **RED KURI** is a hubbard type with a teardrop shape. Two or three fruits, each 4–7 pounds. Red orange. 92 days.

2 **BON BON HYBRID** is a large buttercup type with sweet orange flesh. About four fruits, each 4–5 pounds. Dark green with a gray button on the bottom. 95 days.

3 **SWEET DUMPLING** is a delicata type with teacup-shape fruits with sweet orange flesh. 8–10 fruits, each 4 inches wide. Ivory with dark green stripes. 100 days.

4 **TABLE ACE** is an acorn type with sweet, nutty flavor. Five to seven fruits, each 2–3 pounds. Black-green. 85 days.

5 **TABLE QUEEN** is an heirloom acorn type with golden flesh. The vine is vigorous. Four to six fruits, each 2–3 pounds. Black-green. 85 days.

6 **WALTHAM** is a cylindrical, 9-inch-diameter butternut type with sweet orange flesh. Four or five fruits, each 4–5 pounds. Tan. 105 days.

7 **SPAGHETTI** has flesh that separates into long noodlelike strings after baking. Four or five fruits, each 4 pounds. Ivory maturing to yellow. 88 days.

SMALL-SPACE SOLUTIONS

Bush-type plants make it easy to grow most varieties of summer squash in small spaces. Vining small-fruited winter squash and pumpkins can be trained onto a trellis. Avoid trellising large-fruited varieties as the weight of the fruit will stress the trellis and the vine. Train a vine to grow up a sturdy trellis by weaving the growing tips gently between the openings every few days. Here are a few excellent small-fruited winter squash and pumpkins for growing on a trellis.

Winter Squash

'Cream of the Crop'
'Delicata'

Pumpkin

'Baby Boo'
'Jack-be-Little'
'Lumina'
'Munchkin'
'Small Sugar'

Sweet potato

(Ipomoea batatas)

Easy-to-grow sweet potatoes require a long, frost-free growing season to mature large roots. The plant's thick storage roots, which grow from nodes on trailing stems, are high in vitamin A and can be stored into the winter.

YOU SHOULD KNOW

In the supermarket "yam" and "sweet potato" are used interchangeably, but they are the roots of two different plants. In North America, virtually all roots by these names are sweet potatoes.

Best site

Plant in full sun and well-drained soil. Sweet potatoes grow well in moist soil but quickly languish in soggy, poorly drained soil. Grow plants in a raised bed if soil drainage is poor.

Planting

Sweet potatoes are normally started from small plants called slips that are planted in the garden two weeks after the last average frost date. Create a 6- to 12-inch-high raised bed, and amend the soil with a 2- to 3-inch-thick layer of compost. Plant certified disease-free sweet potato slips 12 to 18 inches apart in rows 4 feet apart for vining plants, and 30 inches apart for bush types.

In cool-summer areas lay black plastic over the raised bed two weeks before planting time to warm the soil, and plant the slips into holes poked in the plastic at the appropriate spacing.

Growing

Keep the area around plants weed free until the vines begin to run and can crowd out competing plants. Then mulch around plants with a 2- to 3-inch-thick layer of organic material. Keep the slips well watered for the first few weeks and consistently moist until the last month of growth. Reduce watering three to four weeks before harvesting to avoid root rot.

Harvest

Most sweet potato varieties can be harvested beginning 90 days after planting. Harvest after the vines are lightly frosted and the leaves show a little yellowing. Plants left in the ground too long will either rot from the cold soil temperatures or, in warmer areas, continue to grow larger roots. With a garden fork, carefully dig up the vines and separate the sweet potato roots.

Cure sweet potatoes for one to two weeks in a room with high humidity and a temperature of 80° to 90°F. Store cured roots wrapped in newspaper in a dry location at 55° to 60°F. Allow the roots to sit for a few weeks before you begin eating them. Starches begin converting to sugar in storage, but it takes six to eight weeks of storage for sweet potatoes to develop their full characteristic sweetness.

Pests and diseases

Avoid root rot disease by not planting sweet potatoes in the same ground more than once every three years, cleaning crop debris well in fall, and growing certified disease-free slips.

varieties:

1. **CENTENNIAL** is a fast-maturing vining type with red skin and orange flesh. This variety is good for Northern gardens. 90 days.
2. **GEORGIA JET** is a productive vining variety with red skin and orange flesh. 100 days.
3. **VARDAMAN** is a bush variety with golden skin and deep orange flesh. 95 days.

Tomatillo, husk tomato

(Physalis ixocarpa)

A relative of tomato, tomatillo is a Central America native that has been used in cooking for thousands of years. It is a key ingredient in stews, moles, and salsas.

YOU SHOULD KNOW
Tomatillo's sweet, tart, and somewhat citrusy flavor is often used to counteract the hottest of chili peppers in many dishes.

Best site

Plant in full sun and moist, well-drained soil. Tomatillos grow best in nutrient-rich soil. Amend the planting area with a 2-inch-thick layer of compost prior to planting.

Tomatillos do well in containers. Grow this top-heavy plant in a large, sturdy container.

Planting

Set transplants in the garden after the last average frost date. Promote a sturdy plant by pinching off the lowest leaves and burying the stem of the transplant so only the top leaves are aboveground. Roots will emerge along the buried stem.

Space transplants 36 inches apart. Tomatillos can also be started from seeds planted eight weeks before the last average frost date.

varieties:

1. **TOMA VERDE** is an early variety with green fruits that turn yellow at maturity. 60 days.
2. **PURPLE,** which stores well, features purple skins and very sweet purple-tinged flesh that makes unique color salsa. 65 days.
3. **DE MILPA** is an heirloom with small green fruits blushed with purple. 70 days.

Growing

Keep the soil well weeded and moist. Mulch with a 2- to 4-inch-thick layer of organic mulch, such as straw, after the soil has warmed to suppress weeds and maintain soil moisture. Mature plants are drought tolerant.

Fertilize plants with a complete low-nitrogen fertilizer such as 5-10-10 at planting. Use the same fertilizer to side-dress plants once the fruits form and then fertilize monthly. Tomatillo plants benefit from trellising. They naturally sprawl across the soil. Use a tomato cage or stake to keep the branches and fruits off the ground.

Harvest

For the best flavor, harvest tomatillos when the papery husk changes from green to tan while the fruit is still green. Use a sharp knife to harvest the fruits. In cool-summer areas, remove the whole plant if frost is forecast, suspending it upside down in a sheltered place to mature the remaining fruits.

Store harvested tomatillos in their husks for up to two weeks in the refrigerator.

Pests and diseases

Tomatillos are vulnerable to the same pests as tomatoes. Avoid diseases by practicing crop rotation. Do not plant tomatillos in the same ground that tomato-family plants (eggplant, peppers, potatoes, and tomatoes) were grown in the previous three years.

Tomato *(Lycopersicon esculentum)*

Whether you enjoy them sliced, stuffed, grilled, dried, juiced, or simply fresh off the vine, the flavor of homegrown tomatoes can't be beat. Easy to grow, tomatoes are the most popular garden vegetable. Grow them in a container on your balcony or in your perennial border, or plant a row of heirlooms in your vegetable garden. Four tomato plants often provide enough fruit for a family of four.

Best site

Plant in full sun and well-drained soil. Tomatoes need at least eight hours of direct sunlight a day to produce fruit. Plants need consistent moisture, but they do not tolerate waterlogged soil. If your soil is slow to drain, plant tomatoes in a container or raised bed.

Soil rich in organic matter produces the best tomatoes. Mix a 2-inch-thick layer of compost into your planting site in early spring.

Avoid diseases by not planting tomatoes or other members of the tomato family (eggplant, pepper, potato, and tomatillo) in the same location more than once every three years. Do not plant tomatoes near walnut trees. Tomatoes are particularly susceptible to juglone—a chemical compound found in walnut roots, leaves, and twigs.

Types of tomatoes

Tomato plants vary in their growth habit. Scientists label these habits determinate and indeterminate, which you may see on plant tags.
Determinate tomatoes are small, compact plants. They grow to a certain height, stop, then flower and set all their fruit at once. Since all their fruit ripens within a week or two, determinate varieties are good for preserving.
Indeterminate varieties grow, flower, and set fruit until they are killed by frost. Harvest from an indeterminate variety usually extends over a two- or three-month period, and the yield is generally greater than in determinate varieties.

So, what type should you choose? If you are growing tomatoes for immediate enjoyment, choose an indeterminate variety, such as 'Early Girl' and many of the heirlooms, for a long, delicious harvest. If you plan to make and can salsa, plant a few determinate plants, such as 'Celebrity', to ensure you have many tomatoes ripe at one time.

While growth habit designations are useful, a more helpful classification system for this favorite summer fruit is based on taste, fruit size, and growth. The following pages include groups of tomatoes prized for these endearing factors.
Heirloom tomatoes offer unique taste, shape, and texture and vary widely from the standard red orb tomato that was popular for many years. Heirlooms often perish quickly after harvest, but when eaten at perfect ripeness, their flavor trumps that of nearly any other tomato variety.

Thanks to their recently rediscovered delicious taste and lovely shapes and colors, heirloom tomatoes are becoming easier to find. Mass merchants often carry a limited line of heirloom species. Local garden centers are also a good place to look for heirlooms. If you don't see what you are looking for, don't hesitate to ask the staff to grow some heirlooms next season.

The Internet is rife with heirloom tomato seedlings. For a diverse selection of seedlings, visit these sites: seedsavers.org and territorialseed.com.
Slicers are a group of tomatoes with medium to large fruits that are often sliced horizontally for topping burgers and sandwiches. Often red, but also available in yellow and green varieties, slicers tend to be disease resistant and easy to grow. Some of the most popular backyard tomatoes, including 'Better Boy' and 'Celebrity', are in the slicer group.
Small-fruited tomatoes, also called grape and cherry tomatoes, make perfect snacks. These bite-size tomatoes are packed with flavor and sweet tomato juice. Available in shades of red and yellow, small-fruited tomatoes are often very prolific. One plant can produce several pounds of fruit from midsummer until frost.

YOU SHOULD KNOW
Heirloom tomatoes offer an exciting new culinary experience for tomato lovers everywhere. Heirloom varieties are available in many different colors and shapes and have unique flavors too. Nearly as easy to grow as modern tomatoes, heirlooms will produce several pounds of perfectly ripe fruit.

heirloom varieties

1 **BRANDYWINE** is a popular, pink-skinned tomato with soft flesh and full flavor. It has yellow and red versions. 12–16 ounces. 80 days.
2 **CHEROKEE PURPLE** is a Tennessee heirloom with flavorful, soft-textured, rose-purple skin and red flesh. Highly perishable. 10–12 ounces. 72 days.
3 **YELLOW PEAR** bears small pear-shape fruits with a sweet flavor. 1–2 ounces. 78 days.

Paste tomatoes are typically used for canning whole or making ketchup, paste, and sauces. Their solid, meaty, low-moisture flesh simplifies preserving. Paste-type plants are usually short and set many fruits that ripen all at once. **Container tomatoes** are short, stocky plants that are easy to grow in hanging baskets and pots. These productive plants often produce small to medium-size fruit, and some varieties require staking to remain upright when loaded with fruit late in the season.

Planting

Plant transplants in the garden after the last average frost date. Although seeds can be directly sown in the garden and plants grown to maturity in warm areas, most gardeners buy transplants or start seeds indoors six to eight weeks before their average last frost date.

When shopping for tomato plants at your local nursery, look for short, stocky plants with dark green foliage. The foliage should be free of blemishes. Avoid tall, lanky plants as they have been growing in their container too long and will take longer to establish in the garden.

Plant small bush varieties 24 inches apart and larger varieties, especially sprawling indeterminate plants, 36 to 48 inches apart in rows 36 inches apart.

Tomato transplants should be planted deeper than other vegetables. While most plants are transplanted so the top of the soil in their container is level with surrounding garden soil, tomatoes, and their relatives tomatillos, are unique. They can form roots along their stems. The extra roots help anchor the plant and provide more opportunity for water and nutrient uptake, which is especially helpful when starting with tall, leggy transplants.

Prune off the transplant's bottom leaves and set the root ball in a planting hole deep enough so that only the top cluster of leaves is showing aboveground. If the transplant is exceptionally tall, try laying the stem horizontally along a 4- to 6-inch deep trench in the soil. Turn the uppermost portion of the stem vertically so the top cluster of leaves pokes out of the soil.

1

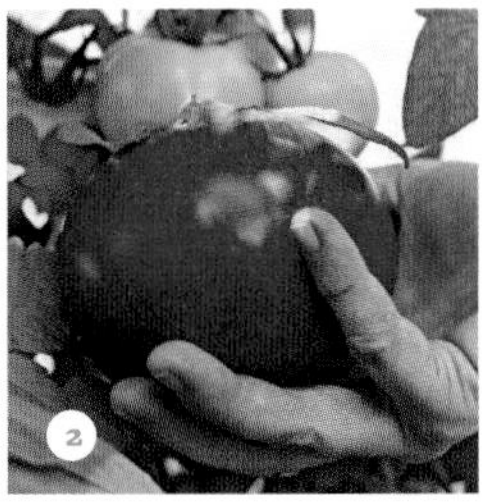
2

3

4

slicer varieties:

1 **SOLDACKI** is a Polish heirloom variety with intense flavor. It has dark pink flesh and produces massive fruits. 24–32 ounces. 80 days.

2 **CELEBRITY** is a productive and widely adapted cultivar with meaty, red fruits that ripen uniformly. It is good for canning and preserving. A bush form is available. 8–12 ounces. 72 days.

3 **DELICIOUS** has extra large, meaty fruit with very few seeds. Each crack-resistant tomato is more than 1 pound. 77 days.

4 **BIG BEEF** is grown for its large yields of uniform red fruit. It produces until frost and has great disease resistance. 10–12 ounces. 73 days.

EARLY GIRL is dependable and widely adapted with large yields of solid, red fruit. 4–6 ounces. 52 days.

Growing

After planting, stake or cage all tomatoes with the exception of small bush or patio varieties, which can often support themselves. Waiting a few weeks after planting to install stakes or cages can injure the plant's roots. Cages and stakes keep tomatoes off the ground, helping to prevent fruit rot and numerous diseases.

Tomato cages are typically made of heavy-gauge wire and stand 5 to 6 feet tall. Purchase tomato cages at a garden center or fashion your own out of heavy wire fencing. Firmly anchor the cages to the ground with stakes to keep the plants from blowing over and uprooting themselves during storms. They should have openings wide enough for your hand to reach inside to harvest.

Stakes are another way to help tomatoes stand tall. They need to be at least 8 feet high and 1 inch wide. Pound the stake at least 12 inches into the ground and 4 inches from the plant. Attach the stem to the stake with garden twine, self-adhesive fabric, or strips of cloth.

If desired, fertilize plants monthly with a balanced plant food such as 5-5-5 when the first tomatoes are about the size of golf balls.

After the soil has warmed, mulch plants with a 2- to 3-inch-thick layer of organic mulch, such as straw or finely shredded wood chips, to prevent weeds and to maintain soil moisture. Mulch is also valuable for preventing soil and soilborne diseases from splashing onto leaves when it rains. At the end of the season, enrich the soil by tilling in the mulch. It will decompose and add valuable nutrients for next season.

Tomatoes grow best when they have consistent moisture. If it rains less than 1 inch per week, supplement by watering. To prevent diseases, avoid wetting the foliage. Use a watering can or wand to deliver water directly to the root zones or use a drip irrigation system.

1

2

3

small-fruited varieties:

1 **SUPER SWEET 100** is an improved version of the classic cherry variety. This vigorous plant has large yields. 1 ounce. 65 days.

2 **GOLD NUGGET** produces seedless golden fruits on a compact plant. It is a good choice for containers. 1–2 ounces. 60 days.

3 **BLACK CHERRY** is an heirloom with large cherry-size fruits. It has striking black-red skin and flesh and a complex flavor. 2–3 ounces. 65 days.

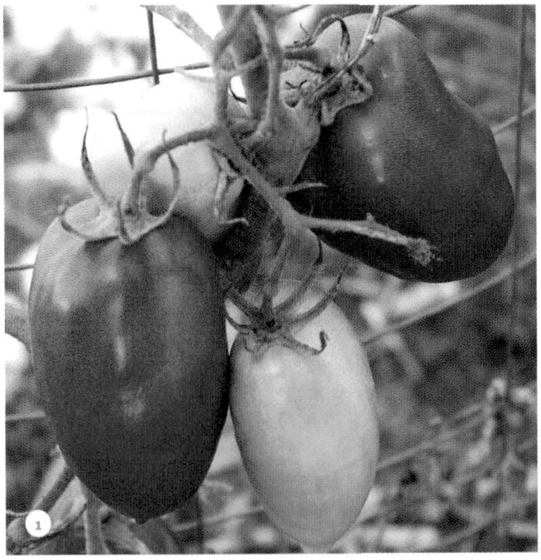

Harvest

Pick fruits when they are firm, full size, and fully colored. Tomatoes mature and ripen best at temperatures close to 75°F. When the temperature rises about 90°F, the fruits soften and develop poor color. Tomatoes will ripen when picked at their green mature size.

Before a killing frost, harvest all but the greenest fruits and bring them indoors to a 60° to 65°F room, and wrap them individually in a sheet of newspaper. Check the fruits once a week for ripeness and remove any tomatoes that are decayed or not showing signs of ripening. Also, whole plants can be uprooted and hung in a warm, sheltered location, where the fruits can continue to ripen.

Once picked, ripe fruits can be stored for up to two weeks at 55°F. They can also be stored in the refrigerator but will not taste as good as those stored at cool room temperature.

Freeze or can tomatoes in summer and lend your wintertime meals garden-fresh taste. Canning tomatoes involves sterilized jars, a hot water bath, many pounds of tomatoes, and a few hours of your time. Freezing, on the other hand, is a relatively quick and easy process and is an efficient way to preserve four or 40 tomatoes.

Whether you choose to freeze or can tomatoes, the skins are generally removed prior to preservation. To easily peel a fresh tomato, dip the fruit in near-boiling water for about 1 minute, depending upon the skin thickness. Remove the tomato from the water and allow it to cool slightly. The skin should easily peel away.

paste varieties:

1 **AMISH PASTE** is an heirloom paste variety with juicy, meaty fruits prized for their intense flavor. 5–7 ounces. 85 days.

2 **ITALIAN HEIRLOOM** is a popular canning tomato that is easy to peel and has few seeds. Unlike other paste tomatoes, it does not have a plumlike shape. The meaty fruit is large and round. 10–12 ounces. 75 days.

3 **ROMA** is a standard paste tomato with meaty fruit. It is widely adapted and easy to grow. 2–3 ounces. 78 days.

VIVA ITALIA is an Italian paste variety with a high sugar content. It has good heat tolerance. 3 ounces. 75 days.

PRINCIPE BORGHESE produces small, plum-size tomatoes that have few seeds. This variety is especially good for drying. 1–2 ounces. 80 days.

Pests and diseases

Tomatoes are affected by many insects, diseases, and physiological disorders. Use cardboard collars around tomato transplants to discourage cutworms. Handpick and destroy Japanese beetles. Spray *Bacillus thuringiensis* (*Bt*) to control tomato hornworms and pinworms. Spray insecticidal soap to control white flies.

Diseases such as verticillium and fusarium wilts and tobacco mosaic virus stunt plant growth and cause plants to die young. Control these diseases by planting resistant varieties. Foliar disease, such as early blight, late bight, and septoria leaf spot, cause leaves to yellow and drop prematurely.

The fruits are also affected by environmental conditions that cause cracking, sunscald, and blossom-end rot.

Although it might sound challenging, growing healthy, pest- and disease-free tomato plants is relatively simple. When a pest or disease does strike a healthy plant, it will have trouble getting a foothold and causing damage. Grow healthy tomatoes with these tips.

Rotate crops. Don't plant tomatoes or members of the tomato family (eggplant, pepper, potato, or tomatillo) in the same planting space more than once every three years. Pests and diseases overwinter in the soil and will infect the following year's crop.

Plant disease-resistant varieties. Disease resistance is often noted on plant tags and seed packets as an abbreviation. Some of the most common disease abbreviations are BST (bacterial spot), CMV (cucumber mosaic virus), EB (early blight), LB (late blight), PM (powdery mildew), and V (verticillium wilt).

Space plants properly, allowing at least 24 inches between mature plants. Adequate air circulation prevents many fungal diseases. Proper spacing allows foliage to dry before fungal spores can flourish.

Mulch plants with a 2- to 3-inch layer of organic compost to prevent soil and potential diseases from splashing onto the leaves.

Water as needed to ensure the plants receive at least 1 inch of water per week. Lack of water stresses plants, making them more vulnerable to pest and disease infestations.

container varieties:

1 **PATIO** produces medium-size red fruits on a 2-foot-tall plant. This variety has excellent flavor. 3–4 ounces. 72 days.

2 **BUSH EARLY GIRL** is a compact, 2-foot-tall version of the popular 'Early Girl' with the same size fruit and excellent productivity. 6–7 ounces. 54 days.

3 **TINY TIM** grows just 18 inches tall. It produces grape-size red tomatoes that are excellent for salads. 1 ounce. 60 days.

BUSH BIG BOY produces the classic 'Big Boy' fruit but on a plant that is half the height. 10–11 ounces. 72 days.

Turnip

(*Brassica rapa* Rapifera group)

Large, round turnip roots are smooth on the outside and meaty on the inside. Flavor is best when turnips mature in cool weather, so plant the crop in early spring or late summer to take advantage of cool soil temperatures. Eat turnips fresh in salads and cooked in side dishes.

YOU SHOULD KNOW
Don't discard turnip tops. They boast rich vitamins and are often cooked and eaten as greens. 'Shogoin' has particularly tasty greens.

1

Best site
Plant in full sun or part shade and well-drained soil. Turnips grow best in fertile soil. Mix a 2-inch-thick layer of compost into the garden bed before planting. Loose, rock-free soil produces the best turnips.

Planting
Sow turnip seeds in the garden four weeks before the last frost date in spring for an early summer crop, and 60 to 70 days before the first frost in fall for an autumn crop. For the best flavor, plant turnips in midsummer for a fall crop. The roots will sweeten in the cool weather.

Plant seeds ½ inch deep and 2 inches apart for large roots and 1 inch apart for small roots in rows 12 inches apart.

2

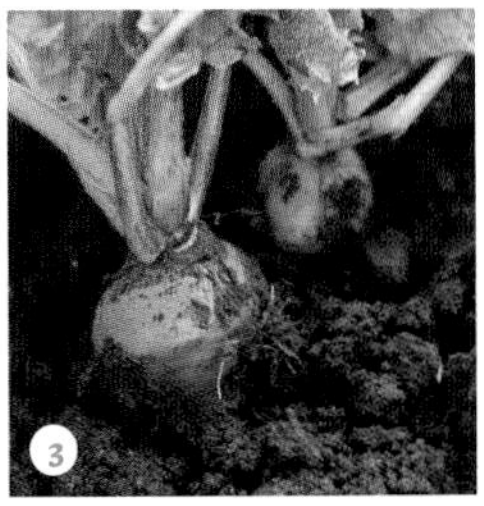

3

varieties:

1 **SHOGOIN** has tender, mild greens and tasty young roots. 42 days.

2 **PURPLE TOP WHITE GLOBE** is a 3- to 4-inch round root that's white below the soil line, purple above it. It has tender, crisp, white flesh. 50 days.

3 **SCARLET QUEEN RED STEM** produces slightly fattened, red-skinned roots with mild white flesh. Its red stems are attractive in salads, and it also has a green-stem variety. 43 days.

Growing
Thin turnip seedlings to 3 to 4 inches apart when they are 4 inches tall. The thinnings can be eaten as greens.

Keep the soil evenly moist, applying at least 1 inch of water a week. Cultivate lightly when the roots are young, and apply a 2- to 3-inch thick layer of organic mulch, such as straw, around the roots to maintain soil moisture, keep the soil cool, and deter weeds.

Harvest
If you plant turnips for greens, harvest the tops as needed when they are 4 to 6 inches tall. Leave the growth point in the center when you're picking individual leaves and the plants will continue to produce greens and roots. Harvest sweet young turnip roots for salads when they are 2 inches in diameter. Allow some roots to mature to 3 to 4 inches in diameter for cooking and winter storage. Turnip roots taste sweeter when exposed to a light frost.

To store turnip roots, trim off the foliage with a sharp knife to within 1 inch of the crown. The roots can be stored for two to four months at 35°F and in high humidity. You can also store turnips directly in the garden until the ground freezes by mulching the beds with a 6- to 8-inch-thick layer of straw in fall.

Pests and diseases
Rotate crops and do not plant this or another cabbage-family crop in the same ground for three years to avoid disease such as club root, anthracnose, and root rot. Control aphids and flea beetles with strong sprays of water or by applying insecticidal soap.

Watermelon

(Citrullus lanatus)

Watermelon is one of summer's sweetest treats. A long, warm growing season especially favors this crop, but gardeners in northern areas can grow melons when they choose early varieties and start the seeds indoors or set out transplants in late spring.

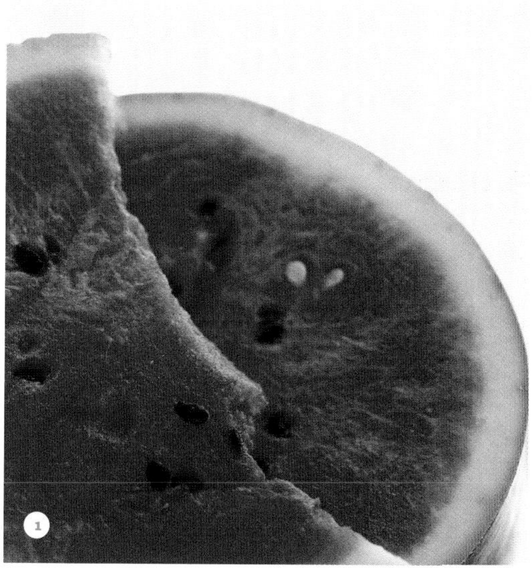

Best site

Plant in full sun and well-drained soil. Watermelons grow best in highly fertile soil. Incorporate a 2-inch-thick layer of compost in the soil before planting.

Planting

If your growing season is long and hot, sow seeds directly in the garden two weeks after your last average frost date in spring when the soil temperature is at least 70°F or warmer. Sow seeds in hills 6 feet apart, with six seeds per hill. Sow seeds ½ inch deep.

In a cool-weather climate, start seeds indoors in peat pots four to six weeks before the last average frost. Set outside two weeks after the last frost, planting three plants per hill.

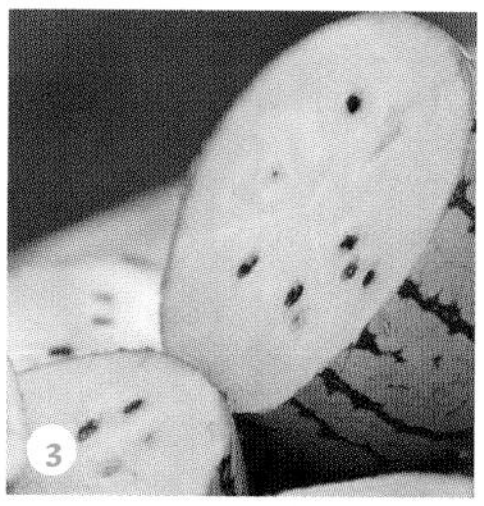

varieties:

1. **CRIMSON SWEET** is an oval melon with sweet red flesh. 15–25 pounds. 85 days.
2. **MOON AND STARS** is an heirloom with very sweet red flesh and green skin with a yellow moon and stars. 25 pounds. 100 days.
3. **YELLOW DOLL** has yellow flesh and short vines. Its small fruit is easy to store in the refrigerator. 5–8 pounds. 75 days.

Growing

Thin direct-seeded plants to three plants per hill after the first set of true leaves forms. When the vines are 12 to 24 inches long, thin again and keep only one or two of the most vigorous vines per hill. Keep plants well watered, applying at least 1 inch per week and more water during hot, dry, windy periods. The most critical watering periods are when the vines are flowering and fruiting. Hand weed until the leaves are big enough to shade out weeds.

Keep ripening fruits off the ground by setting them on cardboard, upside-down pots, or pieces of wood. You can hasten ripening by removing vine tips and new flowers when nights grow cool.

Harvest

Watermelons should be harvested when they are perfectly ripe because they will not ripen off the vine. Use a combination of the following indicators to pick the perfect melon. First, the light green, curly tendrils on the stem near the watermelon usually turn brown and dry when it is ripe. Also, the surface color of the fruit becomes dull. The rind hardens, is resistant to penetration by the thumbnail and is rough to the touch. Finally, the underside of the melon turns yellow when the fruit is ripe.

Pests and diseases

Cucumber beetles, squash bugs, and aphids are the main pests for melons. Aphids and cucumber beetles damage young seedlings, flowers, and fruits and transmit devastating mosaic virus and bacterial wilt diseases to melon plants.

YOU SHOULD KNOW

Since seedless melons do not funnel energy into producing mature seeds, they are often sweeter than normal seeded types. 'Ruby Seedless' and 'Orange Sunshine' are popular, easy-to-grow seedless cultivars.

fruit encyclopedia

Sweeten your table with fruit crops. From apple to strawberry, the following pages are filled with tips for growing sweet treats in your landscape.

HARDY FRUIT TREES

Dwarf and semidwarf cultivars make it possible to grow hardy fruit trees in even the smallest landscape. These long-lived plants begin producing fruit about five years after planting.

SMALL FRUITS, BERRIES

Easy to grow and requiring little maintenance, small fruits such as strawberries, blueberries, and brambles are good choices for first-time gardeners.

TROPICAL FRUITS

Citrus, mangoes, and other tropical fruits thrive in sultry, long growing climates. Check out the tips and techniques for growing a juicy crop.

Apple *(Malus domestica)*

Apples are the most widely adapted deciduous fruit trees. This favorite crunchy snack fruit thrives from freezing Zone 3 to nearly tropical Zone 10. The long-lived trees have fragrant spring flowers and dense, leafy canopies, valuable additions to the landscape. With careful selection and good care practices, you can harvest bushels of deliciously ripe apples with little pruning or pesticide sprays.

Best site

Plant in full sun and well-drained soil. Apples thrive in sandy loam and languish in heavy soil or clay. Amend slow-draining soil with plenty of compost before planting.

Ample sunlight is also essential. Plant an apple tree where it will receive at least eight hours of direct sunlight per day. Take the growth of nearby trees into consideration. Apple trees can live 50 years or more; do not plant them where nearby trees will cast shade in years to come. Apples are hardy in Zones 3 to 10.

Prevent spring frost damage by choosing a site near the top of a hill or slope. Avoid "frost pockets" or low-lying areas where cold air accumulates, such as at the bottom of a hill or near a hedgerow or woodland. An area with good air circulation will also help prevent cold air from accumulating and damaging tender buds.

Types of apples

Apples are divided into three groups based on when their fruit ripens. Early season varieties are some of the first apples to ripen in mid- to late summer. Midseason apples follow in early fall. Late season apples are the last to ripen, in mid- to late fall. Late season apples often store well; some keep for up to six months in a cool, humid location.

Standard apple trees grow 20 to 40 feet tall and wide. Scientists have developed dwarfing rootstocks that prevent apple trees from growing to such heights. For easy harvest and pruning, choose a 10-foot-tall dwarf apple cultivar or a 15-foot-tall semidwarf cultivar. Bred to be shorter than standard varieties, dwarf and semidwarf apples produce the same size fruit as standard varieties but often fruit earlier and are easier to care for and harvest. Most common apple varieties are available in these smaller forms.

Generally, apples are considered self-incompatible, meaning they cannot pollinate themselves or any flowers of the same variety. The best fruit is harvested when cross-pollination occurs.

Ensure cross-pollination by planting two different apple trees that bloom at the same time and have compatible pollen. Two early season varieties usually pollinate each other well as do two midseason varieties and so on. There are some exceptions. A few varieties, such as 'Winesap', 'Mutsu', and 'Stayman', produce sterile pollen and will not pollinate themselves or any other apple, but other apple trees can pollinate them. The variety descriptions on the following pages include pollinator recommendations.

Planting

Plant bare-root trees in late winter or early spring. Plant container-grown trees anytime during the growing season.

When shopping for an apple tree, look for a tree that has ample roots for the amount of branches. Opt for a small tree with a large root system rather than a large tree with a small root system. The small tree will establish quickly and most likely fruit before a large tree with few roots. The trunk and branches should be free of scrapes, and the tree should have a pleasing symmetrical form.

To plant a bare-root tree, dig a hole wide and deep enough that the roots are not crowded or bent. Plant so the graft (bulging area low on the trunk) is at least 2 inches above the soil to prevent the stem from rooting. Space trees as far apart as they will be tall when mature, or as close as 6 feet for hedgerows. Refill the planting hole with the excavated soil, forming a basin around the trunk to hold water.

YOU SHOULD KNOW
Apples can be sweet, tart, soft and smooth, or tart and crunchy. Plant a few different varieties and enjoy their unique flavors.

early season varieties:

1 **EIN SHEMER** is a yellow variety with crisp, sweet-tart flesh. Pollinate with 'Dorsett Golden' or 'Ein Shemer'. Susceptible to scab. Zones 8–10.

2 **ANNA**, a very early green apple with a red blush, is crisp and sweet. Pollinate with 'Dorsett Golden' or 'Ein Shemer'. Susceptible to scab, especially in the Southeast. Zones 8–10.

3 **EMPIRE** has dark red skin and creamy white, tart flesh. Pollinate with 'Freedom' or 'Liberty'. Resistant to rust, and fire blight. Zones 4–7.

Plant a container-grown tree by digging a hole as deep as the container and slightly wider. Remove the tree from the pot and place it in the hole so that the graft (bulging area low on the trunk) is at least 2 inches above the soil to prevent the stem from rooting. Using the excavated soil, backfill the planting hole, tamping the soil as you go to prevent air pockets. Build a soil basin around the trunk to hold water.

Growing

Water newly planted trees for at least six weeks after planting, longer if the weather is dry. Aim to moisten soil to the depth of 12 to 18 inches.

Apples grow best when the area under the canopy is free of grass and weeds. Vegetation competes for water and nutrients, slowing the growth of the tree. Skim away the sod as the canopy expands. To control weeds, spread a 2-inch-thick layer of organic mulch, such as wood chips or compost, in a circle under the tree canopy. Be sure to keep the mulch away from the trunk where it could cause rot. Replace the mulch annually.

In early summer when apples are about the size of a golf ball, thin them by hand to one apple per cluster or about one for every 6 inches of stem. Thinning will produce large, more uniform fruit and prevent branches from breaking from excess fruit production.

If necessary, support fruit-laden branches through summer and until harvest with a sturdy post. The post will prop up the branch and prevent it from breaking under the weight of the developing fruit.

Apple trees don't require fertilization for good growth, but fruit yield can be improved with an annual application of compost or a balanced fertilizer. If using compost, spread a 2-inch-thick layer of compost over the soil under the canopy in early spring. Or fertilize using a 10-10-10 fertilzer product applied at the rate of 1 pound for one-year-old trees, 2 pounds for two-year-old trees, and so on until 5 or 6 pounds are applied per year.

Annually in late winter or early spring, prune the tree, removing any broken, crossing, or rubbing branches. If you would like, increase fruit production by pruning trees to a specific form as outlined on pages 128 and 129.

1

2

3

4

5

midseason varieties:

1 **HONEYCRISP** is a popular variety that has a distinct flavor and stores well. Pollinate with 'Empire', 'Liberty', or 'Gala'. Susceptible to fire blight. Zones 3–7.

2 **GALA** has crisp, fragrant flesh. It is a good variety for fresh eating and storage. Pollinate with 'Golden Delicious' or 'Liberty'. Susceptible to rust and fire blight; resistant to mildew. Zones 4–9.

3 **PRISCILLA** produces crisp, mild flavored apples that last well on the tree. Pollinate with 'Honeycrisp'. Excellent disease resistance. Zones 5–8.

4 **GOLDEN DELICIOUS,** prized for its excellent flavor, bears young and annually. It is a self-fertile variety that is a good pollinator to others. Susceptible to many diseases. Zones 5–9.

5 **LIBERTY** is the most disease-free apple. Very productive, it often requires fruit thinning. Pollinate with 'Honeycrisp' or 'Liberty'. Zones 3–5.

Harvest

Expect to wait three to five years after planting for your first apple harvest. Fruits ripen 70 to 180 days from bloom depending on the variety. A ripe apple separates easily from the fruiting spur and has firm flesh. A soft apple is overripe but can still be used in cooking. Late varieties are best for long-term storage at cool room temperature.

The best place to store apples is the crisper drawer of the refrigerator, where a cool temperature and high humidity will prevent the fruit from spoiling for many weeks. Do not store apples near vegetables since ripening fruit gives off gas that may spoil vegetables.

Pests and diseases

Apples are prone to many diseases and insect pests. Some of the common diseases that attack apple trees are apple scab, powdery mildew, black rot, rusts, collar rot, sooty blotch, and fire blight. Some common insects that attack apples are apple maggot, codling moth, plum curculio, San Jose scale, European red mite, and aphids.

For exceptional fruit production, pesticide sprays are usually necessary. But disease-resistant cultivars will produce quality fruit, perhaps not a massive quantity of fruit, without pesticides. Make disease resistance a priority when you are selecting apple cultivars.

Prevent problems by cutting out diseased and damaged branches as soon as you notice them. When removing diseased twigs, disinfect pruners with a 10-percent bleach solution before and after pruning and between trees. At the end of the season, rake fallen leaves and fruit to prevent the spread of diseases.

Good growing conditions—full sun, fertile soil, and adequate water—will go a long way toward producing bushels of tasty apples.

late season varieties:

1 **WINESAP** has an intense sweet-tart aroma. This heirloom is a heavy producer and widely adapted. Pollinate with 'Empire', 'Liberty', or 'Honeycrisp'. 'Winesapp' has sterile pollen and will not pollinate other varieties. Zones 5–8.

2 **WINTER BANANA** is a reliable producer with fruits that have a distinct flavor. Pollinate with 'Keepsake' or 'Liberty'. Zones 5–9.

3 **GOLDEN RUSSET** is an heirloom with very sweet flesh. It produces good cider. Pollinate with 'Golden Delicious'. Zones 4–5.

4 **MUTSU** produces large apples that are good for baking and storage. Pollinate with 'Empire' or 'Liberty'. Mutsu has sterile pollen and will not pollinate other varieties. Zones 4–8.

5 **KEEPSAKE** is a good dessert apple that stores well. Pollinate with 'Honeycrisp', 'Liberty', or 'Gala'. Resistant to fire blight and rust. Zones 3–6.

Apricot

(Prunus armeniaca)

Apricots are fast-growing small trees. One tree reliably produces more than 100 pounds of fruit in moderate climates. New cultivars make it possible to have fruit in cool climates too. Most apricots are self-fruitful and do not require pollination by another tree.

YOU SHOULD KNOW
Jams and jellies are two ways to preserve a small crop of apricots. Tie a simple bow around a jar of garden-fresh jam and share your garden's bounty with a friend.

Best site

Plant in full sun and well-drained soil. Apricots bloom in early spring, and flowers are often nipped by frost in cold climates. Prevent frost damage by planting in a site that is protected from winds and frost. A north-facing slope, because it is slow to warm up in the spring and revive dormant trees, is best if spring frosts are a factor. Apricots are hardy in Zones 4 to 10.

Planting

Plant bare-root trees in late winter or early spring. Plant container-grown trees anytime during the growing season. When selecting an apricot, be sure to choose a cultivar that is hardy in your climate. Space standard-size trees about 25 feet apart, semidwarfs 15 feet apart, and dwarfs 6 feet apart.

varieties:

1. **HARCOT** is a very productive variety with good disease resistance. The medium to large fruits have an excellent flavor. Zones 6–7.
2. **MOONGOLD** is exceptionally hardy and bears medium-size sweet, tangy fruits. It requires another variety for pollination. Zones 4–8.

Growing

Prevent late spring frost damage by covering trees with tarps or sheets if a frost is predicted. Apricot trees do not tolerate drought. Keep the soil consistently moist but never waterlogged. Water deeply every week during warm weather.

Apricots grow best when the area under the canopy is free of grass and weeds. Vegetation competes for water and nutrients, slowing the growth of the tree. Skim away the sod as the canopy expands. To control weeds, spread a 3-inch-thick layer of organic mulch, such as wood chips or compost, in a circle under the tree canopy. Be sure to keep the mulch away from the trunk where it could cause rot. Replace the mulch annually.

After normal fruit drop, thin to the healthiest fruit on each spur and leave about 3 inches between fruits.

Harvest

The apricot harvest season occurs for two or three weeks anytime from late spring through early summer depending on the apricot variety, weather, and regional climatic conditions. For the richest flavor, let the fruits ripen on the tree and pick them once they develop full color with the flesh just starting to soften slightly.

Pests and diseases

Avoid most diseases by choosing resistant varieties and practicing clean cultural habits. Prune out diseased and damaged wood immediately, and keep the ground around trees clear of dropped fruit and other plant debris, which harbor pests and encourage diseases.

Avocado

(Persea americana)

When grown in a moderate to tropical climate, full sun, and well-drained soil, an avocado tree will produce an abundant harvest of rich, buttery fruit. Enjoy its yellowish white flowers as part of the edible landscape. Leathery foliage provides year-round shade.

Best site

Plant in full sun and well-drained soil. Avocados are hardy in Zones 9 to 11.

Types of avocados

The various types of avocado are Mexican, Guatemalan, and West Indian as well as hybrids of these groups. The **Mexican, Guatemalan, and hybrids** are best adapted to California and the Southeast. **West Indian** varieties are best adapted to south Florida and Hawaii. **Guatemalan** avocados are restricted almost exclusively to frost-free Zone 10.

Planting

The best time to plant avocados is in early fall once the air temperature has begun to cool but the soil is still warm. Or plant at any time of the year except in the high heat of midsummer. Space trees so that their canopies will not touch when they reach their mature size.

Growing

Fertilize trees with a transplant starter at planting time. Water young trees frequently until well established, then water only during times of drought. In winter prune plants to control size. Spread a 3-inch-thick layer of organic mulch under the tree canopy to suppress weeds and prevent soil moisture loss. Be sure the mulch does not touch the trunk.

Harvest

Trees usually bear fruit one to five years after planting. Depending on the avocado variety, ripening occurs 6 to 18 months after fruit sets. Because the trees bloom over a long period, fruits will not mature all at once. Use external coloring as a guide to ripeness. Pick the largest, fullest avocados first, using hand pruners to cut the stems. Fruits will soften at room temperature in 5 to 10 days.

Pests and diseases

Avocado root rot is a problem in California. Select certified disease-free plants and avoid planting where avocados previously grew or where soil drainage is poor. In Florida and Hawaii fungus diseases such as scab, anthracnose, and powdery mildew are common. Check with your county extension service for control measures.

YOU SHOULD KNOW

At harvest time it's important to know the mature color of the avocado variety you are growing. Depending on the variety an avocado might be medium green, dark green, deep purple, or black when fully ripe.

varieties:

1. **PINKERTON** is a heavy producer that bears small to medium, excellent-quality fruits on a medium, upright tree. Zones 9–11.
2. **GWEN** is a dwarf tree, growing just 12 to 14 feet tall and bearing small fruits with good flavor. Zones 9–11.
3. **HASS** is a popular hybrid that produces small to medium fruits with a nutty flavor. Zones 9–11.

Blueberry (*Vaccinium* species)

Flowers in spring, purple berries in summer, and red and yellow color in fall make blueberries an ideal plant for the edible landscape. Use these low-growing or tall woody plants as a hedge or colorful shrubs in a foundation planting or mixed border. They grow best in areas with cool, moist, acidic soil. Growing a crop of blueberries may require adjusting the soil pH; the extra effort is worth it for a large crop of juicy berries.

Best site

Plant in full sun and moist, well-drained, acidic soil. Blueberries require an acid soil with a pH of 4.0 to 5.5. Test your soil to learn its pH. Note that you would like to grow blueberries on the testing form. A quality soil-testing lab will provide soil test results and recommendations to lower soil pH if necessary. The lab will likely suggest that you incorporate a specific amount of sphagnum peat moss or sulfur to acidify the soil. Blueberries are hardy in Zones 3–9.

Types of blueberries

The three main kinds are highbush blueberry (*V. corymbosum*) rabbit-eye blueberry (*V. ashei*), and half-high hybrids of highbush and lowbush (*V. angustifolium*).

Highbush blueberries produce the berries found in most markets. Most varieties grow to 6 feet high or more, though there are varieties that are much lower growing. These blueberries thrive in the East (particularly around the Great Lakes), the Northeast, and the Northwest. The fruits ripen from late spring to late summer depending on variety.

Half-high hybrids grow 2 to 4 feet high and wide and have greater cold tolerance than highbush berries. They are best adapted to northern climates.

Rabbit-eye blueberries are grown in climates that are too warm for highbush blueberries, mainly in the Southeast. The fruit has thicker skin and less flavor than highbush berries.

Both rabbit-eye and half-high varieties require cross-pollination. Plant at least two varieties of these types of blueberries for best fruit set.

Planting

Plant blueberries in early spring where winters are cold and in fall where winters are mild. Plants are available either bare root or in containers. Space highbush and rabbit-eye varieties 6 feet apart, lowbush 2 feet apart, and half-high 3 to 4 feet apart.

Growing

Blueberries are very susceptible to drought. In warm areas without regular summer rainfall, water blueberries weekly, moistening the top 18 inches of soil.

Prune blueberries annually to remove old canes. In the first two years of growth remove weak, diseased, and damaged canes only. In subsequent years remove weak, diseased, and damaged canes along with some of the oldest canes. Remove excess young canes to encourage the growth of others, and prune to reduce the density of branches at the top of plants. Each mature plant should have 15 to 25 canes of varying ages. Canes decline in productivity after five to six years. Rabbit-eye blueberries need little or no pruning.

Fertilize plants every year at flowering time with compost or a low-nitrogen plant food for acid-loving plants, such as one designed for azaleas and rhododendrons.

Harvest

Blueberries turn from green to pinkish red to blue, but not all blue ones are fully ripe. Hold a container in one hand and use your other hand to gently loosen ripe berries from the cluster so they drop into the container. Store blueberries unwashed in the refrigerator.

Pests and diseases

Blueberry plants usually aren't troubled by pests seriously enough to require control.

YOU SHOULD KNOW
Blueberries are easy to freeze. Arrange them in a single layer on a tray. Put the tray in the freezer and as soon as the berries are frozen, place them in containers and put them back in the freezer. Frozen berries will store well for up to one year.

varieties:

1 **BLUECROP** is a highbush variety and the most popular blueberry. It is more cold hardy and drought tolerant than other varieties. Zones 4–8.

2 **COVILLE** is a vigorous, productive highbush with very large, aromatic, slightly tart berries that hold well on the bush. Canker resistant. Zones 4–8.

3 **ELLIOTT** produces medium-size, firm, light blue fruit. This dense, highbush is great for the landscape too. Zones 4–8.

4 **PATRIOT** is a highbush with large clusters of flavorful berries. Its berries are slightly smaller than others. Zones 4–8.

5 **JERSEY** is an easy-to-grow highbush with medium-size firm fruit that resists cracking and keeps well. Zones 4–8.

6 **NORTHCOUNTRY** is a half-high bush that produces fruit with sweet, wild blueberry flavor. It is good for northern regions and has sky blue flowers. Zones 3–7.

7 **NORTHBLUE** is a half-high cultivar that produces large, dark blue fruit that is superior to many highbush varieties. It grows less than 3 feet tall and has attractive, ornamental qualities. It is self-fertile but yield improves if planted with 'Northcountry'. Zones 3–7.

Brambles: blackberry, raspberry (*Rubus* species)

A small patch of brambles—blackberries and raspberries—will easily provide enough berries for a family of four for fresh eating, baking, making jams, and freezing. These productive plants are sometimes unruly, but when rigorously maintained, they are exceptionally productive.

Best site

Plant in full sun and moist, well-drained soil. Althought brambles tolerate a wide range of soil types, they grow best in soil that drains well. Slow-draining or clay soils promote troublesome root rot and can cause considerable winter damage with the alternate freezing and thawing, heaving roots out of the soil. If a well-drained site is not possible, plant brambles in a raised bed that is at least 10 inches tall.

Brambles thrive in soil that is high in organic matter. Before planting, incorporate a 2-inch-thick layer of compost into the site.

Brambles are most productive when they receive 1 to 2 inches of water per week. Consider placing your berry patch near a water source. They are hardy in Zones 4 to 9.

Types of brambles

Red and yellow raspberries are genetically similar plants with 7-foot-long semierect canes. The average plant produces 2 to 3 pounds of tender, juicy fruit in summer or fall, depending on the variety. Red raspberries send out underground shoots and slowly spread from the original planting spot.

Black raspberries, or blackcaps, are borne on trailing thorny canes that reach 8 feet long; these are the least cold-hardy and productive raspberries, and they are more susceptible to diseases. Black raspberries generally do not spread like red raspberries. They produce about 2 pounds of fruit per plant.

Purple raspberries are hybrids of red and black raspberries with canes 7 to 8 feet long. Like black raspberries, they do not spread and they produce about 2 pounds of fruit per plant.

Blackberries produce fruit on their two-year-old canes and may be either erect or trailing canes. Blackberries are some of the most productive brambles, producing 5 to 7 pounds of fruit per plant. Blackberries differ from raspberries in that the core is attached to the center of the berry. Raspberries have a hollow center; the core remains on the plant.

Trailing blackberries include marionberry, boysenberry, loganberry, youngberry, and thornless evergreen. These lesser-known berries often have a unique flavor.

Planting

Plant certified disease-free plants or root cuttings in early spring. Shop local garden centers and specialty fruit nurseries for a diverse selection of brambles.

Brambles are often planted in hills or hedgerows. Plants grown in hills are spaced 4 to 10 feet apart and weeds are controlled by cultivation between and within the row. Plant black and purple raspberries and blackberries in hills.

Hedgerows are a good choice for red and yellow raspberries. A hedgerow is a continuous row about 12 to 24 inches wide. Brambles are spaced 24 to 26 inches apart within the row. This space-saving planting method is especially good for plants that produce many suckers. Cultivate both sides of the hedgerow to control the brambles' outward spread.

In cold-winter regions plant brambles 1 inch deeper than they were grown at the nursery. In mild-winter regions, plant them at the same depth they were previously grown. After planting, cut the canes back to 6 inches tall to spur root growth. The plants will not fruit the first season, but they'll produce a small crop the second season after planting. Water new transplants well after planting to settle the soil and nourish the roots.

YOU SHOULD KNOW
Rich in antioxidants and vitamin C, bramble fruits not only taste good but are good for you. One of the most popular brambles, red raspberries are costly at the supermarket and farmer's market but inexpensive to grow in your backyard.

blackberry varieties:

1 **CHESTER** has large, very sweet fruit. The plant is thornless, upright, productive and resistant to cane blight. It grows well in the South. Zones 5–9.
2 **ROSBOROUGH** bears large, glossy blackberries. This erect, thorny shrub grows well in extreme heat and is drought tolerant. Zones 5–9.
3 **THORNFREE** has large, tangy, tart blackberries on thornless, semierect stems. It grows best when trellised. It is disease free. Zones 5–9.
4 **LOGAN** has light red, tart berries that are prized for their unique flavor. This trailing berry grows best when trellised. Zones 5–9.
5 **MARION** produces large berries with a mild blackberry flavor for weeks on end in midsummer. The trailing canes have many large thorns. It is popular in Washington and Oregon. Zones 7–10.

Growing

Spread a 2-inch-thick layer of mulch around the plants to reduce weeds and keep the plants moist. For best fruiting, provide brambles with at least 1 inch of water per week. Water plants with a drip hose to prevent the foliage from getting wet and developing fungal diseases.

Blackberries and raspberries are biennial. Their canes grow one year, bear fruit, and then die at the end of year two. New canes emerge the following season. Canes of primocane fruiting raspberries, called everbearing (fall-bearing) begin fruiting the first year in the garden and die the second year.

Managing the growth and dieback of the canes through pruning promotes a pest-free patch that is easy to harvest and produces abundant fruit. Annual pruning is essential. The most common downfall of a backyard bramble patch is lack of pruning. In short order the canes ramble out of control.

Each type of bramble has a unique pruning requirement. They are most often pruned in early spring and late summer. Begin pruning all brambles by removing the weak, diseased, and damaged canes at ground level.

Next, remove two-year-old canes called floricanes. These canes produced fruit and will die soon if they are not already dead. They will be quickly replaced by new canes called primocanes. You can tell the difference between primocanes and floricanes by the color of the stem. Young primocanes are green or light brown. Floricanes have brown peeling bark.

For a complete summary of how, when, and what to prune, see page 130.

For easy harvest, train trailing brambles, (purple and black raspberries and blackberries) to a V-shape trellis. Set 6-foot trellis posts so that they are 36 inches apart at the top, 18 inches apart at the bottom. String two wires between the posts and allow the fruiting canes to grow freely in the middle of the V. Tie the nonfruiting canes to the top and bottom wires.

everbearing raspberries:

1 **HERITAGE** is widely adapted with firm, mild-flavored berries. Cut canes to the ground in spring for a heavy late summer or fall crop. Exceptionally productive, it has strong, upright stems and produces suckers. Zones 4–9.

2 **AUTUMN BLISS** bears large, firm berries with a mild flavor. It is earlier fruiting than many other raspberries, bridging the gap between summer and fall crops. It is considered superior to 'Heritage' by some. Zones 3–8.

3 **FALL GOLD** has large, sweet, soft fruit on upright stems. It is an excellent all-purpose choice best in the Upper South and nearby mountains. Zones 4–8.

summer-bearing black raspberries:

1 **ALLEN** produces a large crop of glossy, sweet black raspberries. The plants are disease free. This easy-to-grow cultivar is widely adapted, especially in the Northeast. It is good for jam and jelly. Zones 4–8.

2 **JEWEL** has large, firm, juicy fruit on vigorous canes. This disease-resistant cultivar is a reliable producer and is considered the best all-purpose black raspberry by many. Zones 4–8.

Harvest

Harvest ripe berries when they taste sweet and are easy to pull from the plant, preferably in the early morning when fruits and plants are dry and cool. Ripe blackberries are easy to identify: They're glossy, soft, and deeply colored. A blackberry's small, soft green core separates from the plant when the fruit is ready to pick. Ripe raspberries will have full color (red, yellow, purple, or black) characteristic of the variety.

Carry harvested berries in shallow trays because they are easily crushed. They also are highly perishable, so keep picked berries in the shade and move them to a cool location as soon as possible. Harvest often to keep insects such as sap beetles and wasps from infesting fruit.

Blackberries fruit the first year following planting and are productive for about 10 years. Raspberries bear a small crop the second year after planting and a full crop the third year; they remain productive for five to eight years.

Pests and diseases

Purchase certified disease-free stock, as opposed to taking a division or cutting from a neighbor's berry patch, which could be infested with pests or diseases. Uproot and destroy virus-infected plants so that aphids don't transmit the disease to healthy plants. Black raspberries are the most susceptible of the brambles to viruses.

If spider mites are a problem in hot, dry weather, dislodge them with a strong spray of water from the garden hose. Wilted tips are a sign of borers; cut out and destroy the canes. Avoid using insect controls that might harm beneficial and pollinating insects.

Blackberries are sometimes susceptible to phytophthora root rot, particularly where soils are wet. Verticillium wilt and Japanese beetles are also particularly troublesome. Rabbits are a problem around thornless varieties.

summer-bearing red raspberries:

1 **KILLARNEY** produces large, high-quality fruit with good flavor. It has strong, thick, upright canes. It is a good all-purpose raspberry. Zones 3–7.

2 **CANBY** bears very large berries on nearly thornless canes. The fruit is excellent preserved or frozen. The plant grows best in the cool summers of the Pacific Northwest and has good disease resistance. Zones 4–8.

3 **REVEILLE** is known for early-ripening berries with outstanding flavor. Vigorous, upright vines produce suckers, requiring annual cultivation to keep the plants within the hedgerow. This variety tolerates fluctuating winter temperatures. Zones 5–7.

summer-bearing purple raspberries:

1 **ROYALTY** has very large, sweet, tangy fruit that ripens late in the season. A vigorous plant, it is immune to the raspberry aphid and resistant to the raspberry fruit worm. It is a good all-purpose raspberry. Zones 4–8.

2 **BRANDYWINE** is a nonsuckering vine with strong, upright stems and large, glossy, reddish purple fruit. It is a popular choice for preserves. Zones 4–9.

Cherry (*Prunus* species)

Whether you like them sweet or sour, cherries are beautiful fruit trees for the home landscape, and their flowers are a harbinger of spring. One or two trees provide a large enough crop for plenty of fresh eating as well as preserves. Both dark- and light-fleshed varieties of sweet cherries are eaten fresh or preserved. Sour, or pie, cherries are used in pies and pastries and for juice.

Best site

Plant in full sun and fertile, moist, well-drained soil. If late spring frosts are common in your area, choose a cool, north-facing location if possible to help keep the trees dormant until frost danger is past. Cherries are hardy in Zones 3 to 9.

Types of cherries

Sweet cherries are more challenging to grow than sour ones. The trees can be big, up to 30 feet tall and wide or more, making maintenance and harvest difficult.

Sweet cherries grow best in mild climates. Spring frosts sometimes damage flower buds, and summer heat over 100°F stops fruit growth. Many sweet cherry varieties require cross-pollination. Be sure to plant two different varieties if necessary.

Sour cherry trees are smaller than sweet cherries, topping out at 15 to 20 feet tall and wide. They regularly survive temperatures as low as -35°F and, because they bloom later than sweet cherries, are less likely to be damaged by spring frosts. Sour cherries are self-fruitful and, unlike sweet cherries, do not require a second cultivar planted nearby for fruit production. Both sour and sweet cherry trees are available grafted onto dwarfing rootstocks.

Planting

Cherry trees are available as bare-root trees or container plants. Plant bare-root trees in early spring and container-grown plants anytime during the growing season.

When shopping for a cherry tree, look for a tree that has ample roots for the amount of branches. Opt for a small tree with a large root system rather than a large tree with a small root system. The tree should have a pleasing symmetrical form.

Space standard varieties 25 to 40 feet apart, semidwarfs 15 to 25 feet apart, and dwarfs 8 to 12 feet apart.

Growing

Water newly planted trees until they are well established. Conserve soil moisture and keep the area under the tree canopy weed free by blanketing the area with a 3-inch-thick layer of organic mulch, being careful not to allow the mulch to touch the trunk.

Prune cherries annually in late winter to remove dead branches or branches that are crossing or rubbing. Cherries can be trained to a central leader or an open center, but it is not essential to good fruit production.

Harvest

Sweet cherries begin best production in their fifth year and bear fruit in July. Sweet cherries are enjoyed fresh and as a favorite addition to baked goods and preserves.

Sour cherries begin to bear fruit three to four years after planting. Fruits ripen about 60 days after bloom, from late May to early July. Sour cherries are normally used only for cooking and are too tart to eat fresh from the tree. But a few varieties will become sweet if left on the tree until completely ripe. Store ripe cherries for up to a week in the refrigerator.

Pests and diseases

Humidity and heat encourage fusarium wilt, rots, and molds. Clean cultural practices are essential to the health of cherry trees. Remove and destroy diseased fruits, leaves, twigs, and branches. Choose varieties bred for your weather and soil conditions and with resistance to pests and diseases in your area.

YOU SHOULD KNOW
Invest in a cherry pitter, available at specialty food shops, and make quick work of pitting a gallon of fresh-picked sweet or sour cherries.

varieties:

1 **BING** is a favorite sweet cherry in the West. LIght bearing, it has large, purple, firm, meaty fruit with excellent flavor. Pollinate with 'Montmorency', 'Rainier', or 'Stella'. Susceptible to cracking. Zones 5–9.

2 **STELLA** is a self-fertile sweet cherry with dark red, juicy fruit. It is vigorous and productive. Moderate crack resistance. Zones 5–9.

3 **SWEETHEART** has large, sweet, bright red fruit with outstanding flavor. It is self-fertile and very crack resistant. Zones 5–9.

4 **ULSTER** produces sweet, juicy, high-quality fruit. Pollinate with 'Hedelfingen'. Moderate crack resistance. Zones 5–9.

5 **DANUBE** is a vigorous sour cultivar producing large crops of juicy, dark red fruit with red juice. It is self-fertile. Zones 4–9.

6 **MONTMORENCY** is a sour cherry with medium to large, bright red, firm, tangy fruit. It is the standard pie cherry and ripens over a long season. The tree is self-fertile. Zones 4–9.

7 **NORTHSTAR** produces small, sour cherries on a naturally dwarf tree that grows 8–12 feet tall. Self-fertile, it is a good choice for cold regions. Crack resistant Zones 4–9.

Citrus (*Citrus* species)

Requiring about 12 months to ripen, citrus fruit will test your patience. You'll be tempted to pluck it from the tree long before it is ripe, but hold off. The wait is worth it. The long-lasting plants product juicy, sweet or tart fruit right outside your door in numerous varieties that are rarely available at the market. In addition to producing fruit, citrus trees have glossy evergreen foliage and fragrant flowers.

Best site

Plant in full sun and well-drained soil. Citrus trees are adaptable to many soil types but grow best in light, well-drained soil.

In desert climates plant citrus where they receive some light shade during the hottest part of the day. The shade will prevent the fruit from getting sunburned. In cool climates plant in the warmest possible microclimate such as against a light-color south-facing wall. Avoid low spots where cold air can accumulate. Citrus trees are hardy in Zones 8 to 11.

Types of citrus

Sweet oranges are the most popular citrus. Select early, mid-, and late season varieties and enjoy fruit continuously from early November to July. Two or three orange trees produce ample fruit for one family to eat and share. Sweet oranges include common orange, navel orange, and blood orange.

Grapefruit trees are exceptionally productive, and the fruit they produce stores well. One grapefruit tree is usually so prolific that it is all that is needed in a home landscape.

Mandarins, including tangerines and hybrids of tangerines, grapefruit, and oranges, are a good choice if space is limited. Many varieties grow into 10-foot-tall mature trees.

Lemons are easy to grow in the home landscape or even as indoor plants. The vigorous trees respond well to pruning to keep their size manageable. They grow best in dry climates where disease problems are less severe.

Limes are more sensitive to cold than most other citrus. Small-fruited Mexican, West Indian, and Key limes are easy to grow in the home landscape. Large-fruited Persian, or Tahiti, limes are the types most often grown commercially.

Planting

Where winters are mild and summers are hot, plant citrus in fall. Elsewhere the optimum planting time is early spring after the last frost. Citrus trees are usually sold as container plants.

When shopping for a citrus tree, look for a tree that has ample roots for the amount of branches. Opt for a small tree with a large root system rather than a large tree with a small root system. The small tree will establish quickly and most likely fruit before a large tree with few roots. The trunk and branches should be free of scrapes, and the tree should have a pleasing symmetrical form.

Plant a container-grown tree by digging a hole as deep as the container and slightly wider. Remove the tree from the pot and place it in the hole so that the graft (bulging area low on the trunk) is at least 2 inches above the soil to prevent the stem from rooting. Using the excavated soil, backfill the planting hole, tamping the soil as you go to prevent air pockets.

Using soil, form a 3- to 4-foot-diameter basin around the tree. The basin will help hold water, keeping the tree moist longer after watering, and is especially helpful during the weeks right after planting as the tree is establishing roots.

To plant a bare-root tree, dig a hole wide and deep enough that the roots are not crowded or bent. Plant so the graft (bulging area low on the trunk) is at least 2 inches above the soil to prevent the stem from rooting. Space trees as far apart as they will be tall when mature, or as close as 6 feet for hedgerows. Refill the planting hole with the excavated soil, tamping the soil as you go to prevent air pockets. Form a 3- to 4-foot-diameter basin around the trunk to hold water.

YOU SHOULD KNOW
Orange, the most popular citrus fruit, is available in many more varieties than you find at the typical grocery store. Choose a unique cultivar and enjoy tangy sweetness from your own backyard.

orange varieties:

1 **PARSON** is a juice orange that ripens very early and has large, seedy fruit. It is best in Florida.
2 **VALENCIA** bears medium-size, sweet, juicy fruit on a large, upright tree that tends to bear heavy crops every other year. It is widely adapted in all citrus-producing regions.
3 **HAMLIN** produces small, usually seedless, tender, juicy fruit very early in the season. The medium to large tree bears heavily. It grows well in the desert Southwest, Florida, and the Gulf Coast.
4 **CARA CARA** is a navel orange with large, seedless, pink-fleshed fruit with excellent flavor. It grows well in all citrus regions.
5 **SUMMER NAVEL** is a flavorful navel orange that ripens late in the season. The tree is vigorous and spreading. It grows well in California.
6 **TAROCCO** is a medium to large, firm, juicy, blood orange with few seeds. Its flesh is variable and often dark red. It grows best in interior California.
7 **MORO** is a blood orange with violet or burgundy flesh and a distinctive aroma. It is almost seedless and ripens very early. The medium-size tree is vigorous with a spreading habit. It tends to bear in alternate years and grows well in California or the Gulf Coast.

Growing

Most citrus trees are easy to care for, requiring minimal pruning and infrequent pest control. Regular watering and fertilizing is usually all they require for years of good fruit production.

The plants need adequate soil moisture for healthy growth. Drought during bloom causes flowers to drop, resulting in poor, if any, fruit set. Lack of moisture during the growing season causes fruit drop and low yields. Prolonged drought will defoliate and eventually kill a tree. At the other extreme, standing water and poorly drained soils are almost always lethal to citrus. Plant citrus in well-drained soil and water regularly during dry periods, supplementing natural rainfall so that trees receive about one inch of water per week.

Citrus trees grow best when they are fertilized two or three times from February through September. Use 1 pound of 10-10-10 fertilizer per application per tree the first two years, gradually increasing the amount each year to between 5 and 7 pounds after about eight years. Spread the fertilizer evenly over the tree's root zone. Water well after fertilizing to leach nutrients into the tree's root zone.

Soils in some areas are deficient in micronutrients. In these cases the tree will need foliar sprays of micronutrients such as copper, zinc, manganese, and boron. Look for these products at your local garden center. Don't overfertilize.

Citrus trees naturally self-regulate the amount of fruit they set and regularly drop small fruit in June, hence the term "June drop." Well-watered and fertilized trees usually drop some fruit, but excessive fruit drop might be an indicator of a problem. Keep trees in good health and well irrigated to minimize fruit drop.

Most citrus trees require little pruning, though you might want to prune lemons and other vigorous trees to control their size. Pruning to remove dense growth and open the center of a citrus tree is also a good way to keep the tree bearing throughout the canopy and prevent the buildup of insect pests. Most citrus

mandarin varieties:

1 **CLEMENTINE** has red-orange, sweet, juicy fruit that peels easily. A small tree with an attractive weeping habit and dense foliage, it needs a pollinator such as 'Dancy' for best production. It grows well in all citrus-producing areas.
2 **DANCY** is the traditional winter tangerine that peels and segments easily and has few to many seeds. The medium to large tree is vigorous and has few thorns. It grows best in Florida.
3 **GOLD NUGGET** produces rich, sweet, seedless fruit late in the season. The medium-size, upright tree tends to bear alternate years. It is best in California.
4 **SATSUMA** produces mild, seedless, sweet fruit on a slow-growing, spreading tree. Very cold-hardy. It is best in California, Florida, and the Gulf Coast.
5 **PAGE** has rich, sweet fruit with few to many seeds. The attractive tree is almost thornless. It grows well in all citrus-producing areas.

types tolerate shearing into a hedge or being trained flat as an espalier.

The bark of citrus trees is thin and susceptible to overheating and sunburn, especially after heavy pruning. Paint exposed branches and trunks with diluted water-base plant (1 part paint to 1 part water) or commercially available whitewash after heavy pruning. Also protect the bark of newly planted trees by using trunk wraps (available at garden centers) or by painting the trunks with diluted water-base white paint.

Citrus trees vary in their sensitivity to cold, but many are vulnerable when temperatures fall to 29°F for 30 minutes or longer. Protect young frost-sensitive trees by wrapping them with an insulating material, such as cardboard, palm fronds, or cornstalks.

Cover the trunks from ground level up to the main branches. Frost will rarely kill a mature citrus tree. If the leaves or twigs show signs of frost damage, be patient and wait until the spring flush of growth to determine the damage.

Growing citrus in containers

In cold climates, grow citrus trees in pots and enjoy perfectly ripe oranges, juicy lemons, and many other citrus fruits from your own trees. Because citrus reacts well to pruning, you can maintain a small, productive tree in a container for many years. Small types of citrus, such as calamondin, limes, kumquats, lemons, and limequats are best suited to container culture.

Begin by selecting a pot. Citrus trees grow well in containers when their roots are somewhat constricted, so choose a smaller pot rather than a larger one. A pot about 15 inches wide and 15 inches deep is a good size for a young citrus tree. As the tree grows, you'll need to either transplant it into a larger pot or prune the roots and foliage and replant it in the same pot. If you choose to transplant the tree to a larger pot, increase the pot size by no more than 25 percent.

Fill the pot with a well-drained potting mix and plant the citrus tree as you would when growing it outside. The final soil surface should be 2 to 4 inches below the container rim to allow

1

2

3

4

grapefruit varieties:

1 **DUNCAN** produces large, seedy, very juicy fruit with white flesh. The fruit has excellent flavor, and the tree is large, vigorous, and productive. One of the most cold-tolerant grapefruits, it is best in Florida and the Gulf Coast.

2 **OROBLANCO** is a pummelo-grapefruit hybrid with large, seedless, extremely juicy fruit with white flesh. It is best in California and the desert Southwest.

3 **RED BLUSH** produces medium-size fruit with red-tinged flesh and rind. The fruit requires heat to develop good red coloring. The tree is large, vigorous, and productive. It grows well in all citrus regions.

4 **STAR RUBY** is a popular, medium-size, seedless, juicy grapefruit with deep red flesh that ripens in midseason on a medium-size tree with an attractive open habit. Weeks of hot weather are essential for best flavor. It grows well in all citrus regions.

for easy watering. You can add a thin layer of mulch on top of the soil to help conserve soil moisture.

The most challenging aspect of growing citrus trees in cold climates is providing them with enough light indoors. In fall acclimate trees to indoor lighting by progressively moving them to shadier and shadier spots for about three weeks prior to taking them indoors. Reverse the process in spring as you acclimate the trees to more intense outdoor lighting.

Container-grown citrus trees have exacting watering requirements. Most watering mistakes involve overwatering. Wait until the top inch or two of soil is dry to the touch, and then water by thoroughly moistening the soil.

Dark green leaves indicate that a citrus tree is healthy and has adequate nutrition. Fertilize off-color trees with a balanced water-soluble product according to label directions. Maintain healthy trees by fertilizing them with a slow-release product every two months. Look for a mix that includes micronutrients.

Citrus trees rely on bees for pollination. When your tree is in bloom, be sure it is outside where bees can pollinate it. If that's not possible, pollinate the flowers by whisking a small artist's brush over the yellow pollen-covered stamens until the brush is coated with pollen. Touch the brush to the flower's central pistil.

Citrus trees in containers often produce more fruit than they should. Just after the fruits form, thin them to just four to six fruits per tree in the first year. In subsequent years, increase the number of fruits left on the tree by one or two each year.

Harvest

Citrus fruits mature at various times of the year. Early varieties of oranges and mandarins ripen in October or November of the year in which they bloom. Late varieties of oranges, mandarins, and grapefruits mature from February to May of the following year.

In hot, humid regions such as Florida and South Texas, the fruits mature slightly before the same varieties grown in the hot, dry desert

1

2

3

4

lemon varieties:

1 **IMPROVED MEYER** is a favorite hybrid because of its excellent flowery flavor. It is orange-yellow when mature and holds well on the tree. The small to medium tree, which is nearly thornless, moderately vigorous, and spreading, is good for hedges and containers. It grows well in all citrus-producing regions.

2 **LISBON** produces highly acidic, juicy fruit with few seeds. It is best picked ripe as it loses acidity if left on the tree. The most productive and cold hardy of lemons, it grows best in California and the desert Southwest.

3 **PONDEROSA** is a lemon-citron hybrid with grapefruit-size, juicy, acidic fruit. Good for containers and hedges, it grows well in all citrus-producing regions.

4 **VARIEGATED PINK EUREKA** has very acidic, juicy fruit with few seeds. The tree is eyecatching with dark green leaves variegated white. It grows best in the desert Southwest and the Gulf Coast.

regions of the Southwest and well before fruits in the cool coastal areas of California.

The only sure way to determine maturity is to taste the fruit. Color is a poor indication of ripeness because many fruits have fully colored rinds months before they can be eaten. Lemons, limes, and other acidic types of citrus are an exception. They can be picked whenever they reach acceptable size and juice content.

Once mature, most citrus fruits can be stored on the tree for several weeks and picked as needed. Mandarins are an exception. When mandarins have been on the tree too long, they lose their juice and the pulp dries out. A puffy rind is another indication that the fruit is overly mature and should be tossed in the compost pile.

Most citrus fruits can be stored in the refrigerator for at least two or three weeks. Under dry conditions at room temperature, fruits develop an off-flavor, wither, and become unattractive within 10 days.

Pests and diseases

Citrus plants are sensitive to a variety of environmental problems, the most serious of which are wind and water damage. Well-drained soil, ample sun, and consistent but not too much moisture are keys to their success.

Citrus plants are susceptible to leaf miners, aphids, scales, mites, and other pests as well as a host of diseases including viruses, rots, molds, and anthracnose.

Tristeza is a virus disease that kills citrus trees quickly, particularly those growing on a sour orange rootstock. This devastating disease has made it illegal to transport citrus trees across state lines in some areas. Learn more about citrus tristeza virus by contacting your local county extension office.

Varieties sold for use in your geographic area are bred and grafted to reduce the likelihood of pest attack. When insects and diseases strike, ask your local county extension agent or a nursery owner for spraying guidelines specific to your plants and follow directions carefully when using pesticides.

1

2

3

lime varieties:

1 **BEARSS** has small to medium, acidic, very juicy limes that are yellow at maturity. They do not hold well on the tree and should be picked before turning yellow. The medium-size, spreading tree with fragrant blossoms is hardier than 'Mexican'. It grows well in all citrus-producing regions.

2 **MEXICAN** produces very small, juicy, acidic limes with a distinctive aroma. Known as the bartender's lime, it is yellow when mature but is picked green. The medium-size, twiggy tree with a dense canopy of small leaves and many short thorns, grows well in all citrus-producing regions.

3 **RANGPUR** has small to medium, very acidic, juicy fruit that holds well on the tree. The medium-size tree is vigorous and spreading and has few thorns. Very cold-tolerant, it is not a true lime but a good lime substitute. 'Otaheite' is a low-acid semidwarf form. It grows well in all citrus-producing regions.

Currant, gooseberry, Jostaberry (*Ribes* spp.)

Currants, gooseberries, and jostaberries are all hardy fruiting shrubs that grow well in cool, humid regions of North America. They grow well in partial shade and produce large crops of tart fruit.

YOU SHOULD KNOW
Currants and gooseberries aren't nearly as common or popular as they might be, primarily because of their potential to carry and spread white pine blister rust, a devastating disease that kills white pine. Check with your local extension service before planting currants or gooseberries in your area. Jostaberries are immune to the disease and can be planted without worry.

1

Best site
Plant in full sun or part shade and moist, well-drained soil. All are hardy in Zones 2 to 9.

Types of *Ribes*
All types of currants and gooseberries are self-fruitful, but yields improve when two varieties are planted for cross-pollination.
Currants grow 3 to 5 feet tall and wide and have attractive 3-inch-wide leaves on thornless stems. In early fall the foliage turns brilliant orange or red. Clusters of creamy white flowers in early spring are followed by midsummer fruits that ripen to red, white, or black.
Gooseberries are similar to currants in every regard but their large, tart fruits and thorny stems. The fruits are often harvested while still green. Mature fruits are purple.
'Jostaberry', a hybrid of black currant and gooseberry, has more in common with currant.

2

3

varieties:

1. **ROVADA** is a popular, productive red currant that is good for preserves. Zones 3–7.
2. **POORMAN** is a long-time favorite gooseberry that produces large amounts of fruit. Zones 4–6.
3. **JOSTABERRY** is a fast-growing cross of black currant and gooseberrywith reddish black fruits. The thornless plant is more vigorous and earlier bearing than either parent, and it is resistant to both mildew and white pine blister rust. Zones 4–7.

Planting
Plant in late winter or early spring as soon as the soil is workable, or set out plants in fall if they are available.

Growing
The plants produce well only when watered adequately and regularly. Provide about 1 inch of water per week. Spread a 2-inch-thick layer of mulch around plants to conserve soil moisture and stifle weeds. Plants benefit from fertilization. Apply a nitrogen fertilizer annually in fall or early spring.

During the dormant season after the first year's growth, select six to eight of the strongest and best-positioned stems and remove the others to the ground. A year later choose three or four good one-year-old shoots and remove the rest; also choose four or five of the best two-year-old shoots and remove the rest. After the third year select shoots so that the bush has three or four shoots each that are one, two, or three years old. In subsequent years remove shoots that are four years old or older.

Harvest
When all the berries in a cluster attain full color, they're considered ripe. They gradually become sweeter with ripening.

Pests and diseases
Prune out and destroy diseased or damaged wood, watching for signs of cane borers. To control currant worms, pick off any you see or apply *Bacillus thuringiensis* (*Bt*).

Elderberry, sweet elder

(Sambucus nigra canadensis)

Easy to grow and productive, elderberry's only downside is its enthusiasm—it spreads fast. In early summer elderberry is covered with clusters of purple-black berries.

Best site

Plant in full sun and moist soil. Elderberry thrives in moist soil but will not grow in soil that is poorly drained or boggy. The plant grows best in fertile soil. Mix a 2-inch-thick layer of compost into the soil before planting.

Be sure to plant where elderberry has plenty of space to spread. Each plant should have at least 6 square feet of growing space. Elderberry is hardy in Zones 3 to 9.

Planting

Plant container-grown plants in early spring. Space them 6 to 10 feet apart. Elderberries are self-unfruitful, requiring two cultivars planted within 60 feet of each other for fruit set. Water shrubs well after planting.

varieties:

1 **ADAMS NO. 1** and its close relative, 'Adam's No. 2', are strong, vigorous, productive, and hardy varieties that bear large fruit clusters. They ripen late and have been the standard since 1926. Zones 4–9.

YORK is often more productive than the Adams series and the berries tend to be larger. Zones 4–9.

Growing

Elderberry is easy to grow. It responds well to fertilization. Spread a 2-inch-thick layer of compost over the root zone in early spring or fertilize with a balanced fertilizer product, such as 10-10-10, according to package directions.

Weeding is one of the most challenging aspects of growing elderberry. Because it has a very shallow root system, cultivating around plants with a hoe or tiller is not a good idea. Instead, hand pull weeds and mulch plants with a 2-inch-thick layer of organic mulch.

Prune annually to prevent elderberry from spreading vigorously. Cut out dead branches as they appear. Keep plants dense by pruning hard in late winter, removing oldest stems completely and shortening others. Rejuvenate overgrown elderberry plants by cutting off all stems just above ground level.

Harvest

Pick berries once they're ripe by raking through the clusters with your open fingers. Use the berries at once for juice, jelly, syrup, or pie, or freeze them for later use.

Pests and diseases

Birds watch the fruit as closely as you do and are good at getting to the ripe ones first. Deploy bird protection just as the berries approach ripening. Wrap the shrubs with bird netting or use bird scare devices. Varieties that ripen late often suffer the least bird damage.

YOU SHOULD KNOW

Purple-black elderberries have a flavor similar to that of blueberries. Both the flowers and fruit are famous for making wine, and the berries are also used for juice and pies.

Fig (*Ficus carica*)

Figs are remarkably adaptable. They are productive with or without heavy pruning. Even if the plant freezes to the ground in winter, it can often spring back and bear fruit the following summer. The silvery gray branches add drama to the landscape and the fruit is a unique addition to the table.

YOU SHOULD KNOW
Peeled or unpeeled, perfectly ripe homegrown figs are delicious fresh. If you have a large crop, they will add sweetness to a variety of baked goods.

Best site
Plant in full sun and well-drained soil. Figs will grow in sandy soil, provided they are watered regularly. Ample sunlight is key to good fig production. Site the tree where it will receive at least eight hours of direct sunlight per day. Figs grow 10 to 30 feet tall and wide; plant them where they have plenty of space to expand. Fig trees are hardy in Zones 8 to 10.

Planting
Plant container-grown fig trees in fall. Set the trees 2 inches deeper than they grew in the nursery container. Space them 10 to 25 feet apart, depending on the fig variety.

In climates where temperatures fall below 18°F, grow a fig in a 10- to 15-gallon half barrel or other large container so you can move it to a protected location for winter. Fill the container with a well-drained potting mix enriched with 2 to 3 gallons of compost.

varieties:

1. **BROWN TURKEY** produces a spring crop of brownish purple fruits. Zones 8–10.
2. **LSU GOLD** fruits have yellow skin and pink-red flesh. The figs are very large and sweet. This variety produces best in the South. Zones 8–10.
3. **CELESTE** bears small figs with purplish brown skin and reddish amber flesh. It has good cold hardiness and pest resistance. Zones 8–10.

Growing
Fig roots are close to the surface and the trees dry out quickly. Water plants during hot, dry weather to prevent premature fruit drop, but avoid allowing the trees to stand in water. Spread a 3-inch-layer of mulch over the tree's root zone to conserve moisture.

Because they fruit on new wood, fig trees normally fruit the first year after planting. Shade young trees from the hot midday sun. Apply low-nitrogen plant food twice a year to inground trees or use fruit tree fertilizer spikes for trees in containers.

When the trees are dormant in fall or winter prune heavily to remove buds of the breba (spring) crop and to increase the main crop. Fig trees are fruitful for up to 15 years.

Harvest
Unripe fruits are gummy with latex, which can irritate the skin, so wear gloves when working with your trees. Most varieties bear two crops each year; the breba, or spring, crop is generally inferior in quality to the main crop. Ripe fruits become soft. Protect ripening figs from birds.

Pests and diseases
Protect fig trees from root-knot nematodes with a thick layer of mulch. Prolonged high humidity or drought may invite scale insects.

Grape (*Vitis* spp.)

There are grape varieties for all regions. These easy-to-grow vining plants do well on simple trellises or rambling over pergolas in the home landscape. The handsome large green leaves provide bold texture in summer; in fall they turn red or yellow, often contrasting beautifully with the color of the grape clusters.

YOU SHOULD KNOW
Fully ripe grapes vary from extremely sweet to slightly tart and from strong to subtle in flavor depending on the grape variety. Grow a few different cultivars to experience the many unique flavors.

Best site

Plant in full sun and well-drained soil. Grapes will adapt to a variety of soils, but they thrive in deep, sandy loam.

Late spring frost is a threat to some cultivars. Choose a sheltered location near your home or outbuilding if you are a growing a tender cultivar. Choose a south- or east-facing slope in an area with good air circulation to prevent mildew, rot, and fungal diseases.

Choose the planting site carefully; when properly cared for, grapes can thrive for 50 to 100 years. They are hardy in Zones 4 to 10.

Types of grapes

American grapes, also called fox grapes or Concord grapes, grow well in all but the hottest climates and are adaptable to many soils. The fruits are slipskin—a tough skin that separates easily from the pulpy flesh. American grapes are susceptible to disease and require spraying to obtain high yields of good-quality berries.
European grapes—varieties of *V. vinifera*—are grown for wine. Choose certified disease-free planting stock grafted to American grape rootstock to prevent grape phylloxera damage.
European-American hybrid grapes are grown primarily for making wine but also are good eaten fresh. These cold-hardy, disease-resistant cultivars combine the best attributes of American and European grapes.
Muscadine grapes are the best choice for the South. They are not as hardy as other grapes but are highly disease resistant, in part because of the high concentration of resveratrol, a natural compound with various health benefits that is found in the skin of red grapes.

Planting

The best time to plant grapes is late winter or early spring. Dig a planting hole 1 foot in diameter, leaving adequate room to place a stake, post, or trellis before the roots are positioned. Position the lowest bud on the trunk even with the soil line. Tamp the soil lightly over the roots and flood the hole with water, repeating until the soil settles at ground level.

At planting time, prune the top growth to a single cane. Tie the cane to a stake to keep it off the ground and prevent damage. Mulch the area around the vine with a 2-inch-thick layer of organic mulch and water as needed so plants receive at least 1 inch of water per week for the first eight weeks after planting.

varieties:

1. **CONCORD** is an American grape that is popular for making juice. It is dark blue, seedy, and fruits in large bunches. Zones 4–8.
2. **NIAGRA** produces yellow-green, seedless, large, thick-skinned grapes. This American grape has a sweet, strong “foxy” flavor. Zones 4–8.
3. **SCUPPERNONG** is a muscadine with large, speckled, bronze, thick-skinned fruit. Use it fresh and for wine. It requires a pollinator. Zones 7–9.

Growing

Avoid fertilizing grapes with a commercial product. Highly fertile soil often detracts from the flavor of grapes, especially wine grapes. An annual 2-inch-thick layer of well-rotted compost or manure spread around the root zone will provide sufficient nutrients.

Train grapevines to a trellis, sturdy fence, or arbor. An arbor is a particularly good choice for a small garden as it is a way to use vertical space for ornamental and edible purposes.

To grow vines on an arbor, train and tie one strong cane up a post as a trunk and prune out the side canes. When the trunk reaches the top of the arbor in the second or third season, select a single cane from it to develop as a cordon, or main branch, across the top of the framework. Then begin pruning to train two-bud spurs across the top. Cut back all the vines in late winter to a few buds per cane. (Prune muscadines in early winter to reduce sap bleeding.) For large arbors grow vines up opposite posts and train canes to cross one another over the framework.

Annual pruning is essential in growing good grapes. Homeowners commonly don't prune severely enough. About 90 percent of the twigs must be removed each year to spur the formation of large, healthy fruit clusters.

Vigorous vines overproduce; thinning fruit bunches helps the remaining grapes to grow large and sweet. Table grape clusters must be thinned to produce large grapes free from rot and insect damage. Thin to one or two bunches per shoot by removing clusters when the grapes are no more than ⅛ inch in diameter. To learn more about pruning and training grapes, see page 132.

In cold-winter areas, spread mulch around the base of the vines for winter protection. In extremely cold regions untie the vines and bend them to the ground, then cover them with soil or straw. Uncover and retie the plants to their supports in spring. Provide a windbreak in exposed areas. Rake back the mulch in spring, add a new 2-inch-thick layer of well-rotted compost or manure, and replace the mulch.

1

2

3

american fresh grape varieties:

1 **CANADICE** is a red, seedless, medium-size grape with a spicy flavor. It ripens very early and is eaten fresh and used to make juice. The vine is hardy and productive. Prune hard or thin the crop. Zones 5–7.

2 **HIMROD** bears gold-yellow, seedless, large grapes in long clusters. Deliciously spicy-sweet, this very early-ripening grape is good fresh or dried and stores well. Moderate disease resistance. Zones 5–8.

3 **RELIANCE** produces pale red, seedless fruit in large clusters. It has a mild flavor and is good for eating fresh and for juice. The vines are productive and resist powdery mildew, downy mildew, and anthracnose. Zones 4–8.

1

2

european table grape varieties:

1 **THOMPSON SEEDLESS** is a popular pale green-gold, seedless, sweet grape. It is eaten fresh or dried and grows well in regions of the West and Northwest with long, hot, dry growing seasons. Thin clusters for larger fruit. Zones 7–9.

2 **PERLETTE** bears pale green, small to medium, seedless grapes with a thin, crisp, juicy skin. More productive than comparable varieties with less heat, it ripens early. Zones 6–10.

Harvest

Most grapevines bear a small crop of fruit the second or third year after planting. American grapes and European table grapes are ready to harvest when they reach full variety size and color, usually in about 150 to 165 days. Leave raisin grapes on the vines to ripen completely before picking.

The best time to pick wine grapes depends on the type of wine to be made. Both the sugar (Brix) level and the pH are determining factors. 'Concord' juice grapes are ready to harvest when the sugar level is about 15° Brix; use a digital wine refractometer to measure the level. Muscadine grapes are ready for harvest in about 200 days.

Clip grape clusters from the vines with sharp scissors and handle them as little as possible to avoid damage. Picking bunches with grapes of varying degrees of ripeness is desirable for making jelly and jam. Pick grapes for fresh eating and juice two or three times over a period of several weeks as the grapes ripen. Store them in the refrigerator for up to two weeks.

Pests and diseases

Many grape diseases can be prevented with good air circulation and clean cultural practices. Black rot overwinters on infected vines, leaves, and unpicked grapes. Keep vines pruned and trellised so that air circulates well.

Choose varieties resistant to botrytis bunch rot, downy mildew, and powdery mildew. Remove and destroy infected plants immediately.

Copper and sulfur fungicides are effective disease controls but may damage the vines. Choose grape varieties resistant to gall phylloxera and pretreated for crown gall. Pick and destroy grape berry moth cocoons and infested grapes and leaves. Pick and destroy Japanese beetles. Scrape off loose bark to expose mealybugs. Prune out old wood to control scale.

Use netting to discourage birds or enclose whole bunches of ripening grapes in paper bags.

1

2

3

european wine grape varieties:

1 **CHARDONNAY** is a high-quality, white grape that ripens late in the season. It is somewhat cold hardy, but less than 'White Riesling'. It does not grow as vigorously as other cultivars and has a relatively high susceptibility to botrytis bunch rot. Zones 7–9.

2 **CABERNET SAUVIGNON** produces red grapes with a strong, distinctive flavor. It ripens very late and requires a long, warm season. Zones 7–9.

3 **WHITE RIESLING** is one of the hardiest European wine grape varieties. Its green-yellow, small, speckled grapes ripen late and are prized as high-quality wine grapes. Zones 6–9.

1

2

3

european-american hybrid wine grape varieties:

1 **DE CHAUNAC** is a blue-black grape that produces good-quality red wine. It is a good choice for beginning wine grape growers. Zones 6–8.

2 **NORTON** has small, black grapes that produce good-quality wine. It needs a long, warm growing season. Zones 5–8.

3 **VIDAL BLANC** has small, white fruit in medium to large clusters. The vines are very productive, vigorous, and mildew resistant. Zones 7–9.

Kiwi, hardy kiwi

(*Actinidia* species)

These egg-shape fruits with shimmering, emerald green flesh and delicious berry flavor are making inroads in home gardens. The vigorous, heavy vines need sturdy support and heavy annual pruning. Train the vines over a pergola to shade a patio.

YOU SHOULD KNOW
Also called Chinese gooseberry, kiwi has a fuzzy brown skin that is removed before eating. Hardy kiwi has edible skin and is eaten unpeeled like a grape.

Best site

Plant in full sun and well-drained soil. Kiwis thrive in deep, fertile loam. Enrich the planting site with a 2-inch-thick layer of compost. Plants are susceptible to damage from frost and wind, so locate them in a protected area near your house or an outbuilding. Kiwi is hardy in Zones 8 to 11, and hardy kiwi in Zones 5 to 9.

Types of kiwi

The **familiar kiwi** has 5- to 8-inch dark green leaves that are round with a fuzzy white underside. Both male and female plants must be present for pollination.

Hardy kiwi plants look similar, but the fruit is smaller and its skin is edible. Some hardy varieties may not require a male, but fruiting is better if a male and female plant are present.

varieties:

1. **HAYWARD** is the most common kiwi in North America. Zones 7–9.
2. **VINCENT** is a kiwi that is ideal for mild climates as it requires little cold weather to produce fruit. Zones 8–9.
3. **ISSAI** is a hardy kiwi that is self-fruitful, but produces better with a pollinator. Zones 5–9.

Planting

Plant kiwi in fall once summer temperatures begin to moderate. Plant hardy kiwi in early spring as soon as soil is workable. Space plants 15 to 20 feet apart, and be sure to leave space to erect a trellis.

Growing

The vines require plenty of water. Irrigate deeply and often when the vines are blooming or fruiting. Mature vines need 10 pounds of 10-10-10 fertilizer every year. Because young vines are sensitive to excess fertilizer, apply about 4 ounces the first two years, and increase the amount as the vine grows. Spread fertilizer evenly under the entire canopy. Feed plants in spring through midsummer.

Kiwi vines need regular pruning to prevent them from becoming a tangled mess. Let young plants grow with minimal pruning for a year or two after planting.

Harvest

Fruits mature in late fall or early winter. Pick them while they're still hard and let them ripen off the vine like pears. A change of color from greenish brown to brown is a sign the fruit is almost ripe.

Pests and diseases

Various insects such as leaf roller caterpillars and scale insects can be troublesome. Treat leaf-rolling caterpillars with *Bacillus thuringiensis* (*Bt*). Treat scales with neem oil. Careful preparation of a well-drained planting site and proper watering are the best ways to avoid root rot and other stress-related diseases.

Mango (*Mangifera indica*)

Mangoes have a bold presence in the landscape. Their thick, leathery, pointed leaves are 1 foot or more long and 3 inches wide. Their fruits dangle at the ends of 6- to 8-inch-long stalks. Mangoes grow only in frost-free climates. Where they thrive, mangoes produce hundreds of pounds of juicy fruit.

Best site

Plant in full sun and moist, well-drained soil. Enrich the soil before planting by incorporating a 3- to 4-inch-thick layer of compost into the planting site. In the desert, plant trees in part shade to protect fruit from sunburn. Mangoes are hardy in Zones 10 to 11.

Planting

Plant container-grown mango trees in the fall when daytime high temperatures become more moderate. When shopping for a tree, look for a small tree in a large container, as opposed to a large tree in a small container. A large tree in a small container usually has constricted roots that will inhibit future growth. Wear gloves while working around mango trees; sap in the leaves and fruit skins can irritate skin.

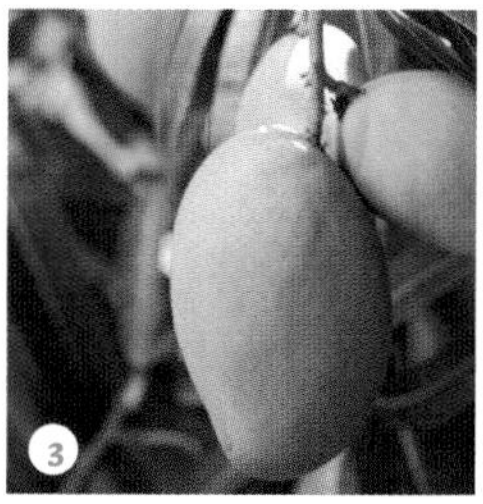

varieties:

1. **AH PING** has large, yellow and orange, fiberless fruits with small seeds. It ripens in July and grows best in Hawaii.
2. **KENT** bears large green, red, and yellow fiberless fruit with small seeds. It ripens in July and August and grows best in Florida.
3. **MANILA** has small to medium yellow fruit that is nearly fiberless. It ripens in late fall and grows best in California.

Growing

Keep the soil around mangoes consistently moist until the fruit is harvested. Weekly irrigation is required during warm weather, though in the desert trees may need daily watering until harvest. Fertilize a mango tree regularly from February through July; spread a 2-inch-thick layer of composted manure over the tree's root zone once a month until July. A commericial fertilizer product can also be used. Don't overfertilize; too much nitrogen increases the likelihood of disease.

Prune in winter or early spring to control a tree's size and shape. Thin flower clusters and fruits to encourage annual bearing.

Harvest

The fruits mature 100 to 180 days after the flowers bloom. Generally the fruits ripen from May to September in most locations. Mangoes are ripe when they develop a consistent round shape and are slightly soft.

Tree-ripened fruits have the best flavor, but pick all fruits from late-bearing trees if temperatures fall to 40°F. Ripe fruits will keep in the refrigerator for up to three weeks.

Pests and diseases

Mangoes experience few problems in the home landscape. Anthracnose and powdery mildew are primarily problems in summer-humid Florida. Choose resistant varieties and plant trees in areas with good air circulation.

YOU SHOULD KNOW

To peel a mango, begin by slicing the flesh away from the hard core. Soon you'll have chunks of flesh with peel attached. Slide a knife between the flesh and peel to separate the two.

Peach, nectarine *(Prunus persica)*

Few fruits say summer like a perfectly ripe homegrown peach or nectarine. These are among the smallest deciduous fruit trees. Properly pruned standard-size trees are easily maintained at 12 to 16 feet tall. Peach and nectarine trees are compact and bushy and beautiful in bloom. Plant them in the landscape or grow them in containers. The trees thrive in sunny, hot weather but are adaptable to many climates.

Best site

Plant in full sun and rich, moist, well-drained soil. In the South and parts of the West, peaches and nectarines are simple to grow. They thrive in sunny, hot weather. Growing peaches elsewhere takes some skill and a little bit of luck, but these adaptable plants can be grown in many regions.

In cool climates choose a protected site—a south-facing slope is best, although a spot on the north side of your property is good if late spring frosts are a problem in your area. Peaches and nectarines are hardy in Zones 5 to 10.

Planting

Plant dormant, bare-root trees in late winter or early spring as soon as the soil is workable. Container-grown trees should go into the ground in fall in hot-summer areas, but they can be planted anytime where summers are cooler. If your soil drains slowly or is high in clay—the trees do poorly in either situation—plant on a mound of soil or in a raised bed. Plant trees so the graft union (swelling on main trunk above the roots) is several inches above the soil surface. Allow 18 to 24 feet between standard-size trees, and 5 to 8 feet between dwarfs.

Growing

Of all the deciduous fruit trees, peaches and nectarines benefit most from regular applications of nitrogen fertilizer. A yearly application of 1 to 1½ pounds of actual nitrogen ensures vigorous growth and annual renewal of fruiting wood. Avoid unnecessary feeding because it causes excess succulent growth, which is susceptible to frost damage and pests.

Peaches and nectarines need heavy pruning every year to stimulate the new growth that will bear fruit the following season. Early each spring as the new growth is just starting, take time to remove up to two-thirds of the shoots that fruited the previous year and leave the thicker of the new growth, cutting the longer shoots back about halfway. Prune more in the upper, outermost parts of the tree to force fruiting on stouter wood. Since lower shoots on peach trees are easily killed by shade, thin the branches so that ample sunlight reaches the interior of the canopy.

Thin fruits to 6 inches apart once they reach 1 to 1¼ inches in diameter and after normal fruit drop. Thin early varieties and heavy producers to 10 inches apart. Use stakes to prop up any sagging fruit-laden limbs to keep them from breaking under the heavy fruit load.

Harvest

Peach and nectarine trees begin bearing two to three years after planting. Fruits ripen from midsummer to midautumn depending on the peach or nectarine variety and your zone. Pick them when all green coloration is gone. Peaches and nectarines can be stored in the refrigerator for a few days.

Pests and diseases

Prune out diseased and damaged wood immediately, and keep the ground around the trees cleared of dropped fruit and prunings, which potentially harbor pests and diseases. Avoid most diseases by choosing resistant varieties, and practice clean cultural habits to prevent pest infestations. If necessary, spray dormant oil during winter to control serious infestations of peach tree borer, scale, and mites; spray *Bacillus thuringiensis* (*Bt*) at bloom time and in summer to control caterpillars, and lightly cultivate the soil around the tree to destroy their pupae. To protect beneficial bees and other pollinators, avoid using insect control products while the trees are in flower.

YOU SHOULD KNOW
Nectarines are simply smooth-skin peaches. Both nectarines and peaches are rich in vitamins A and C and potassium.

varieties:

1 **BRIGHTON** is a semifreestone, round, juicy peach. Vigorous, productive, and an early ripener, it is prized for its high-quality fruit. Zones 6–8.
2 **ELBERTA** is a good all-purpose, freestone peach. It is widely grown, available, and adaptable. The tree is vigorous and compact. Zones 5–9.
3 **VETERAN** produces large, freestone, round peaches that peel easily. It produces reliably in cool, wet weather and is a good all-purpose peach. The tree is large and vigorous. Zones 5–9.
4 **RARITAN ROSE** is a striking reddish, freestone peach. The medium to large, tender, juicy, fruit ripens early in the season. Zones 6–8.
5 **MERICREST** bears dark red, freestone nectarines. The medium-size fruit with yellow flesh is juicy. It is the hardiest nectarine. Zones 5–8.
6 **DURBIN** produces large, semifreestone nectarines with sweet, yellow flesh. The tree has very good disease resistance. The fruit quality is excellent. Zones 5–9.
7 **NECTACREST** bears medium-size freestone nectarines with sweet white flesh. The very dwarf trees grow only 10 feet tall and are exceptionally productive. Zones 6–8.

Pear (*Pyrus* species)

A soft, perfectly ripe pear is hard to share, but a productive pear tree will produce bushels of juicy ripe fruit, giving you plenty to eat and share. Pears are easy to grow where spring is warm and dry. In areas where spring is warm and wet, primarily east of the Rocky Mountains, pears are challenging to grow because they are susceptible to fire blight, which thrives in warm, wet weather.

Best site

Plant in full sun and well-drained soil. Choose a north-facing location to delay blooming in areas where late spring frosts are possible. Pears are hardy in Zones 3 to 9.

Types of pears

All pear trees are attractive garden trees with bright green, leathery leaves and brilliant white spring flowers. All are more productive if another, compatible variety is nearby for cross-pollination. Pear trees usually mature at about 25 feet high and wide. A tree on a dwarfing rootstock is one-half to one-quarter as large.

European pears generally are productive in the South and mild-winter West, and others are hardy in cold climates.

Asian pears are less susceptible to fire blight than their European pear counterparts. Asian and European pears differ in shape and skin texture too, but perhaps their greatest difference is flesh texture. European pears are variously described as soft, creamy, and smooth while the flesh of Asian pears is crisp.

Asian hybrids or **hybrid pears**, are hybrids between European and Asian varieties, and are also available. They are similar in appearance to pears of European heritage but are generally more fire blight-resistant.

Planting

Plant dormant bare-root trees in late winter or early spring. Plant container-grown trees anytime during the growing season. Space standard-size varieties 16 to 20 feet apart, and dwarf varieties 10 to 12 feet apart.

Growing

Keep the soil consistently moist; lack of moisture causes fruit to drop. Fertilize only if a soil test indicates the need because excess nitrogen encourages succulent growth that is susceptible to fire blight. Train young pear trees to either a central leader or an open center form. An open center is easier and may reduce the extent of damage in the event fire blight strikes.

Like apple trees, pears produce fruit on stubby branches called spurs that remain productive for five to seven years. Prune mature trees to control their height, and thin out the branches so that light can reach the fruiting spurs. Remove crossing limbs, dead wood, and watersprouts. Prune hardest in the upper, outermost parts of the tree so that most fruit is borne on the lower, stronger limbs. After normal fruit drop, thin the remaining fruits to one fruit every 6 to 8 inches for best size.

Harvest

Standard pear trees begin to bear fruit five or six years after planting, dwarf trees in three or four years. The fruits ripen in August through September. Pick pears by hand before they are completely ripe, except for Asian pears which are best picked when fully ripe and their stems separate easily from the tree.

Pick European pears and hybrids when they reach full size but are still hard and green, and ripen them off the tree at room temperature. If they are left on the tree too long, they become soft and mushy around the core before the outside is ready to eat.

Pests and diseases

Pears are susceptible to pear scab, mildew, bacterial blossom blast, and fire blight. Only fire blight is a serious problem. Insects such as codling moth and pear psylla are serious pests. Controlling these insects with sprays requires exact timing.

YOU SHOULD KNOW

Pears that ripen early are called summer pears. Eat summer pears right away because they don't store well. The pears that ripen later and can be held in cold storage are called winter pears.

varieties:

1 **BARTLETT** is a productive and popular European pear. It is partially self-fruitful and can be pollinated with several other varieties. Zones 5–8.

2 **BOSC** produces medium to large, brown-tinged European pears. The tender and juicy fruits develop on slow-growing trees. It requires a pollinator such as 'Bartlett'. Zones 5–8.

3 **20TH CENTURY** is a very productive Asian pear that is excellent fresh and stores well. It requires fruit thinning and is disease prone. Partially self-fruitful. Pollinate with 'Bartlett'. Zones 6–9.

4 **SHINKO** is an Asian pear with a distinct flavor. It is resistant to fire blight and codling moth. Pollinate with '20th Century' or 'Bartlett'. Zones 5–8.

5 **KIEFFER** is a hybrid pear that is good for canning and cooking. Zones 4–9.

Plum, prune, plum hybrids

(*Prunus* species)

Of all the stone fruits, none is more varied in origin, size, color, and flavor than plum. The many types range from small native plums to comparatively giant Asian varieties. Plum trees can be kept relatively small, growing 12 to 15 feet tall if the tree is pruned annually. Many plums are self-fruitful, but they often produce more fruit when a compatible pollinator is planted.

Best site

Plant in full sun and rich, well-drained soil. If late spring frosts are a problem in your area, plant on the north side of your property; otherwise a south-facing slope is the best site. Plums are hardy in Zones 2 to 9.

Types of plums

European plums are good for canning, drying, or freezing and occasionally eating fresh. They thrive in cold-weather areas and produce small, oval fruit with various colors of skin and flesh.
Japanese plums are the favorite plum for fresh eating and typically produce large, sweet, juicy fruits with red skin. Because Japanese plums flower early, they do not grow well where late frosts occur. They are commonly grown in California and other moderate climates.
Damson-type plums are small, tart fruits that are most often used for cooking and preserves. Compact and cold hardy, they're easy to grow in many climates.
Plum hybrids result from crossing plums with other stone fruits such as apricots and peaches. The results are completely new fruits with different varieties reflecting various degrees of one parent or the other.

Planting

Plant bare-root trees in late winter or early spring. Plant container-grown plants anytime during the growing season. Space standard-size trees 20 feet apart, semidwarf trees 15 feet apart, and dwarf trees and shrubs 8 to 10 feet apart.

After planting spread a 2-inch-thick layer of compost or well-rotted manure under the canopy of the plum tree and cover it with a 2-inch-thick layer of organic mulch, such as wood or bark chips. Repeat this compost and mulch layering every spring.

Growing

Be sure trees receive at least 1 inch of water per week for the first two months after planting, supplementing rainfall with hand watering as needed. Prune trees after flowering to remove dead or diseased wood. The fruits develop on long-lived spurs. Thin interior branches to promote ripening and to make harvest easier.

Thin fruits by hand after normal fruit drop, leaving only the best plum on each spur and 4 to 6 inches between fruits. Red-fruited varieties need more thinning than blue ones, and heavily fruiting branches may need to be propped up.

Harvest

Plums are ready to harvest when they come off in your hand with a gentle twist. Sample a few from different parts of the tree before harvesting a significant amount. European plums must ripen on the tree but should be picked before they are mushy; ripe plums left on the tree will rot. Pick Japanese plums before they are completely ripe; they will continue to ripen off the tree. Damson plums are ready to harvest when they are soft. Store all types of ripe plums for up to two weeks in the refrigerator.

Pests and diseases

Plums are susceptible to black knot, a fungus that produces hard black bumps on twigs and branches. Prune out infected areas in winter by cutting the wood well below the knots and destroying the cuttings; sterilize your pruning tools between cuts. Use a labeled disease control product to prevent brown rot. Prune away diseased and damaged wood immediately, and keep the ground around trees clear of dropped fruit and other plant debris, which harbors pests and encourages diseases.

YOU SHOULD KNOW
Japanese plums are favorite plums for fresh eating. The flesh and skin color vary by cultivar, but the flavor is sweet and intense.

varieties:

1 **DAMSON** is a small, dark blue plum with tart, juicy, yellow flesh. It is self-fruitful. Zones 5–7.
2 **STANLEY** produces medium to large, dark blue European plums with richly flavored flesh. Self-fruitful, it yields best with a pollinator. Zones 4–8.
3 **GREEN GAGE** is a European plum with sweet, juicy flesh. The low-branching, productive tree is self-fruitful but produces best when planted with a pollinator. Zones 5–9.
4 **METHLEY** is favored for its vigorous production of large, juicy, sweet Japanese plums. The early-blooming tree grows well in many soils and bears excellent all-purpose fruit. Self-fruitful. Zones 5–9.
5 **FLAVOR DELIGHT** is a plum-apricot hybrid. It has yellow flesh and a unique flavor. Self-fruitful, it is better pollinated by any apricot. Zones 6–9.

Strawberry *(Fragaria × ananassa)*

Whether you live in Minnesota or Texas or anywhere in between, there is a good chance you can grow a crop of sweet, juicy strawberries. Growing about 6 inches high, strawberry plants have pretty semievergreen leaves and white flowers in spring. Red berries follow the flowers in early summer, or throughout the summer in the case of some berries, making them a good plant for edible landscaping.

Best site

Plant in full sun and loose, well-drained soil. Loam or sandy loam is preferred. Good drainage is especially important because ripening berries will quickly rot in standing water. If your soil is predominately clay, plant berries in raised beds at least 6 inches deep. Wherever you plant strawberries, mix a 2-inch-thick layer of compost into the soil prior to planting. Strawberries are hardy in Zones 3 to 10.

Types of strawberries

Strawberry are either **June-bearing** (also called spring-bearing) or **day-neutral** (also called everbearing). June-bearing types respond to the lengthening days and shorter nights of spring by flowering and setting a crop that matures in late spring or early summer. In some climates June-bearers may also set another small crop during the short days of fall. This type of strawberry is best for jams, jellies, and preserves because a large crop of berries ripens at once.

Day-neutral strawberries flower and produce fruit anytime the temperatures are between 35° and 85°F. Instead of one main crop in early summer, the harvest is spread through the summer into fall.

Planting

Grow strawberries from bare-root or container-grown plants. Bare-root plants are easy to establish and more economical than container-grown plants.

Before purchasing bare-root plants, inspect them for signs of winter injury, mold, and root rot. If plants are moldy or have brown or orange coloration on leaves and stems, don't purchase them. Store healthy bare-root plants in the refrigerator until you are ready to plant.

Plant strawberries in early spring where winters are cold and in either late winter or fall where winters are relatively mild. Before planting, apply 1 pound of a 10-10-10 fertilizer per 100 square feet and dig it into the soil at least 6 to 8 inches deep.

To plant bare-root plants, dig a hole large enough so that the roots can extend, then cover the plants with soil to just below the crown (the place on the main stem where the leaf shoots emerge). Do not bury the crown; this is where stems, called runners, emerge to produce new plants. If the roots are exceptionally long, cut them back to 4 inches before planting.

Plant container-grown plants at the same depth they were growing in the container.

Plant June-bearing strawberries in rows 3 to 4 feet apart. Space plants 12 to 24 inches apart within the rows. This planting pattern is called a matted row, and soon runners and daughter plants will fill in between the original rows. Mulch plants with a 2-inch-thick layer of straw right after planting. Remove the flowers the first season to encourage the growth of runners and daughter plants. Choose six to eight daughter plants to fill out a row 12 to 18 inches wide; remove additional daughter plants.

Because day-neutral strawberries do not send out as many runners as June-bearers, manage them differently. Plant them in either single rows or staggered double rows. For single rows, space plants 5 to 9 inches apart in rows about 42 inches apart. For double rows stagger plants 10 to 18 inches apart in two 8-inch-wide rows that are 42 inches apart. Mulch plants with a 2-inch-thick layer of straw after planting. To maximize the yield of berries, remove all runners that form the first season. Remove flowers until the end of June, and then after that date allow the flowers to remain to set fruit for a small crop of berries in late summer.

YOU SHOULD KNOW
Ounce for ounce, strawberries have more vitamin C than citrus fruit. Mix strawberries with bananas and yogurt for a good-for-you smoothie to start the day or top a spinach salad with sliced strawberries for added nutrients at lunch.

june-bearing varieties:

1 **HONEOYE** produces large, bright red, slightly tart berries on vigorous plants. Fruit ripens early and over a long season. Susceptible to soilborne diseases. Zones 3–8.
2 **ALLSTAR** has large, light orange-red berries with sweet red flesh late in the season. Good disease resistance. Zones 4–8.
3 **EARLIGLOW** is prized for the outstanding flavor of its large, shiny, dark red berries. Disease-resistant. Zones 4–8.
4 **JEWEL** has large delicious, rich red berries. It is widely grown. Susceptible to verticillium wilt and red stele. Zones 4–8.
5 **LATEGLOW** produces very large, good-quality berries late in the season. Susceptible to leaf blight and anthracnose. Zones 6–8.

Growing

Strawberry plants need about 1 inch of water each week. Water at times other than late evening to avoid keeping the plants wet for long periods and encouraging disease. Soaker hoses are especially useful for watering strawberries. Hoses woven through a strawberry bed will slowly deliver water to the roots without getting the foliage wet.

Strawberry plants are short lived but continually renew themselves. The renewal happens mostly in summer when the plants produce runners and daughter plants. Renewing the patch consists of removing older plants and replacing them with healthy young plants. However, various diseases conspire to wear down plants so that many gardeners simply remove the entire patch and replace it with new plants every four or five years.

Keep the strawberry patch weed free, especially in the first few months after planting. In fall cover the plants with a 3- to 4-inch-thick layer of straw to prevent injury from low temperatures. Apply the straw when nighttime temperatures approach 20°F. Remove the mulch in spring after the threat of severe cold weather has passed. Rake the mulch between the rows to help smother weeds and to keep mud from splashing onto the fruit.

Renovate June-bearers immediately after harvesting to reduce diseases, stimulate vigorous new growth, and prolong the life of your planting. Renovation is as simple as mowing or clipping the plants to a height of 3 inches. Collect your clippings in the mower bag or rake them off and take them to the compost pile. Till between the rows to incorporate the straw. Fertilize with 1 pound of 10-10-10 fertilizer per 100 square feet after renovation. Do not overfertilize. Overfertilization will cause excessive leaf growth and make plants susceptible to frost damage. Water the bed well to direct the fertilizer down to the root zone.

Fertilize day-neutral berries with a 10-10-10 fertilizer each month from June through September the first year, and May through September in subsequent years. Day-neutrals produce well for several seasons, especially in mild-winter regions. Overwinter the plants by covering them with straw.

Harvest

Begin harvesting June-bearing strawberries the year after planting—about 14 months from planting in northern climates and 9 months in warmer regions. Day-neutral plants will be ready to harvest about 90 days after planting. The highest yields will come from the youngest plants. The berries ripen about a month after the plants bloom.

Regardless of size, strawberries are ripe when they attain full color for their variety. Ripe berries left on the plants will quickly become overripe and start to decay and attract pests, so collect all the ripe berries each time you pick. Harvest as frequently as every other day at the peak of the season. Fruit harvested in the morning usually has a longer shelf life. Store harvested berries in the refrigerator.

Pests and diseases

Because strawberries carry hard-to-manage virus disease, it's important to buy only dormant, virus-indexed plants from a reliable nursery. Most insects and diseases are easy to manage with smart cultural practices and by planting resistant varieties.

Botrytis fruit rot, also called gray mold, is a fungus disease prevalent during prolonged rainy and cloudy periods just before or during harvest. It causes healthy fruit to rot within two days of picking. Prevent the problem with good weed control and by not overfertilizing with nitrogen.

Red stele causes plants to wilt and die during the first hot, dry weather of the season. It is most common in poorly drained sites. The best way to avoid red stele is to plant only resistant varieties.

Strawberry bud weevel cuts flower buds and severs stems, causing blossom loss. It comes out of hiding in spring when temperatures approach 60°F. Late varieties usually suffer the most harm. Row covers will protect the plants but only until the covers are removed to allow pollinators in. An insect control product may be necessary to stop the pest. Clean up and remove debris at the end of the growing season.

Verticillium wilt causes older leaves to turn reddish or dark brown at the margins and between the veins. Affected plants wilt and die. The best defense is planting resistant varieties.

1

2

3

day-neutral varieties:

1 **TRIBUTE** produces medium-size, bright red berries with a pleasing acid flavor. Good disease resistance. Zones 3–10.

2 **TRISTAR** is similar to 'Tribute' but has smaller and sweeter berries. It is widely available and adapted. Good disease resistance. Zones 3–10.

3 **RUGEN ALPINE** has large flavorful berries. The plant is vigorous, and low growing. It grows in partial sun and does well in containers. Zones 3–9.

herb encyclopedia

Most herbs are exceptionally productive, contributing fresh flavor to your favorite dishes from spring through the first frost.

WHERE TO PLANT

Many herbs are perennial plants, meaning they come back year after year. Choosing the best planting spot is essential to years of fresh snips. Check out planting tips on the pages that follow.

HARVEST TIPS

Unlike vegetables and many fruits, most herbs can be harvested over a long period. The following pages detail the optimal harvest time for the best flavor and texture.

UNIQUE VARIETIES

Have you tried sweet Thai basil with its pronounced anise flavor or lemon thyme with its strong citrus overtones? Wake up your spice cabinet with easy-to-grow varieties.

Basil (*Ocimum* spp.)

Tomato's perfect partner, basil is one of the easiest herbs to grow. Add it to sauces, soups, and salads for a spicy, tangy flavor. The many varieties, from lime basil to Thai basil, have flavors ranging from citrusy to spicy with a touch of anise. Grow a few and explore the different tastes. Basil grows equally well in the garden and in containers, and its clean, long-lasting foliage makes it a great plant for the edible landscape too.

Best site

Plant in full sun and fertile, moist soil. Basil is very adaptable and grows well in a variety of soil conditions. It grows best in moist soil and will tolerate short periods of drought after it has established a strong root system, about six weeks after planting.

Basil also thrives in container gardens. Be sure to use a well-drained potting mix. Combine basil with parsley, thyme, and other favorite herbs in a pot that holds at least 5 gallons of soil. For small containers, choose a compact variety, such as 'Spicy Bush'.

Planting

Start from seeds or transplants. Basil is very tender and grows slowly in cool weather. For early harvest in cool-weather areas, sow seeds indoors in early spring for planting outside after the danger of frost is over. In areas with a long growing season, sow seeds directly in the garden after the threat of frost is past. Thin seedlings to 12 to 36 inches apart.

Transplants are a great way to grow small quantities of several different basil varieties. Transplants are also a good choice for growing basil in a container garden.

Growing

Cover plants with cloches or put them in cold frames in cool regions or anytime frost is predicted. Cut or pinch off flowers as they appear, to encourage bushier growth. Do not fertilize basil; excessive nutrients result in poor flavor. Average garden soil will provide all necessary nutrients. Keep the soil around plants consistently moist and weed free. Spread a 2-inch-thick layer of mulch around plants after they are about 6 inches tall to prevent weed growth and preserve soil moisture.

Harvest

Begin harvesting basil as soon as the plant has at least four sets of leaves. For the most intense flavor, harvest leaves just as the flower buds begin to form. Pinch out the topmost set of leaves and any flowers as needed for use in the kitchen. Store unwashed basil in plastic bags in the refrigerator for a day or two. It can only be stored for a short time; basil begins to decay as soon as it is picked.

Preserve fresh leaves by processing them with oil and storing them in the freezer for up to two years or in the refrigerator for up to three months. Basil can be dried but is not as flavorful and colorful as when it is preserved with oil.

At the end of the growing season in temperate climates, pull up the plants by their roots and harvest any remaining leaves before the first frost. In hot climates cut basil back to 6 inches tall; it will regrow several times in one year before the final harvest.

Pests and diseases

Discourage pests by keeping mulch from touching the plants, and remove and destroy any leaves that look unhealthy. Spray water from a garden hose to knock aphids and mites off plants. Japanese beetles sometimes feed on leaves; remove the pests by hand.

Basil is susceptible to fusarium wilt in hot, humid weather; look for cultivars bred for resistance and plant them in soil that drains well. Remove and destroy infected plants, including the roots and surrounding soil.

YOU SHOULD KNOW
A few full-size basil plants provide plenty of leaves to make a batch of pesto, a paste made of basil, garlic, nuts, and oil. Use pesto on pasta, pizza, and bread and freeze some to enjoy in the winter.

varieties:

1 **GENOVESE** grows 24 to 36 inches tall and 24 inches wide. It has a spicy flavor and is slow to develop flowers. 68 days.

2 **SPICY BUSH** has a neat and tidy habit and grows 12 inches tall and wide. It is ideal for growing in containers. 70 days.

3 **PESTO PERPETUA** has variegated foliage and forms a columnar plant to 36 inches tall. It seldom blooms. 70 days.

4 **PURPLE RUFFLES** is prized for its purple-black leaves and clovelike flavor. It grows 12 to 24 inches tall. 85 days.

5 **SWEET THAI** has a pronounced spicy, anise flavor and pretty reddish-purple stems. It grows 12 to 24 inches tall. 59 days.

Chives (*Allium* species)

Chives are grassy, clump-forming onions with hollow leaves, essentially tiny onions grown for their leaves, not their bulbs. Fragrant pinkish purple flowers that appear in spring are also edible and can be used as a garnish. Grow this perennial herb in the garden, a landscape bed, or a container.

YOU SHOULD KNOW
Just before serving, sprinkle egg and potato dishes with a few freshly chopped chives for a subtle zip of onion flavor.

Best site

Plant in full sun and average, well-drained soil. Hardy in Zones 3 through 10, chives can be counted on to be productive for many years. Chives will tolerate light shade, but they grow best in an area that receives six to eight hours of sun a day. Chives do best in soil that is rich in organic matter. Incorporate a 2-inch-thick layer of compost into the soil before planting.

Chives grow well in containers. Plant them in a well-drained potting mix. In late summer transplant the chives into the garden to give them time to establish a strong root system. They will emerge the following spring. Or treat container-grown plants as annuals, discarding them at the end of the season.

varieties:

1. **FORESCATE** is a vigorous variety with pretty rose red flowers.
2. **RUBY GEM** has gray-green foliage and purplish red flowers.
3. **GARLIC CHIVES** grow taller than common chives, produce flat leaves and white flowers, and can be invasive. As the common name suggests, the leaves have a mild garlic flavor.

Planting

For quick establishment, plant divisions or nursery transplants anytime during the growing season. They usually produce flowers and foliage that can be harvested the first year. Chives can also be planted from seeds in early spring or, in mild-winter areas, in fall. Seed-grown plants may require a full year of growth before leaves and flowers can be harvested.

Growing

Chives are somewhat drought tolerant and don't require fertilizer or much attention besides regular cutting. The plants are evergreen in warm climates but die back to the ground in cooler zones in winter. The clumps eventually become overcrowded, so dig and divide them every few years and plant the divisions in new locations. Deadhead the spent flowers to prevent chives from self-seeding and spreading throughout the garden.

Harvest

Snip the leaves of established chive plants as needed by cutting through them just above the soil with scissors or a sharp knife. Chives can be dried but retain their color and flavor better when frozen.

Pests and diseases

Few insects or diseases seriously affect chives. They may experience some of the same pests and diseases as onions.

Cilantro, coriander

(Coriandrum sativum)

Cilantro is notable for two different flavors it contributes to foods. One is the pungent, distinctive tang of its leaves that some people love and others abhor; the other is the spicy-citrus taste of its ground seeds. The ground seeds, coriander, are common in Middle Eastern foods.

YOU SHOULD KNOW
An essential ingredient in Mexican and south Asian cuisine, cilantro is a cinch to grow in a pot right outside your door for quick and easy harvest.

Best site
Plant in full sun and well-drained soil. Cilantro will tolerate partial shade. It grows well in containers filled with well-drained potting soil.

Planting
Start from seeds or transplants. Sow seeds in early spring after the last frost. Where winters are mild and summers are extremely hot, sow seeds in fall. Plants that become established and are allowed to scatter seeds will self-sow; seedlings are easy to pull out if they pop up where you do not want them to grow. Cilantro is also easy to grow from purchased transplants.

Growing
Water cilantro during dry weather. Plants tend to bolt in hot, dry conditions, so make successive plantings two to four weeks apart to maintain a steady crop all summer long. In warm climates plant cilantro again in autumn for spring harvest. Try overwintering some cilantro in a cold frame in northern gardens. It will also grow well indoors sown directly into deep pots.

Harvest
Thin out whole plants as needed, or begin picking leaves from the lower part of the plant when several stems have developed. The lower leaves look similar to flat-leaf Italian parsley and have more of the desired spicy flavor than the upper foliage, which resembles dill. The tiny, white or lavender flowers are edible; however, their presence indicates that the plant is past its flavor peak. Add leaves to cooked food just before serving; heat dissipates the flavor. The leaves can be dried, but the flavor is much milder.

Cut the flowers when the seedpods begin to turn brown. Hang the flowers upside down in paper bags to catch the seeds. Use some seeds whole or ground as coriander, and save some for the next planting.

Pests and diseases
Few insects or diseases bother cilantro.

varieties:

1 **SANTO** is among the most popular cultivars for fresh leaves because it is slow to bolt. 40 days.

2 **DELFINO** is an All-American Selections winner with ferny foliage. It tolerates warm weather well and is slow to bolt. 35 days.

Dill *(Anethum graveolens)*

Two or three dill plants produce plenty of tangy foliage—an essential ingredient in dill pickles. In the garden, dill is a 2- to 4-foot-tall, easy-to-grow annual herb with delicate, fernlike leaves and flattish clusters of yellow flowers in summer. The seeds mature in late summer or fall.

YOU SHOULD KNOW
Dill is an important food source for beneficial insects such as lacewings. With dill in the garden, there will be fewer aphids, a favorite main course of lacewings. Dill is also a host plant (along with parsley) to black swallowtail butterfly caterpillars.

Best site
Plant in full sun and moist, well-drained soil. Choose a spot that is protected from high winds because lanky dill sometimes has a tendency to topple. Dill grows best in soil that is rich in organic nutrients. Incorporate a 2-inch-thick layer of compost in the soil before planting.

Planting
Start dill from seeds or transplants. In spring—or in fall in hot-summer areas—sow seeds where you want the plants to grow. Plant seeds ¼ inch deep and cover them with a fine layer of sifted compost. Sow seeds once a month for a continuous supply of ferny new growth. Set purchased transplants outside after the threat of frost has passed.

varieties:

1. **BOUQUET** is the most commonly grown variety; it has large seedheads. 50 days.
2. **LONG ISLAND MAMMOTH** is widely grown for both leaves and seeds. 45 days.
3. **FERNLEAF,** a dwarf blue-green variety with high leaf yield, is excellent in kitchen gardens and containers. 40 days.

Growing
Water plants as needed for about four weeks after planting. Dill can tolerate short periods of drought once it has established a strong root system. Mulch plants with a 2-inch-thick layer of organic mulch to help conserve soil moisture.

Dill does not require fertilizing. Generally, average garden soil provides all the necessary nutrients for vigorous growth.

Thin plants when they are 6 to 8 inches tall to use in the kitchen. Remove flowers to encourage foliage and prevent self-sowing, or let some plants flower and go to seed for a new crop. Tolerant of cool weather, dill is often the last herb standing in the late autumn garden.

Harvest
Dill is ready for leaf harvesting 30 to 55 days after seeding. It goes to seed in 75 to 100 days. Snip leaves as needed or harvest whole stems.

To save seeds, cut the stem 4 inches below the flowerheads when the seeds are turning brown, and hang the heads upside down inside paper bags to catch the seeds as they ripen. Leaves can be air-dried or frozen for long-term storage.

Pests and diseases
Parsley worms, caterpillars of the swallowtail butterfly, feed on dill, but they're worth leaving alone. Handpick them if absolutely necessary.

Edible Flowers

Use edible flowers as garnishes and to add color to foods. Flavor is a bonus; edible flowers often contribute distinct new tastes to well-known dishes. Many kinds of flowers are technically edible, including all flowers of culinary herbs; the following is a selection of favorites.

1

2

3

4

5

1 **BEE BALM** (*Monarda didyma*) Bee balm flowers have a minty, sweet-hot flavor. The plant is a perennial (Zones 4–8) that grows 36 inches tall and wide and produces pink, lavender, or flaming red, shaggy flowers that are quite aromatic. Bee balm doesn't grow well where winters are warm and humid. It tolerates some shade but prefers full sun and grows best in rich, moist soil. Bee balm is slow to start from seeds, so buy container-grown plants. Prune plants almost to the ground in fall.

2 **CALENDULA** (*Calendula officinalis*) The flowers of this annual are slightly bitter, but its yellow or orange color adds brilliance to salads. Calendula enjoys a long flowering season: In warm regions it blooms in winter and spring, and elsewhere in summer and fall. The plant produces angular, branched, hairy stems to 24 inches tall with 4-inch-wide flowers. Flowers of hybrids are in the same color range but richer. Sow seeds or grow from purchased transplants. Plant in full sun and ordinary soil.

3 **NASTURTIUM** (*Tropaeolum* species) Peppery-tasting flowers of this climbing or sprawling annual make colorful additions to summer salads. The pungent leaves are also edible, and the buds and seeds can be pickled as substitutes for capers. The spurred blossoms come in orange, yellow, red, and creamy white. Grow nasturtium in full sun and well-drained soil. If the soil is too rich, plants will produce much lush foliage but few flowers. Do not fertilize. Watch for aphids, which seem to thrive on nasturtiums, and spray plants with a strong blast of water to remove the pests. Grow from seeds.

4 **PINK, CARNATION** (*Dianthus* species) The clovelike quality in the scent of these species, most of them perennials, is also expressed in their flavor. Plant choices range from low-growing miniature pinks with small flowers to the tall florist's carnation. They are perennial and hardy in Zones 3–9. The flowers come in every shade of pink and red as well as white. Carnation (*D. caryophyllus*) also blooms in shades of yellow, orange, and purple. Both pinks and carnations are available with striped and variegated petals. The evergreen foliage is often gray-blue. All need full sun, although some will bloom in partial shade. The soil should be well drained and slightly alkaline.

5 **SWEET VIOLET** (*Viola odorata*) The flowers of this hardy perennial (Zones 3–10) brighten salads in spring. Sweet violet spreads from creeping roots and forms an attractive groundcover of heart-shape leaves with crinkled edges. Flowers of deep violet, pink, or white appear in late spring. The species is native to wooded areas and should be planted in partial shade and fairly rich soil that is kept evenly moist.

French tarragon

(Artemisia dracunculus sativa)

A classic French herb used to season fish and many other foods, the name "tarragon" is derived from the French word for little dragon, which refers to the plant's bold flavor. It is a low, perennial shrub with glossy leaves on slender stems that sprawl outward before sending up shoots.

YOU SHOULD KNOW

Citrus and licorice flavors mingle together in the leaves of French tarragon, giving it a pronounced, vibrant flavor. Use it in sauces, dressings, and marinades.

Best site

Plant in full sun and well-drained soil. French tarragon does not grow well in clay or other slow-draining soils. It tolerates drought well and is a good choice for a low-water garden. It will tolerate partial shade but grows best in six to eight hours of direct sunlight. Hardy in Zones 5 to 9, it thrives in nutrient-rich soil. Mix a 2-inch-thick layer of compost into the site before planting.

French tarragon grows well in containers. Plant it in a pot filled with a well-drained potting mix. In late summer transplant it into the garden so it can establish a strong root system before winter. New shoots will emerge the next spring. Or treat container-grown plants as annuals, discarding them at the end of the season.

1

2

varieties:

1 **FRENCH TARRAGON** is a versatile herb with a pronounced citrus and licorice flavor. Sometimes difficult to find, it is often available at local garden centers that have extensive herb collections. There are no notable varieties of French tarragon.

2 **RUSSIAN TARRAGON** almost impossible to visually distinguish from French tarragon, Russian tarragon has notably poor flavor.

Planting

Start from transplants purchased at your local garden center. French tarragon rarely flowers so seeds are uncommon; instead, plants are propagated by stem cuttings. When purchasing plants, be sure not to confuse French tarragon with its relative Russian tarragon, an inferior, flavorless plant.

Set out container-grown plants in spring, or do so in fall in areas with mild winters. Space plants 18 to 24 inches apart.

Growing

Encourage foliage growth by removing any flowers that form. Plants will grow vigorously if cut regularly. Cut them back in fall and mulch with a 4- to 6-inch layer of organic mulch for winter protection. The short-lived plants must be replaced every few years. Propagate new plants by dividing plants in spring and replanting the divisions.

Harvest

Begin harvesting leaves and stems as soon as the plant establishes a strong root system, about four weeks after planting. Snip leaves as needed from the tops of the stems. To enjoy the most flavor, add leaves just before serving hot foods. For long-term storage, submerge leaves in vinegar or freeze them.

Pests and diseases

Few insect pests or diseases bother either type of tarragon.

Horseradish

(Armoracia rusticana)

The pungent roots of horseradish are a flavorful addition to the culinary garden. The plant has glossy green leaves and profuse small white flowers. It's a hardy perennial. Plant where its spread is retained; it will become an invasive weed if left unattended.

YOU SHOULD KNOW
Harvested horseradish roots turn green quickly if exposed to light. To keep their white color, store them wrapped in black plastic in the refrigerator.

Best site

Plant in full sun and moist, well-drained soil. Horseradish grows very well in sandy loam soil. Hardy in Zones 3 to 9, it adapts to nearly any location and grows so vigorously that it can become invasive. For best growth, mix a 2-inch-thick layer of well-decomposed manure or compost into the soil before planting.

Planting

Start plants in early spring from root cuttings purchased at your local garden center or a mail-order source. The root pieces should be one finger width in diameter and 12 to 18 inches long. As soon as the soil can be worked, plant root cuttings horizontally, laying them in a trench that is 3 inches deep. Plant the roots 18 inches apart in rows that are 36 inches apart.

varieties:

1 **COMMON** is a crinkle-leaf type that is easy to find and is grown for its large roots. It is susceptible to some viruses and rusts.

2 **BOHEMIAN** is popular because of its hardiness and high-quality roots.

WASABE (*Wasabia japonica*), a distant relative that produces highly aromatic, spicy rhizomes used in Asian foods, is grown in streams in mild climates.

Growing

Water root cuttings well for about four weeks after planting. Established plants will tolerate short periods of drought.

To encourage large taproots, remove a few inches of topsoil in midsummer and trim the fine lateral roots off the main root, then replace the soil. Start new plants from lateral root cuttings taken from near the top of the large taproot. Thin overcrowded plants in fall by harvesting.

Harvest

Cuttings planted in spring produce mature roots in 6 to 8 months, but for the best flavor leave the roots in the ground until after a few frosts have sweetened them. Roots may need two or more seasons to reach usable size.

Loosen the soil with a pitchfork and pull up the roots by hand, using those that are 6 to 12 inches long and replanting the smaller ones. Save some cuttings for next year's crop, or simply leave the plants in the ground and mulch them for winter protection.

Store unwashed harvested roots in black plastic bags in the refrigerator. Horseradish roots are usually processed by peeling, dicing, and mincing with a blender.

Pests and diseases

Few insects or diseases seriously affect horseradish.

1

Lavender (*Lavandula* spp.)

Lavender is a bushy shrub. The smooth-edged silver-gray leaves grow to 2 inches long, and the small lavender-purple to deep purple flowers bloom on 6- to 8-inch-long stems for a month or more in summer. The whole plant is aromatic, and on a warm day the scent will waft through the garden.

YOU SHOULD KNOW
Lavender flowers are sweet with lemon and citrus flavors. The stems and leaves can be used in place of rosemary in most recipes.

Best site

Plant in full sun and well-drained soil. Lavender thrives in sandy loam and doesn't tolerate wet or boggy sites. It grows best in moderately fertile soil; it is best not to incorporate compost or well-rotted manure.

Lavender is a perennial, returning year after year. Plant it in a mixed border with other perennials and shrubs. It is also easy to grow in a container. Plant it in a pot filled with a well-drained potting mix. In late summer transplant lavender into the garden so it can establish a strong root system before winter. New shoots will emerge the following spring. Or treat container-grown plants as annuals, discarding them at the end of the season.

2

3

varieties:

1 **MUNSTEAD** English lavender is a popular culinary variety with purple-blue flowers and green leaves. Zones 5–10.

2 **ALBA** is a vigorous white-flowering form of French lavender. Zones 6–10.

3 **SPANISH LAVENDER** (*L. stoechas*) has dark purple flowers on short stems and is very fragrant. It grows 24 to 36 inches tall. Zones 5–10.

Planting

Start lavender from nursery-grown plants in spring or, where winters are mild, in fall. Be sure to water fall-planted transplants well to encourage fast root growth. Space transplants 24 to 36 inches apart, depending on the variety.

Growing

Lavender tolerates drought, heat, and wind, but not high humidity, wet soil, or poor drainage. Even though lavender is drought tolerant, it benefits from regular watering during the first six weeks after transplanting.

Shear plants after bloom to remove spent flowers and to promote density and repeat blooms. In spring wait until new growth has begun before cutting plants back. Never cut them down to the ground; instead reduce the stem length by about one-third.

Harvest

Cut flower stalks when about half of the flower buds are open. Cut stems in the morning if possible as the oils are most concentrated then. To dry, hang small bundles of lavender upside down in a dark, airy place.

Pests and diseases

Occasionally lavender is troubled by root rot or southern blight, particularly when it's not in an ideal site. Mulch plants with pea gravel to promote rapid drying around the crown.

Lemon balm
(Melissa officinalis)

This old-time favorite bears leaves that give off an intense minty lemon fragrance, and its flowers attract bees. Lemon balm complements cooked vegetables and fruit salads, and it can also be used to make tea. The plant is bushy with heavily veined, heart-shape foliage.

1

YOU SHOULD KNOW
Use lemon balm as a garnish. Place a couple of sprigs of this citrus-flavor alternative to mint in a glass of iced tea.

Best site
Plant in partial shade or full sun and moist, rich, well-drained soil. Lemon balm grows best in a site that receives five to six hours of direct sunlight a day, but it will tolerate more sun if planted in moist, rich soil. It is a perennial and is hardy in Zones 3 to 10.

For the most succulent foliage, boost the soil nutrient content before planting by incorporating a 2-inch-thick layer of compost in the planting site.

When choosing a site, keep in mind that lemon balm spreads freely and self-seeds readily. If not kept in check it can quickly become a weed. Rein it in by growing it in a container garden instead of in the ground. Plant it in a pot filled with well-drained potting mix.

2

varieties:

1. **LEMON BALM** is available in only a handful of varieties. The species is an excellent choice and very productive. Zones 4–10.
2. **AUREA** is a vigorous variety with gold-tinged leaves and white flowers. Zones 3–7.

Planting
Plant nursery-grown plants or divisions in early spring. Space plants 24 inches apart. Lemon balm is also easy to grow from seeds planted in early spring or fall. Since the seeds are very small, cover them with a fine layer of potting mix or sifted compost.

Growing
Plants may be thin the first year but will fill out quickly. Lemon balm reseeds and spreads readily, sometimes to the point of becoming a weed. Cut plants back in midsummer to prevent self-sowing. In areas where the ground freezes in winter, mulch lemon balm with a 4- to 6-inch-thick layer of organic mulch.

Harvest
Collect leaves as you need them for fresh use. The best time to harvest leaves is just before the plant blooms. Preserve harvested leaves by drying, although dried leaves lose much of their fragrance. To keep the leaves from turning black, dry them quickly on a rack and store the dried leaves in an airtight container.

Pests and diseases
Powdery mildew is occasionally a problem, particularly in sites with poor air circulation.

Lemon verbena
(Aloysia triphylla)

A tropical shrub, lemon verbena has a sharp, intensely lemony fragrance and flavor. The semievergreen plant's narrow, almost viney branches are covered in pale green leaves. It grows 6 feet tall and sprawls.

YOU SHOULD KNOW
Lemon verbena leaves are tough. Finely chop them before adding them to baked goods or sauces, or use them whole and remove them prior to serving.

Best site
Plant in full sun and average soil. Lemon verbena adapts to many soil types. It grows well in both wet clay soil and quick-to-drain sandy loam. Do not enrich the planting site with compost; lemon verbena grows best in soil that has few nutrients.

Lemon verbena is a perennial, coming back year after year, in Zones 9 and 10. It is grown as an annual elsewhere. Where it is hardy, add it to shrub borders and landscaping beds to begin creating an edible landscape.

This herb grows well in containers. Plant nursery-grown plants in pots filled with well-drained potting mix. Container growing is a great choice for gardeners in cold zones; in fall the pot can be moved indoors where lemon verbena will overwinter.

varieties:

(1) **LEMON VERBENA** There are no notable cultivars of lemon verbena. The species is productive and easy to grow.

Planting
Plant container-grown plants in spring after the soil has warmed and the threat of frost is past. Look for lemon verbena at specialty nurseries and online sources. It may be hard to find in the marketplace.

Growing
Provide plants with about 1 inch of water per week for the first six weeks after planting. Lemon verbena may drop leaves during winter chills. Minimize leaf drop by wrapping the plant in burlap when cool temperatures are predicted. In spring, prune plants as needed to maintain the plant's shape and size.

In northern regions move container-grown plants indoors before the first frost. Place them in a bright, sunny window and water as needed during winter. Fertilize container-grown plants in summer.

Harvest
Lemon verbena can be harvested any time. Collect leaves as needed for recipes, and chop them finely when using fresh. Preserve leaves by drying them.

Pests and diseases
Few insects or diseases affect lemon verbena.

Lovage
(Levisticum officinale)

Lovage is a relative of celery and, on casual comparison, it looks like a robust form of the vegetable. Unlike celery, lovage is a hardy perennial. Though its leaves and stems die to the ground in winter, its roots persist and produce new growth the following spring.

YOU SHOULD KNOW
Lovage leaves are a popular ingredient in tomato sauces in northern coastal Italy. It can often be used in place of parsley, but in limited quantities. A little lovage goes a long way.

Best site
Plant in full sun and deep, fertile, consistently moist soil. Unlike most herbs, lovage grows well in wet soil. It is a good choice for clay and other slow-to-drain soils. Lovage grows best where soil nutrients are plentiful. Mix a 2-inch-thick layer of compost into the soil before planting.

Select a planting spot where this 2- to 4- foot tall and wide plant has room to expand. Count on it to add interest to the landscape—in summer the dark green leaves are topped with small pale yellow flower blossoms that attract beneficial insects. Lovage is hardy in Zones 3 to 9. It will grow vigorously for about four years, and then growth will slow but the plant will continue to produce many stems and leaves.

varieties:

1 **LOVAGE** There are no notable cultivars of lovage. The species is productive and easy to grow.

Planting
Start from seeds or divisions. Sow seeds directly in the garden in fall or early spring, or sow them indoors in late winter for transplanting in spring. Plant seeds in fall if possible for the best germination.

Lovage can also be started by the division of established lovage plants in spring or fall. Be sure to water divisions well at planting time to ensure a strong root system forms before winter.

Growing
Prevent self-seeding by removing flowers as soon as they appear. Mulch lovage with a 4- to 6-inch-thick layer of organic mulch for overwintering in cold climates.

Harvest
Begin collecting lovage leaves about three months after sowing seeds. After plants are a year old, harvest the tender leaves and stalks anytime during the growing season and use them fresh in salads. Removing flowers as they appear will give you more leafstalks. Letting some flowers develop will invite beneficial insects into the garden and allow you to collect dried seeds.

When dried or frozen, the leaves hold their flavor about one year. Collect seeds by cutting off the nearly mature seedheads and hanging them upside down in bunches in paper bags.

Pests and diseases
Maintain adequate space between plants to help avoid blights. If any stems rot or leaves turn yellow or reddish, pull and destroy the whole plant and sow seeds in another location.

Marjoram, sweet marjoram

(Origanum majorana)

Like its relative oregano, marjoram is a primary herb in Italian cuisine, but marjoram leaves have a sweeter, milder flavor and aroma than those of oregano. Use them in soups and egg dishes and to flavor vegetables.

YOU SHOULD KNOW
The most tender of the *Origanum* species, marjoram is grown as an annual beyond mild-winter regions.

Best site

Plant in full sun and well-drained soil. Marjoram is adaptable to many soil types but grows best in light, sandy soil. It is hardy in Zones 8 to 10 and is grown as an annual elsewhere.

The plants are low growing and clump forming, producing tiny white, pink, and red flowers in mid- to late summer. Marjoram grows well in containers filled with well-drained potting mix.

Planting

Set out nursery-grown plants in spring as soon as the danger of frost has passed. Space plants 12 inches apart and water them well after planting. Marjoram is challenging to start from seed; choose nursery-grown plants instead.

varieties:

1. **ERFO** has pale, grayish green leaves with a balsamlike fragrance.
2. **MAX** is a tall, upright marjoram with yellow-green leaves. It grows very well in containers.
3. **ITALIAN OREGANO,** hardy marjoram, sometimes sold by this name, is a cold-tolerant hybrid (Zones 6–9) of wild oregano and sweet marjoram that is both pungent and sweet.

Growing

Marjoram is well suited to container growing and looks especially attractive in hanging baskets. Cut the trailing stems frequently to encourage bushier growth.

Protect plants from midday sun in hot climates. Marjoram dries out quickly, so keep the soil consistently moist but not waterlogged. To stimulate new growth, dig and divide plants every few years when they become woody. Overwinter plants where they are hardy by covering them with a 4- to 6-inch layer of organic mulch, or dig and divide plants in autumn and pot some for use indoors.

Harvest

Pick leaves and stems as needed. Snip freshly harvested leaves into salads or cooked dishes just before serving. To dry, hang small bundles of stems upside down in a cool, dark location with good air circulation. Pull the leaves from the stems when they are completely dry, crumble them, and store them in airtight glass jars. Dried marjoram retains its flavor better than dried oregano. It stores well for about one year.

Pests and diseases

Few insects or diseases affect marjoram.

Mint (*Mentha* species)

As fragrant and flavorful as they are unfussy, mints are welcome members of the garden, especially if you enjoy mint tea or mint julep. Add fresh leaves to brewed tea while it is still hot or snip leaves into fruit salad, ice cream, or sherbet. Mint is such a vigorous plant that it will become invassive unless confined.

Best site

Plant in full sun or part shade and rich, moist, well-drained soil. Mint is adaptable to many soil types and degrees of sunlight. It will grow in average soil but produces the best foliage in soil that has been enriched with a 2-inch-thick layer of compost.

Mint is a perennial. Its hardiness varies by variety. Prevent mint from growing out of control by planting in a container instead of in the garden.

Planting

Mint is easy to grow from container-grown plants set out in spring. Mint readily cross-pollinates. Space different varieties as far apart as possible to avoid cross-pollination.

varieties:

1. **PEPPERMINT** (*M. ×piperita*) has a distinct peppermint flavor. There are many cultivars of peppermint including slightly sweet chocolate. Zones 3–8.
2. **SPEARMINT** (*M. spicata*) is aptly named for its bold spearmint flavor. Zones 5–10. 'Kentucky Colonel' has large, flavorful leaves.
3. **APPLE MINT** (*M. suaveolens*) has a fresh, unique apple and mint flavor. Zones 5–10.

If growing mint in the garden, limit its spread by planting it in a container that is sunk into the soil. Or set edging 12 inches deep in the soil all around the plants.

Growing

Frequent cutting will keep mint looking attractive. Remove flowers as they appear, and pinch back the stems to encourage bushier growth. Keep the area around mint free of weeds and grass, which reduce yields and may affect flavor. Divide mint every few years. Cut the plants to the ground in late fall.

Harvest

Cut the leaves and the flower tops when the plants start to bloom; hang them upside down to dry in small bundles or spread them loosely in a shallow tray. When the stems are brittle, remove the leaves and flowers and store them in airtight containers. Freeze fresh leaves to retain their bright color.

Pests and diseases

Verticillium wilt, mint rust, mint anthracnose, spider mites, flea beetles, root borers, cutworms, root weevils, and aphids are occasionally troublesome. Knock off mites and aphids with a spray from the garden hose, being careful to spray the undersides of leaves. Plant mint in containers to avoid soilborne diseases, such as verticillium wilt. Provide good air circulation to thwart foliar diseases.

YOU SHOULD KNOW

Mint is notorious for vigorous growth and rapid spread. For the simplest care, grow it in a pot so it cannot put down roots and ramble through your landscape.

Oregano

(Origanum vulgare)

An essential ingredient of Mediterranean cuisine, oregano is a low, sprawling shrubby perennial that sports aromatic leaves and small purple, pink, or white tubular flowers. The plants are low growing, producing tiny white, pink, and red flowers in mid- to late summer.

YOU SHOULD KNOW

Unlike many herbs, oregano keeps much of its flavor when dried. In late summer dry a few bunches for use in winter.

Best site

Plant in full sun and well-drained soil. The more sun oregano receives, the more pungent the flavor of the leaves. It will not tolerate wet soil; if your soil is slow draining, plant oregano in a raised bed or in containers filled with a well-drained potting mix.

Oregano is a perennial and is hardy in Zones 5 to 10. Use it as a low-growing groundcover in the edible landscape, planting it at the base of fruiting shrubs or growing it alongside other perennial herbs.

Planting

Set out nursery-grown transplants in spring after frost danger is over. Space plants 24 inches apart. Oregano is tough to start from seed; grow it from nursery-grown transplants instead. Unique varieties of oregano can be difficult to find in the local marketplace. Search online or visit specialty nurseries for unique varieties.

Growing

Avoid root rot by watering only during periods of drought. Divide plants every few years when they become woody or begin to lose their compact, low-growing habit. To obtain two large harvests, cut the whole plant back to 3 inches just before it flowers, then again in late summer.

Harvest

Oregano's flowers attract bees and butterflies, but the leaves are best picked just before the buds open. Cut succulent stems as needed and snip fresh leaves and flowers into salads or cooked dishes just before serving them.

To dry oregano, hang small bundles of stems upside down to dry in a cool, dark location with good air circulation. Pluck the leaves from the stems when they are completely dry, crumble them, and store them in airtight jars. Fresh leaves can also be frozen for later use.

Pests and diseases

Insect pests and diseases rarely affect oregano.

varieties:

1. **AUREUM,** sometimes sold as creeping golden marjoram, has bright yellow-green leaves and white flowers.
2. **COMPACTUM** is a low-growing aromatic and edible groundcover that rarely blooms.
3. **MEXICAN OREGANO** (*Lippia graveolens*) grows 4 feet high and wide and is perennial in Zones 9–11. Its flavor and intensity are similar to those of common oregano.

Parsley

(Petroselinum crispum)

Valued for its vitamin content and mild flavor, parsley has many culinary uses. The dark green leaves are divided into feathery sections and may be flat or curly. Plant this neatly mounding herb along the edge of a vegetable garden or perennial border.

YOU SHOULD KNOW
Harvest fresh parsley in winter by growing it in a cold frame. The plant will continue to produce new leaves until spring.

Best site

Plant in full sun and moist, well-drained soil. Parsley grows well in soil that is rich in organic matter. Incorporate a 2-inch-thick layer of compost into the site before planting. Parsley is grown as an annual but can overwinter in a cold frame or a thick layer of straw in many climates.

Planting

Sow seeds or set out transplants in early spring. Parsley seeds are slow to germinate; use a cold frame over the seeding site to warm the soil and spur germination. Space transplants and seedlings 10 to 18 inches apart.

Growing

When seedlings develop their first leaves, thin them to 10 inches apart. For a steady supply of parsley, sow seeds in spring and fall. Spread a 2-inch-thick layer of mulch around curly parsley to keep soil particles from gathering in the leaf crevices. To keep parsley productive, snip the full length of stems regularly; remove flower stalks as soon as they begin to form.

Harvest

Harvest parsley as needed, and encourage new growth by cutting outer stems about 1 inch above the soil. The whole plant can be cut before winter or mulched for overwintering in the garden. Plants kept in an insulated cold frame will continue to produce new stems until the following spring. Parsley can be stored in the refrigerator for up to one month or dried for one year.

To dry parsley, hang a small bunch of stems upside down or spread them in a single layer on screens in a cool, shady, well-ventilated location. Use leaves, fresh or dried, in cooking. Its mild flavor blends well with many foods.

Pests and diseases

Knock off aphids with a strong spray of water from the garden hose. Parsley attracts swallowtail butterfies. Its caterpillars will eat some parsley leaves, but not enough to damage the plant, so the insects are best admired rather than controlled.

varieties:

1. **'GIANT OF NAPLES'** is a flat-leaf Italian type that is very productive. 60 days.
2. **'MOSS CURLED'** is the most popular curly-leaf parsley. 70 days.

Rosemary

(Rosmarinus officinalis)

Pruned into topiary or allowed to become bushy, rosemary is a favorite of gardeners and cooks alike. It is an evergreen shrub with scaly bark and narrow dark green leaves that have a distinctive, pungent, piney scent. Upright and creeping varieties of rosemary are available.

YOU SHOULD KNOW

A popular ingredient in Mediterranean dishes, fresh rosemary has a pinelike aroma.

Best site

Plant in full sun and well-drained soil. Quick-draining soil is key to good growth; rosemary does not tolerate wet sites. If your soil is slow draining, plant in a raised bed or a pot. Rosemary is drought tolerant.

It is hardy in Zones 6 to 10 and grown as an annual elsewhere. Where it is hardy, rosemary will grow 1 to 6 feet tall and 2 to 6 feet wide. Rosemary grows well in containers both indoors and out. Overwinter rosemary in Zones 5 and below by digging it up at the end of the growing season and transplanting it into a container filled with well-drained potting mix. Place the pot in a bright, sunny window and water it regularly to keep the soil moist but not wet.

varieties:

1. **ARP** has gray-green foliage and blue flowers. Zones 6–10.
2. **ATHENS BLUE SPIRES** grows upright to 6 feet. Zones 7–10.
3. **BLUE BOY** is a dwarf, only 12 inches tall by 8 inches wide; it does well in containers. Zones 8–10.

REXFORD is a warm-climate cultivar with especially good flavor. Zone 9–10.

Planting

Set out transplants or container plants in fall or, in Zones 6 and 7, in spring after frost danger is past. Unique rosemary varieties are often hard to find at local nurseries. Speciality herb nurseries offer a diverse selection.

Growing

In cold climates grow rosemary in containers and bring them indoors in winter. Grow the plants in a greenhouse or place them in a sunny, cool window. Rosemary must have high humidity to overwinter well indoors. Regularly harvest a few stems throughout the season to encourage bushier growth. In mild-winter areas protect rosemary from cold winter winds that may dry it out by wrapping the plant with burlap.

Harvest

Cut a few succulent stems above woody growth as needed throughout the growing season. Strip the resinous leaves from the stems and chop or grind them. Tie harvested stems in small bunches and hang them upside down in a cool, airy space to dry. Dried rosemary leaves are acceptable for culinary use, but fresh leaves have a much more robust flavor and soft texture. Grow plants in pots over winter and enjoy fresh leaves year-round.

Pests and diseases

Root rot is the most common problem plaguing rosemary. It is caused by overwatering and slow-draining soil.

Sage *(Salvia officinalis)*

Sage is the most savory of herbs and a featured favorite in poultry seasoning. It is an evergreen shrub in mild climates and deciduous in cold regions. Some cultivars sport colorful variegated, purple, or yellow leaves. In midsummer mauve-blue flowers bloom on 36-inch-tall stems rising above the leaves.

YOU SHOULD KNOW
For a festive look in the garden and on the plate, plant green-, purple-, and yellow-leaf sage varieties.

Best site
Plant in full sun and moist, well-drained soil. Sage is adaptable to many soil conditions but grows best in rich loam that drains well. Incorporate a 2-inch-thick layer of compost into the soil before planting.

Sage is hardy in Zones 4 to 10 and grows 24 to 36 inches tall and wide. It maintains blemish-free leaves and a neat, upright habit all season, making it a good addition to perennial and shrub borders and frontyard landscapes. Sage is easy to grow in a container filled with well-drained potting soil.

Planting
Transplant container-grown plants or divisions in spring. Space plants 24 to 36 inches apart.

varieties:

1. **ICTERINA** is a variegated green-and-gold variety. Zones 7–8.
2. **EXTRAKTA** has smooth green leaves and is exceptionally flavorful. Zones 4–8.
3. **TRICOLOR** leaves are variegated green, cream, and purple. Zones 6–9.

Growing
After plants finish blooming, trim them as needed to maintain a pleasing shape, but leave the woody stems to resprout new growth. Protect plants in winter by spreading a 4- to 6-inch-thick layer of mulch over the root zone. To have fresh leaves through winter, dig plants in late autumn and pot them in containers filled with well-drained potting mix.

Harvest
To harvest, cut about 6 to 8 inches of succulent growth above the woody stems two or three times before the plant blooms in summer. For the best flavor, cut the stems in the morning after the dew has dried. The fresh leaves are delicious snipped into egg and cheese dishes.

Dry stems in a dark, airy space either by tying them together in small bunches and hanging them upside down or spreading them on screens. Crumble the dried leaves off the stems and store them in airtight jars for up to three years. The dried leaves are outstanding added to poultry stuffing and ground into a dry-rub powder for meats.

Pests and diseases
Sage is rarely troubled by pests and diseases.

Savory, summer and winter

(*Satureja* species)

With a flavor similar to thyme and sweet marjoram, the leaves and flowers of summer and winter savory are harvested for use in bean, egg, vegetable, beef, pork, and poultry dishes. Summer savory is an annual, and winter savory a perennial.

YOU SHOULD KNOW

For a mild savory flavor, choose summer savory. For a stronger flavor and fragrance, plant winter savory.

Best site

Plant in full sun and well-drained soil. Savory is adaptable to most soils.

Summer savory (*S. hortensis*) is a sweet-flavored, upright annual with long, gray-green leaves and small, white or pink flowers. Its flavor is more delicate than that of winter savory (*S. montana*), a semievergreen spreading perennial with trailing stems and petite, white to lavender flowers. Winter savory is hardy in Zones 5 to 8. Both plants bloom in summer.

Planting

Start winter savory from transplants planted in the garden after the soil warms in spring. It can also be started from seeds planted indoors four to six weeks before the last frost date.

Direct-sow the seeds of summer savory after the last frost date in spring in northern climates or anytime during the growing season in mild-winter zones. Plant the seeds ½ inch deep and 1 inch apart.

Growing

Savory thrives when given consistent moisture. Keep the soil around plants moist but not waterlogged. Trim summer savory regularly to encourage new growth. Prune winter savory to a miniature hedge, if desired.

Harvest

Summer savory is ready to harvest in 60 to 70 days after sowing seeds. Winter savory can be trimmed the first time 50 days after planting transplants or 75 to 100 days after planting seeds.

Cut stems from either plant for drying when flowers begin to form. Spread them on screens or tie them in small bunches and hang them upside down in a dark, airy space. When the leaves are completely dry, strip them from the stems, making sure to remove all woody parts. Store the leaves in airtight containers for up to two years.

Pests and diseases

Savory is rarely troubled by pests and diseases.

varieties:

1. **AROMATA** summer savory is a peppery cultivar bred for high leaf yields.
2. **NANA** winter savory is an extremely cold-hardy dwarf variety only 3 inches tall and spreading to 24 inches. Zones 5–8.

Thyme (*Thymus* species)

The biggest decision when growing thyme is which of the 40 or more species and cultivars to plant. All are small, creeping plants with many woody stems. They have tiny aromatic leaves and small bluish purple to pink flowers that open in summer and attract bees. Thyme is an excellent edible groundcover.

1

YOU SHOULD KNOW
Thyme blends well with almost any beef, pork, poultry, or seafood dish and adds a sophisticated flavor to cheese and egg dishes.

Best site

Plant in full sun and well-drained soil. Thyme does not tolerate wet soil. It grows best in moderately fertile soil.

Thyme is hardy in Zones 4 to 10. Use it as a groundcover in the perennial garden or shrub bed. It handles foot traffic well and can be planted in between stepping stones.

Thyme grows well in a container. Be sure to use a well-drained potting mix to ensure roots receive the drainage they require.

Planting

Plant container-grown plants or divisions in spring. Space plants 8 to 12 inches apart. Thyme can also be started from seeds indoors or sown directly into the garden. Seed-grown plants often require a year or more of growth before they can be harvested.

Growing

Water plants when needed to maintain soil moisture, but do not overwater. Shear off the tiny flowers after plants finish blooming to keep energy concentrated in the leaves and stems. Plants may lose vigor and need replacing or division after five to seven years.

To divide thyme, in midspring gently dig up the entire clump and use a sharp spade to sever it into three or four divisions, each with ample foliage and roots.

Harvest

Harvest stems and leaves anytime during the growing season. For a large harvest, trim the entire plant back to 2 inches aboveground in midseason.

Strip the leaves from the stems and use them fresh. To dry thyme, harvest handfuls of the stems, tie small bundles together, and hang them upside down in a cool, airy room. When the leaves are completely dry, crumble them off the stems and store them in airtight glass jars for up to two years.

Pests and diseases

Root rot is the most common problem plaguing thyme. It is caused by overwatering and slow-draining soil.

2

3

varieties:

1. **AUREUS** is a variegated form of lemon thyme (*T. × citriodorus*). The green and yellow coloration is most pronounced in cool regions. Zones 5–9.
2. **CARAWAY** (*T. herba barona*) has a caraway scent, shiny green leaves, and lavender flowers. Zones 5–10.
3. **COMMON** (*T. vulgaris*) has a strong thyme fragrance. Zones 4–7.

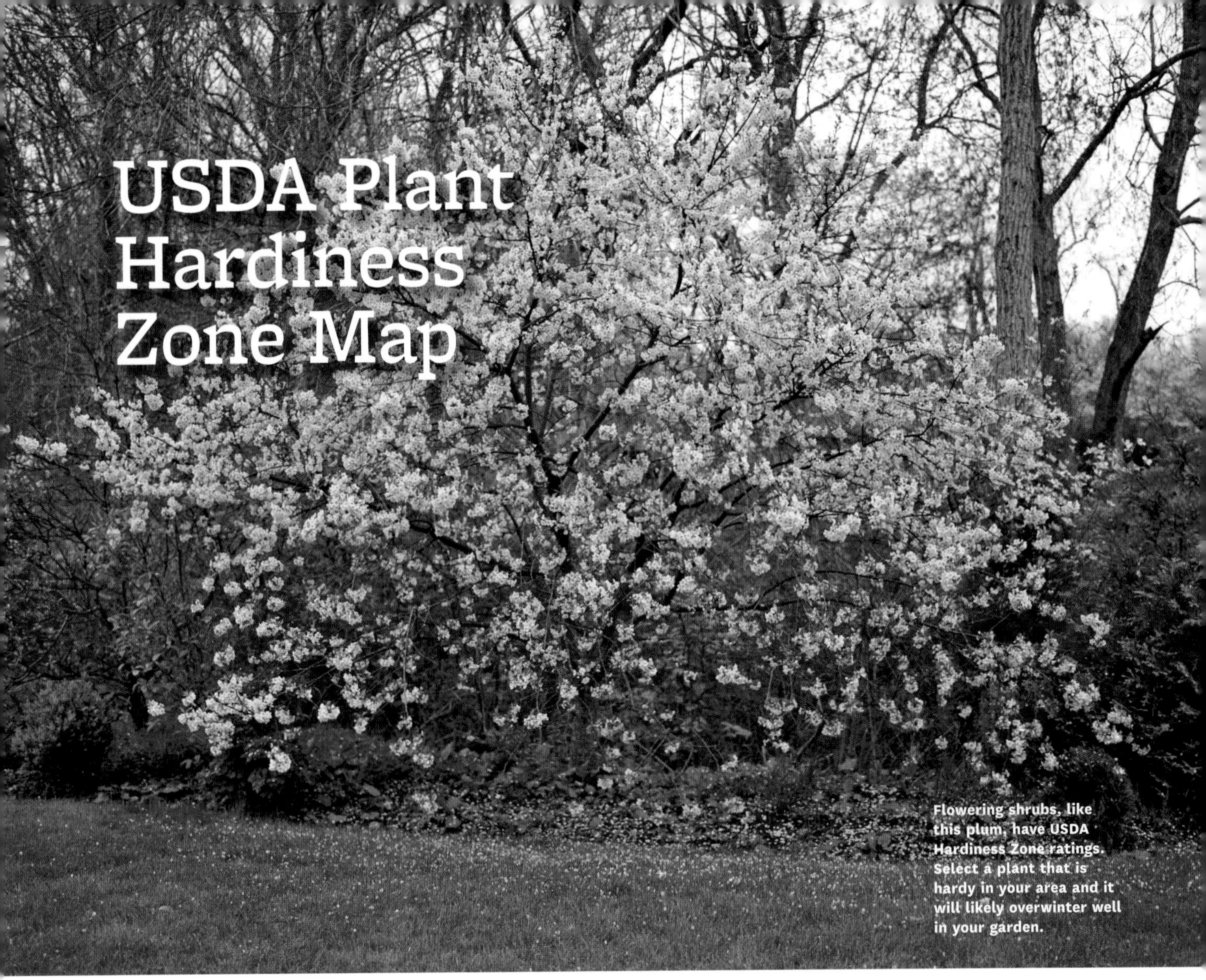

USDA Plant Hardiness Zone Map

Flowering shrubs, like this plum, have USDA Hardiness Zone ratings. Select a plant that is hardy in your area and it will likely overwinter well in your garden.

Each plant has an ability to withstand cold temperatures. This range of temperatures is expressed as a zone—and a zone map shows where you can grow this plant.

Planting for your zone

There are 11 zones from Canada to Mexico, and each zone represents the lowest expected winter temperature in that area. Each zone is based on a 10-degree difference in minimum temperatures. Once you know your hardiness zone, you can choose plants for your garden that will flourish. Look for the hardiness zone on the plant tags of the perennials, trees, and shrubs you buy.

Microclimates in your yard

Not all areas in your yard are the same. Depending on your geography, trees, and structures, some spots may receive different sunlight and wind and consequently experience temperature differences. Take a look around your yard and you may notice that the same plant comes up sooner in one place than another. This is the microclimate concept in action. A microclimate is an area in your yard that is slightly different (cooler or hotter) than the other areas of your yard.

Create a microclimate

Once you're aware of your yard's microclimates, use them to your advantage. For example, you may be able to grow plants in a sheltered, south-facing garden bed that you can't grow elsewhere in your yard. You can create a microclimate by planting evergreens on the north side of a property to block prevailing winds. Or plant deciduous trees on the south side to provide shade in summer.

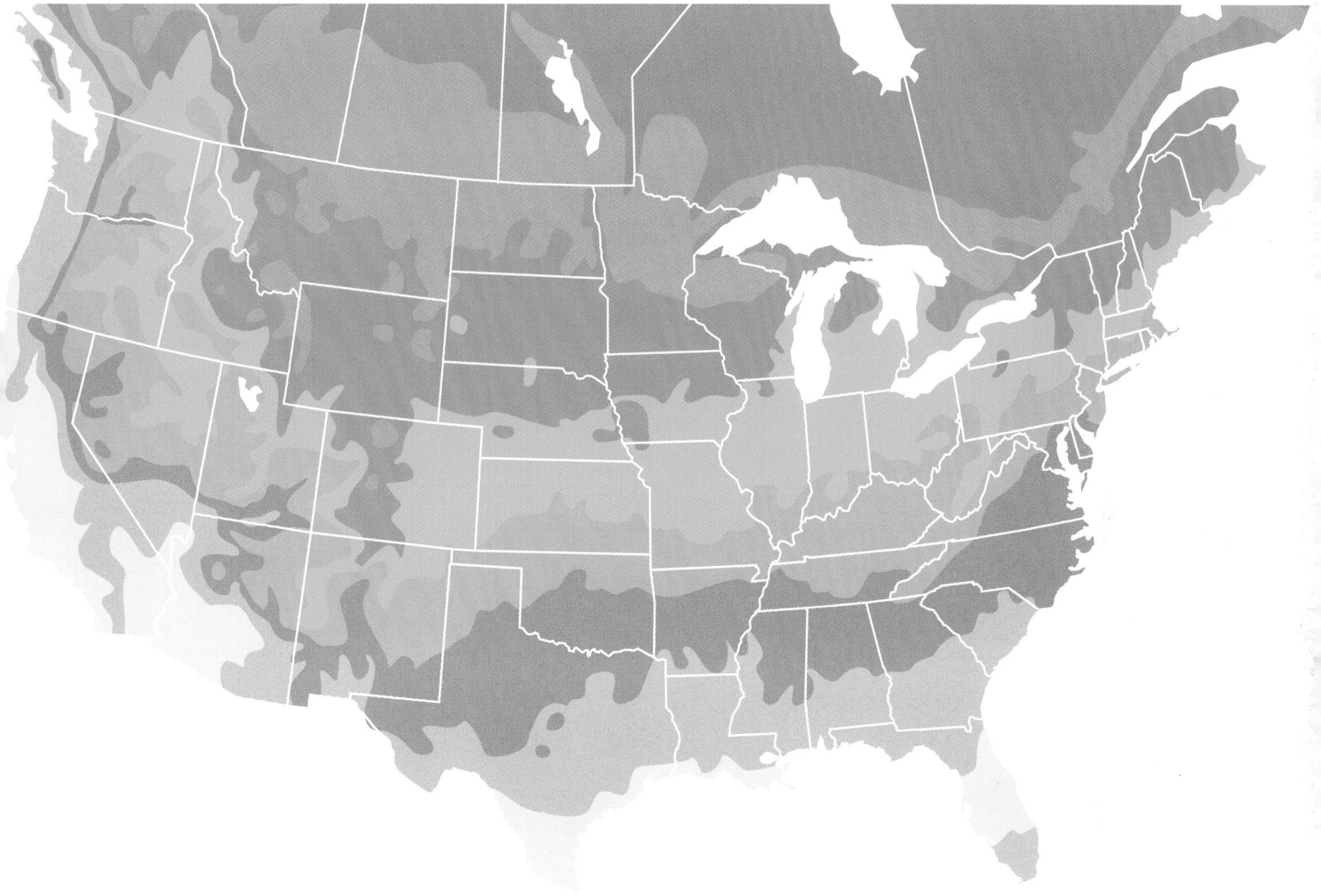

Range of Average Annual Minimum Temperatures for Each Zone

- Zone 2: -50 to -40° F (-45 to -40°C)
- Zone 3: -40 to -30° F (-40 to -35°C)
- Zone 4: -30 to -20° F (-34 to -29°C)
- Zone 5: -20 to -10° F (-29 to -23°C)
- Zone 6: -10 to 0° F (-23 to -18°C)
- Zone 7: 0 to 10° F (-18 to -12°C)
- Zone 8: 10 to 20° F (-12 to -7°C)
- Zone 9: 20 to 30° F (-7 to -1°C)
- Zone 10: 30 to 40° F (-1 to 4°C)

Spring Frost Map

The average date of the last spring frost is a valuable guide for determining when to plant many annual crops.

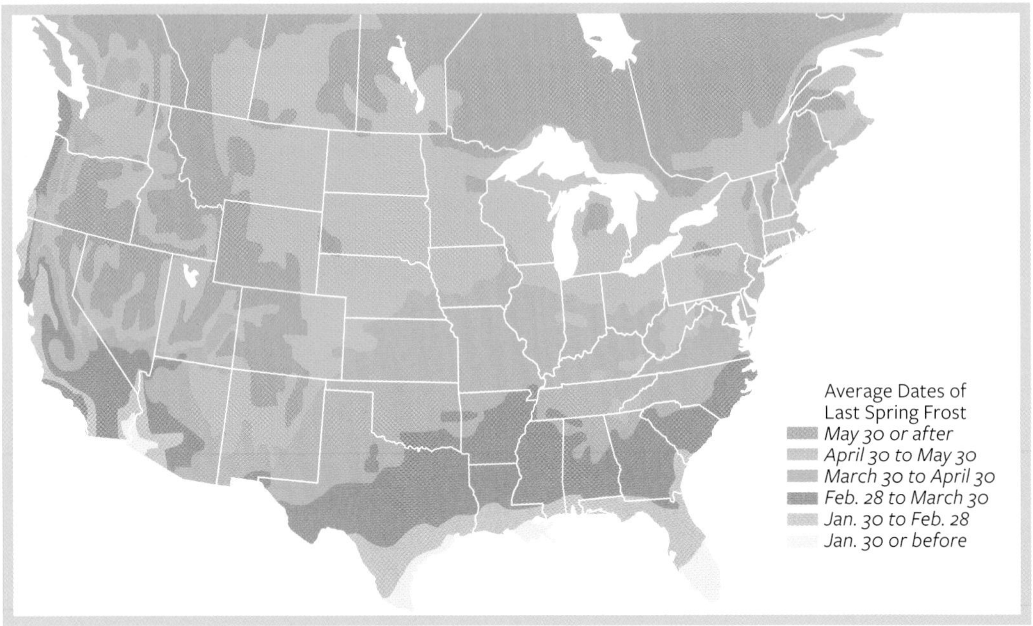

Tomatoes and peppers are usually planted after the last average spring frost. Lettuce and radishes, on the other hand, are often planted three to four weeks before the last average frost date.

Many factors combine to determine the actual date in your garden. Weather combined with the contours and orientation of your land are major contributors. More often than not, if you abide by the average date of last spring's frost for your area, your crops will thrive.

Fall Frost Map

The average date of the first autumn frost is helpful for deciding when to plant late season crops. See page 52 to learn more about growing vegetables in late summer and fall.

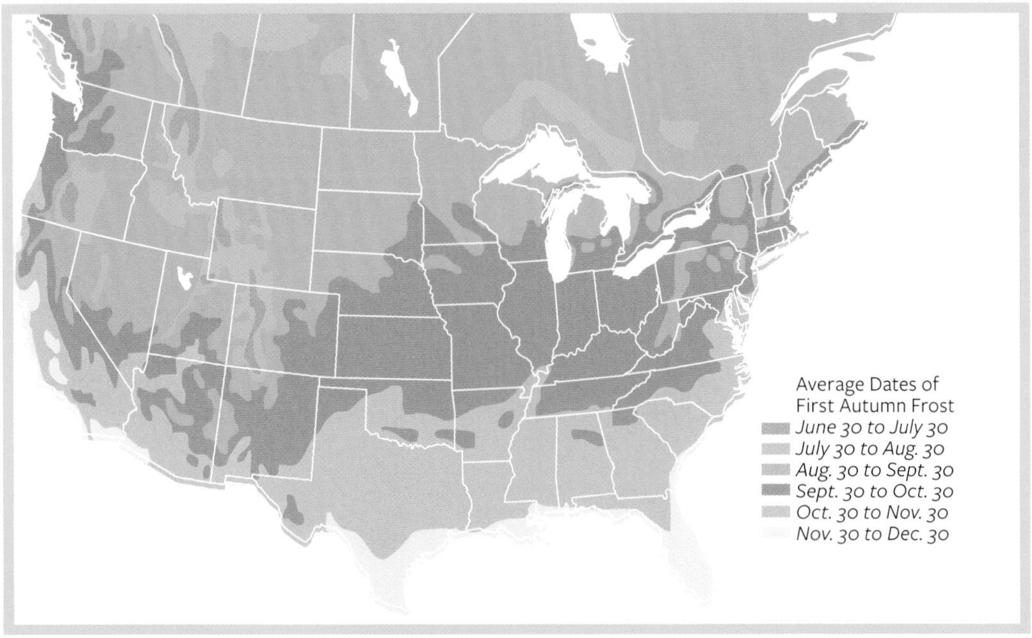

The average first autumn frost date in combination with the average last spring frost date, defines the number of frost-free growing days. Frost-free growing days are particularly important to tender plants such as tomatoes, peppers, and squash. Be sure to choose a cultivar that will mature before the first average autumn frost in your area.

Vegetables and herbs

ANNIE'S ANNUALS
www.annniesannuals.com
888.266.4370
Unique vegetable and herb plants.

BAKER CREEK HEIRLOOM SEEDS
rareseeds.com
417.924.8917
Organic vegetable, herb, and flower seeds. Heirlooms from more than 50 countries.

THE COOK'S GARDEN
www.cooksgarden.com
800.457.9703
Culinary vegetables, herbs, and flowers. Salad mixes.

GURNEY SEED & NURSERY COMPANY
www.gurneys.com
513.354.1491
Vegetable and flower seeds, some fruit trees, and berries.

HENRY FIELD'S SEED & NURSERY CO.
henryfields.com
513.354.1494
Vegetable and flower seeds, some fruit trees, and berries.

JOHNNY'S SELECTED SEEDS
www.johnnyseeds.com
877.564.6697
Vegetable, herb, and flower seeds; and seeds for cover crops.

J.W. JUNG SEED COMPANY
www.jungseed.com
800.297.3123
Vegetable and flower seeds.

NICHOLS GARDEN NURSERY
www.nicholsgardennursery.com
800.422.3985
Vegetable and herb seeds and herb plants.

PARK SEED COMPANY
www.parkseed.com
800.213.0076
Vegetable, herb, and flower seeds and plants.

RENEE'S GARDEN SEEDS
www.reneesgarden.com
888.880.7228
Vegetable, herb, and flower seeds. Many heirlooms.

SEED SAVERS EXCHANGE
www.seedsavers.org
563.382.5990
Heirloom vegetable and herb seeds.

SOUTHERN EXPOSURE SEED EXCHANGE
www.southernexposure.com
540.894.9480
Heirloom vegetable, flower, and herb varieties adapted to the South.

TERRITORIAL SEED COMPANY
www.territorial-seed.com
800.626.0866
Vegetable, flower, and herb seeds and plants.

THOMPSON & MORGAN SEEDSMEN, INC.
www.tmseeds.com
800.274.7333
English vegetable, flower, and herb seeds and plants.

TOMATO GROWERS SUPPLY COMPANY
www.tomatogrowers.com
888.478.7333
Tomato and pepper seeds.

VERMONT BEAN SEED COMPANY
www.vermontbean.com
800.349.1071
Vegetable, herb, and flower seeds, and small fruit plants.

W. ATLEE BURPEE & CO.
www.burpee.com
800.333.5808
Vegetable, herb, and flower seeds and plants.

Fruits

MILLER NURSERIES
www.millernurseries.com
800.836.9630
Fruit trees, berries, and garden supplies.

STARK BROTHERS NURSERY
www.starkbros.com
800.325.4180
Fruit trees and berries.

TYTY NURSERY
www.tytyga.com
800.972.2101
Fruit trees and berries, including some unusual and tropical fruits.

Garden accessories and tools

CAMPANIA INTERNATIONAL, INC.
www.campaniainternational.com

GARDENER'S SUPPLY CO.
www.gardeners.com
800.876.5520

GOODS FOR THE GARDEN
www.goodsforthegarden.com
800.663.3158

KINSMAN CO.
www.kinsmangarden.com
800.733.4146

LEE VALLEY TOOLS
ww.leevalleytools.com
800.267.8735; from Canada: 800.267.8761

Note: Page references in **bold type** refer to Encyclopedia entries. Page references in *italic* type refer to photographs, illustrations, and information in captions.

A

Animal pests, 120–121
in compost, 63
control methods, *96*, *97*, 120
diagnosing problems, 97
integrated pest management, 98–99
Annual plants
defined, 45
flowering, 14
landscaping role, 21, 23
watering, 87
Anthracnose, 114
Aphids, 110
Apple, 216–219
chilling requirement, 47
cultivar selection, *24*
diseases/disorders, 116, 117
dwarf varieties, 25
insect pests, 112
in landscape, 23
nutrients in, 9
Apricot, 220
diseases/disorders, 116, 117
dwarf varieties, 25
heat requirements, 47
in landscape, 23
nutrients in, 9
plum hybrids, **248–249**
Arbors, design role, *21*
Artichoke, 148
climate considerations, 49
insect pests, 113
in landscape, 23
nutrients in, 9
from seeds/transplants, 73
Arugula
climate considerations, 20
for Italian-inspired gardens, 13
Asian-inspired gardens, 12, 13, *13*
Asparagus, 149
climate considerations, 49
insect pests, 111
nutrients in, 9
Automatic timers, for watering, *38*, *91*
Avocado, 221
diseases/disorders, 117
nutrients in, 9

B

Backyard gardens
benefits, 8, 11, 12
donating extra produce, 11
exercising restraint, 13
Bacterial blight, 114
Basil, 256–257
for Asian-inspired gardens, 12
for Italian-inspired gardens, 13
in landscape, 23
removing flower stalks, 137
Beans, 150–153
for Asian-inspired gardens, 12
asparagus, **150**, **152**
climate considerations, *48*, 49, 51
in containers, 37
diseases/disorders, 114, 115, 116, 117
dried, **150**, **153**
fava, 49, **150**, **152**, **153**
growing season, 45
insect pests, 111, 112
juglone susceptibility, 19
lima, **150**, **153**
from seeds, 14, 73
snap, **150–152**
soybeans, **150**, **152–153**
watering, 89
weeds suppressed by, 105
Beds and borders, 22–23, *22–23*
Bee balm, edible flowers, **261**
Beet, 154
climate considerations, 49, 51
in containers, 37
diseases/disorders, 115, 116
insect pests, 113
in landscape, 23
nutrients in, 9
from seeds, 73
Beetles
Colorado potato, **111**
cucumber, **111**
Japanese, **112**
Bermudagrass, 118
Berries
blackberry, 9, 115, 116, 131, *131*, **224–227**
blueberry, 9, 23, *132*, 133, **222–223**
currant, 133, **236**
elderberry, **237**
gooseberry, 133, **236**
jostaberry, **236**
raspberry, 9, 125, 130–131, *130–131*, **224–226**
See also Grape; Strawberry

Better Homes and Gardens *You Can Can*, 11
Birds
as insect predators, 107
as pests, 120
Blackberry, 224–227
diseases/disorders, 115, 116
nutrients in, 9
pruning/training, 130, *130*
See also Brambles
Blood meal, 65
Blossom drop, 114
Blossom-end rot, 115
Blueberry, 222–223
in landscape, 23
nutrients in, 9
pruning/training, *132*, 133
Borers, 110
Boxwood hedges, 22–23
Brambles, 224–227
diseases/disorders, 114
insect pests, 110
pruning/training, 125, *130–131*, 131
Branch collars, defined, 126
Broccoli, 155
climate considerations, 49, 51
diseases/disorders, 103, 115
insect pests, 110
in landscape, 23
nutrients in, 9
from seeds/transplants, 73
Brussels sprouts, 156
climate considerations, 49, 51
insect pests, 110
nutrients in, 9
from seeds/transplants, 73
Buds, types of, 125
Butternut, juglone susceptibility, 19
Buying plants. *See* Selecting and buying plants

C

Cabbage, 157
in beds and borders, *22–23*
climate considerations, 49, 51
diseases/disorders, 103, 115
insect pests, 110, 111
juglone susceptibility, 19
nutrients in, 9
for partial shade, 142
from seeds/transplants, 73

Cabbageworms, 110
Cages. *See* Stakes, trellises, and cages
Caring for plants
- container gardens, 41
- orchard design and, *25*
- overview, 15
- pest control role, 97, 98, *106*
- in traditional vegetable gardens, 20–21, *20*

See also Diagnosing plant problems; Fertilizing; pruning/training; Watering; Weed control
Carnation, edible flowers, **261**
Carrot, 158–159
- climate considerations, 49, 51
- in containers, 37
- ease of growth, *10–11*
- insect pests, 111, 113
- juglone susceptibility, 19
- in landscape, 23
- as row markers, 81
- from seeds, 73
- thinning, *83*

Cauliflower, 160
- climate considerations, *48*, 49, 51
- insect pests, 110
- nutrients in, 9
- from seeds/transplants, 73

Celery, 161
- climate considerations, 49
- diseases/disorders, 114, 116

Central and modified leader training, 129
Chard, Swiss chard, 162
- climate considerations, 49, 51
- in containers, *32–33*
- in landscape, 23
- for partial shade, 142
- from seeds, 73

Cherry, 228–229
- chilling requirement, 47
- diseases/disorders, 116, 117
- dwarf varieties, 25
- juglone susceptibility, 19
- in landscape, 23
- nutrients in, 9
- pollination requirements, 25, *25*

Chickweed, common, **118**
Chives, 258
- growing season, 45
- in landscape, 23
- for Mexican-inspired gardens, 13
- watering, 89

Cilantro, coriander, 259
- for Asian-inspired gardens, 12
- diseases/disorders, 114, 115, 117
- for Mexican-inspired gardens, 13

Citrus, 230–235
- diseases/disorders, 117
- insect pests, 113
- nutrients in, 9
- pruning, *124*

Clay soils
- characteristics, 57, 58
- drainage, 59, *59*
- improving, 67
- nutrient content, 61
- raised beds and, *58*

Climate and seasons, 42–53
- blossom drop and, 114
- fruit crops and, 46, *46–47*
- hardiness zones, 44–47, 276
- microclimates, 45, 47, 51
- produce selection and, 11, 43
- sunscald, **117**
- vegetables and, 37, 48–49, *50–51*, 51, *52–53*, 53
- as watering cue, 87

Cloches, 51, 83
Cold frames, 51, *76–77*
Collards, 163
- climate considerations, 49
- insect pests, 110
- from seeds/transplants, 73

Colorful produce, benefits, 9, *9*
Community gardens, 27
Compost
- applying, *62*, 67, 79, 140
- benefits, 57, *57*, *60*, 63, 93
- calculating amount needed, 67
- for container gardens, 35
- defined, 65
- deterring pests, 63
- heaps, 63
- holding units, 63
- how to make, 63, *63*
- sheet, 63
- trench, 63
- turning units, 63

Container gardens, 28–53
- benefits, 30–31
- caring for, 41
- designing, *32–33*, 33
- fertilizing, 35, 37
- Flowers and Fruit, 139, *139*
- Fresh Snips, 144, *144*
- hanging baskets, 31, 39
- mulching, 41, *41*
- pests and diseases, 41
- planting, 36–37, *36–37*
- plants suited/not well suited to, 33
- site selection, 31
- for small spaces, 26–27, *26–27*
- Small Wonder, 137, *137*
- soil mixes, 14, 34–35, *34–35*
- staking plants, 41
- Taste of Summer, 138, *138*
- watering, 31, 33, 37, 38–39, *38–39*
- window boxes, 31

Containers (pots)
- baskets or wooden crates, 138, *138*
- drainage, 32, 33, *34–35*
- pot size, 35, 37
- for seeding indoors, *72–73*, 74–75, *74–75*
- selection criteria, 33
- self-watering, 39

Coriander. *See* Cilantro, coriander
Corn, 164–167
- climate considerations, *48*, 49
- diseases/disorders, 114, 115
- insect pests, 110, 111, 112, 113
- juglone susceptibility, 19
- for Mexican-inspired gardens, 13
- nutrients in, 9
- from seeds, 73
- weeds suppressed by, 105

Cottonseed meal, 65
Cover crops (green manure), 65, 66, 105
Crabgrass, 118
Crop rotation, 103, 107
Cucumber, 168–169
- for Asian-inspired gardens, 12
- climate considerations, 49
- in containers, 37
- diseases/disorders, 114, 115, 116, 117
- ease of growth, *10–11*
- insect pests, 111, 113
- from seeds, 73
- support for, *32–33*
- weeds suppressed by, 105

Cultivation. *See* Tilling

Currant, 236
pruning/training, 133
Cutworms, 111

D

Damping off, 77, *78,* **115**
Dandelion, 118
Deer, 120
Designing gardens, 16–27
beds and borders, 22–23
container gardens, *32–33,* 33
for diversity, *96*
Flowers and Fruit, 139, *139*
Fresh Snips, 144, *144*
orchards, 24–25
Patio Garden, 142, *142–143*
Salad Bowl, 136, *136*
Seasonal Harvest, 140, *140–141*
for small spaces, 26–27, *26–27*
Small Wonder, 137, *137*
Taste of Summer, 138, *138*
traditional vegetable gardens, 20–21, *20–21*
See also Site selection
Diagnosing plant problems, 94–103
damaged foliage, 109, *109*
damaged fruit, 109, *109*
integrated pest management role, 98–99
no fruit, 109, *109*
plant death, 109, *109*
poor plant growth, 108, *108*
See also Animal pests; Diseases of plants; Insect pests; Weeds
Dill, 260
for beneficial insects, 101
Diseases of plants, 114–117
of container gardens, 41
control methods, 97, 103
diagnosing problems, 97, 108–109
integrated pest management, 98–99
overview, 103
prevention strategies, 107
pruning and, 127, 133
resistant plant varieties, 103, 107
watering and, 77, 89, 92–93, 115
See also specific crops; specific diseases
Downy mildew, 115
Drip irrigation, 38, 39, 90, 91, *91*

E

Easy-to-grow vegetables, *10–11*
Eggplant, 170–171
for Asian-inspired gardens, 12
climate considerations, 49
in containers, 37
diseases/disorders, 114
growing season, 45
insect pests, 111
juglone susceptibility, 19
nutrients in, 9
from seeds/transplants, 73
staking, 139
Elderberry (sweet elder), 237

F

Fences and walls
design role, *21*
to exclude animal pests, 120
microclimates created by, 45
Fennel
for beneficial insects, 101
diseases/disorders, 115
for Italian-inspired gardens, 13
Fertilizers
label information, 64
nutrient sources, 65
organic, 40
slow-release, 37, 40, *60*
synthetic, 65
water-soluble, 40, *64*
See also Compost; Organic matter; Soil amendments
Fertilizing
container gardens, 35, 37, 40–41, *40*
symptoms of excessive, 67
Fig, 238
nutrients in, 9
Fire blight, 114
Fish emulsion, 65
Floating row covers, 101
Flowering plants
design role, *21*
edible flowers, **261**
Flowers and Fruit, 139, *139*
Small Wonder, 137, *137*
Freezing temperatures
to break up clay soil, 67
early vegetables and, *50–51,* 51
hardiness zones, 42–47, 276
impact on fruit trees/shrubs, 47
mulch to protect plants, 53
planting time and, 37
protecting tender plants from, 47, 83, *83*
Fresh Snips garden, 144, *144*
Fruit and fruit trees, 214–253
climate considerations, 45, 46, *46–47*
cold-weather protection, 47
in containers, 27, 37, 41
deciding what to grow, 11
dwarf varieties, *21,* 25, 27, 37, 143
for ethnic cuisines, 11, 12–13, *12–13*
hardy cultivars, 47
insect pests, 110, 112
landscaping role, 23
orchard design, 24–25, *24–25*
pollination requirements, 24–25
pruning/training, 125, *126,* 127–129, *128–129*
space constraints, 25
thinning fruit, 129
from transplants, 73
watering, 87
wind protection, 47
Fruiting shrubs
blueberry, 9, 23, *132,* 133, **222–223**
currant, 133, **236**
elderberry, **237**
gooseberry, 133, **236**
jostaberry, **236**
See also Grape

G

Garlic, 172
climate considerations, 49
for Italian-inspired gardens, 13
nutrients in, 9
Gooseberry, 236
pruning/training, 133
Gophers, 120
Grape, 239–240
climate considerations, *46*
diseases/disorders, 115, 117
insect pests, 112
in landscape, 23
nutrients in, 9
pruning/training, 125, *132–133,* 133
thinning, 133
Grapefruit, 230–234
See also Citrus
Green manure (cover crops), 65, 66, 105
Greens
for Asian-inspired gardens, 12
climate considerations, *106*
mesclun salad mix, **180**
Salad Bowl, 136, *136*
See also Lettuce

H

Hanging baskets, 31, 39
Harvesting
disease-control role, 106
overview, 15
through fall, *52–53*, 53
See also specific crops
Herbs, 254–275
for beneficial insects, 101
bringing inside in winter, 144
in containers, 27, *27*, *30–31*, *32–33*, 33, 37
deciding what to grow, 11
dividing, *145*
for ethnic cuisines, 11, 12–13, *12–13*
Fresh Snips, 144, *144*
landscaping role, 23
low-water crops, 86
for partial shade, 142
perennials, 45
Pretty Herbs, 145, *145*
from seeds vs. transplants, 73
site selection, *18–19*
watering, 87
Hickory, juglone susceptibility, 19
Horseradish, 263
diseases/disorders, 115, 117

I

Insecticides, 101
Insect pests, 110–113
biological controls, 101
chemical controls, 101
of container gardens, 41
control methods, 97
diagnosing problems, 97, 108–109
integrated pest management, 98–99
overview, 100
physical controls, 100–101
prevention strategies, 107
pruning and, 127
resistant plant varieties, 103
See also specific crops; specific pests
Insects, beneficial, 101, 107
Integrated pest management, 98–99
Intercropping (interplanting), 27, *27*
Italian-inspired gardens, 11, 13, *13*

J

Jostaberry, 236
See also Brambles
Juglone, toxicity to vegetables, 19

K

Kale, 173
in beds and borders, *22–23*
climate considerations, 49, *49*, 51
diseases/disorders, 115
insect pests, 110
intercropping, 27, *27*
in landscape, 23
for partial shade, 142
from seeds/transplants, 73
Kiwi, hardy kiwi, 242
in landscape, 23
nutrients in, 9
Kohlrabi, 174
climate considerations, 49
in landscape, 23

L

Lambs quarters, 119
Landscaping. *See* Designing gardens
Lavender, 264
in landscape, 23
watering, 89
Lawns, converting to gardens, 14, 78–79, *79*
Leafhoppers, 112
Leek, 175
climate considerations, 49, 51
harvesting/storing, *53*
in landscape, 23
for partial shade, 142
from seeds/transplants, 73
Lemon, 230–235
nutrients in, 9
See also Citrus
Lemon balm, 265
Lettuce, 176–177
in beds and borders, *22–23*
climate considerations, 49, *49*, 51, *106*
in containers, *30*, *37*
diseases/disorders, 115, 116
insect pests, 110, 111
intercropping, 27, *27*
for Italian-inspired gardens, 13
in landscape, 23
mesclun mix, **180**
nutrients in, 9
from seeds, 73
site selection, *18–19*
watering, *92*
Light (artificial), for seedlings, 75, *77*
Lime, 230–235
nutrients in, 9
See also Citrus
Loam soils, characteristics, 58
Lovage, 267

M

Mandarin, 230–235
Mango, 246
diseases/disorders, 114, 117
in landscape, 23
nutrients in, 9
Marjoram, sweet marjoram, 268
growing season, 45
Melons, 178–179
casaba, **178**
charentais, **178–179**
climate considerations, 49
crenshaw, **178–179**
diseases/disorders, 116, 117, 118
honeydew, **178–179**
insect pests, 111
juglone susceptibility, 19
muskmelon (cantaloupe), **178**
nutrients in, 9
planting tips, 81
from seeds, 73
watering, 89
watermelon, **213**
weeds suppressed by, 105
Mesclun salad mix, 180
Mexican-inspired gardens, 11, 13, *13*
Microclimates
for early vegetables, 51
for fruit trees/shrubs, 47
overview, 45
Mint, peppermint, spearmint, 269
diseases/disorders, 117
for partial shade, 142
Mosaic virus, 116
Mulch
applying, 67
to conserve water, 93, *93*
for containers, 41, *41*
for early vegetables, 51
for frost protection, 53
to improve soil structure, *66*
pest-prevention role, *106*, 107
for seedlings, 82
for weed control, 97, *98*, 105

N

Nasturtium, edible flowers, **261**
Nectarine, 244–245
diseases/disorders, 117
dwarf varieties, 25
juglone susceptibility, 19
nutrients in, 9

Nitrogen
deficiency, 61, **116**
from fertilizers, 64
overview, *64*
Nodes, defined, 127
Nutrient deficiencies
blossom-end rot, 115
symptoms, 61, *64*
Nutrients, in produce, 9, *9*
Nutrients, in soil
plant growth role, 61, 64
plants with low-nutrient preferences, 61
as site-selection criterion, 19
testing, 58, 61, *64*
tips for boosting, 61
Nutsedge, 119

O

Obelisks, 21, *32–33*
Okra, 181
climate considerations, 49
from seeds, 73
watering, 89
Onion, 182–183
for Asian-inspired gardens, 12
climate considerations, 49, 51
in containers, 37
diseases/disorders, 115
ease of growth, *10–11*
green, nutrients in, 9
harvesting/storing, 53
for Italian-inspired gardens, 13
in landscape, 23
nutrients in, 9
from seeds, 73
Open center training, 128–129, *129*
Orange, 230–235
dwarf varieties, 25
nutrients in, 8
See also Citrus
Oregano, 269
growing season, 45
for Italian-inspired gardens, 13
in landscape, 23
Organic matter, 57, *57*
See also Compost; Mulch

P

Papaya, diseases/disorders, 114, 117
Parasites, beneficial, 101
Parsley, 271
for beneficial insects, 101
diseases/disorders, 115
for Italian-inspired gardens, 13
in landscape, 23
for partial shade, 142
removing flower stalks, 137
Parsnip, 184
climate considerations, 49, 51
nutrients in, 9
for partial shade, 142
from seeds, 73
Paths, planning for, 21
Patio garden, 142, *142–143*
Paved surfaces, microclimates created by, 45
Peach, 244–245
chilling requirement, 47
diseases/disorders, 116, 117
dwarf varieties, 25
heat requirement, 47
juglone susceptibility, 19
in landscape, 23
nutrients in, 9
plum hybrids, **248–249**
from seeds, 73
Peanut, 185
climate considerations, 49
from seeds, 73
Pear, 246–247
Asian, **246–247**
chilling requirement, 47
diseases/disorders, 116, 117
in landscape, 23
nutrients in, 9
Peas, 186–187
for Asian-inspired gardens, 15
climate considerations, 49, 51
diseases/disorders, 117
insect pests, 111, 113
nutrients in, 9
for partial shade, 142
Peat pots/pellets, *72–73*, 74–75, *74–75*
Pecan, juglone susceptibility, 19
Pepper, sweet and hot, **188–191**
for Asian-inspired gardens, 12
climate considerations, 49
in containers, 27, *27*, *29*, 33, 37
diseases/disorders, 114, 115, 116, 117
growing season, 45
insect pests, 111
for Italian-inspired gardens, 13
juglone susceptibility, 16
in landscape, 23
for Mexican-inspired gardens, 13
nutrients in, 9
from seeds/transplants, 14, 73
staking, 139
Perennial plants
defined, 45
dividing, *145*
landscaping role, 21, 23
watering, 87
Pest-resistant plant varieties, 103, 107
Pests, 94–121
control methods, *96*, 97
defined, 97
diagnosing problems, 97, 98–99, *99*, 106, 108–109
integrated pest management, 98–99
prevention strategies, 107
See also Animal pests; Diseases of plants; Insect pests; Weeds
Phosphorous
deficiency symptoms, 61
from fertilizers, 64
overview, *64*
Planting, 70–83
container gardens, 36–37, *36–37*
cover crops, 65, 66, 105
exercising restraint, 15
for fall harvest, 52–56, *56*
indoor seedlings, 74–75, *74–75*
intercropping, 27, *27*
marking rows, 81
overview, 15
succession planting, 27, 49
techniques, 81
when to plant vegetables, *50–51*, 51, 81
See also Seeds and seedlings; *specific crops;* Transplants
Plum, 248–249
diseases/disorders, 116
dwarf varieties, 25
hybrids, **248–249**
juglone susceptibility, 19
in landscape, 23
nutrients in, 9
Pollination, planning for, 25, *25*
Pomegranate, climate considerations, *46*
Potassium
deficiency symptoms, 61
from fertilizers, 64
overview, *65*
Potato, 192–193
climate considerations, 46
in containers, 37
growing season, 45
insect pests, 111, 112, 113
juglone susceptibility, 19
nutrients in, 9
Pots. *See* Containers

Powdery mildew, 117
Preserving (canning, freezing, or drying) produce, 7, 11
Pretty Herbs garden, 145, *145*
Prune, 248–249
nutrients in, 9
Pruning/training, 122–133
reasons for, 124–125
terms, 125
tools for, 127, *127*
types of pruning cuts, 127
See also specific crops
Pumpkin, 194–195
diseases/disorders, 115, 116, 117
fall harvest, 52, *52*
insect pests, 110, 111, 113
nutrients in, 9
planting tips, 81
from seeds, 73
weeds suppressed by, 105
Purslane, 119

Q

Quackgrass, 119

R

Rabbits, 121
Raccoons, 121
Radicchio, climate considerations, 51
Radish, 196
climate considerations, 49, 51
diseases/disorders, 115
ease of growth, *10–11*
in landscape, 21
nutrients in, 6
for partial shade, 142
from seeds, 73
Raised beds
benefits, 8, *14, 106*
building and maintaining, 68–69
design role, *26–27*
for early vegetables, 51
site selection, *18–19*
soil drainage and, *58, 68*
soil for, 57
stone building materials, 69
Raspberry, 224–227
nutrients in, 9
pruning/training, *125*, 130–131, *130–131*
See also Brambles
Rhubarb, 197
climate considerations, 49, *106*
growing seasons, 45
in landscape, 26
nutrients in, 9
Rosemary, 272
in containers, *31*
growing season, 45
in landscape, 23
watering, 89
Row covers, floating, 101
Rutabaga (Swede turnip), 198
climate considerations, 49
diseases/disorders, 114, 115, 116
nutrients in, 9
from seeds, 73

S

Sage, 273
diseases/disorders, 115, 117
in landscape, 23
for partial shade, 142
watering, 89
Salad Bowl garden, 136, *136*
Sandy soils
characteristics, 57, 58
nutrient content, 61
Sanitation, pest control role, 107
Savory, summer and winter, **274**
Scab, fungal, **117**
Scale insects, 112
Seasonal Harvest garden, 140, *140–141*
Seasons, growing. *See* Climate and seasons; Freezing temperatures
Seeds and seedlings
acclimating, *76–77*, 77, 83
for container gardens, 37
containers for, *72–73*, 74–75, *74–75*
damping off, 77, *77*, **115**
for fall harvest, 53
germination, 77
outdoor care, 82–83, *82–83*
seed packet information, 81
soil mixes, 75
sowing in garden, *14*, 73
starting indoors, 73, 74–77
thinning, 82–83, *82–83*
Selecting and buying plants
disease- or pest-resistant varieties, 107
dwarf fruit trees, *21*, 25, 27, 37, 143
for fall harvest, 53
pest control role, 99, *103*
small-size cultivars, 137
for specific sites, 23
for specific zones, 44–47
Self-fruitful or self-sterile trees, 25
Shade. *See* Sunlight
Silt soils, characteristics, 57
Site selection
for containers, 31
disease control role, 103
for fall harvest, 53
microclimates, 45, 47, 51
for orchards, 25
overview, 14, *18–19*, 19
Size of garden
as design consideration, 20
exercising restraint, 15
small-size cultivars, 137
Small Wonder garden, 137, *137*
Snails and slugs, 113
Soil
defined, 57
nutrient content, 19, 58, 61
selecting crops suited to, 107
types, 57
Soil amendments
for container soils, 34–35
organic matter, 57, *57*
overview, 19, 65
See also Compost; Mulch
Soil compaction, avoiding, 67, 69
Soil drainage
for container gardens, 33, 34, *34–35*
for fruit trees, 25
overview, 58, 59
for seedling containers, 74
as site-selection criterion, 19
testing, 58, 59, *59*
Soil mixes
for containers, 14, 27, 34–35, *34–35*, 39, 40
for seedlings, 75
Soil preparation, 54–69
overview, 14
for seedbeds, 78–79
workability of soil, 51
Soil temperature, measuring, 51, *51*
Soil testing
drainage, 58–59, *59*
nutrient content, 58–59, 59, 61, *63*
pH, 59
Soil texture
for fruit trees, 25
improving, 19, 66–67, *66*
overview, 58
as site-selection criterion, 19

Soybeans, 150, 152–153
Spacing plants, 20–21, 107
Spinach, 199
for Asian-inspired gardens, 12
climate considerations, 49, 51
in containers, 37
diseases/disorders, 115, 116
nutrients in, 9
from seeds, 73
Spurs, fruiting, 125
Squash bugs, 113
Squash, winter and summer, **200–203**
climate considerations, 49
diseases/disorders, 114, 115, 116, 117
fall harvest, 52, *52*
insect pests, 110, 111, 113
for Italian-inspired gardens, 13
juglone susceptibility, 19
nutrients in, 9
from seeds, 73
weeds suppressed by, 105
Stakes, trellises, and cages
arbors, *21*
for container gardens, 41
obelisks, *21, 32–33*
for small spaces, 27
for tomatoes, *81*, 139
tomato tepees, 83, *83*
Sticky traps, 101
Strawberry, 250–253
in containers, *30*
diseases/disorders, 114, 115, 117
insect pests, 112, 113
in landscape, 23
nutrients in, 9
Succession planting, 27, 49, *140–141*, 140–141
Suckers, removing, 127
Sunlight
changing patterns, 23
for containers, 31
for fruit trees, 25
for indoor seedlings, 75, 77
as site-selection criterion, 19
sunscald, **117**
vegetables for partial shade, 142
Sunscald, 117
Sweet potato, 204
climate considerations, 49
nutrients in, 9

T

Tarragon, French, **262**
diseases/disorders, 115, 117
Taste of Summer garden, 138, *138*
Thinning branches, 127
Thinning fruit, 129, 133
Thinning seedlings, 82–83, *82–83*, 127
Thyme, 275
in containers, 31, *36–36*
growing season, 45
for Italian-inspired gardens, 13
in landscape, 23
watering, 89
Tilling (cultivation)
disease control role, 103
techniques, 79
tools for, *79*
for weed control, *20*
Tomatillo (husk tomato), 205
climate considerations, 49
in landscape, 23
for Mexican-inspired gardens, 13
from seeds/transplants, 73
Tomato, 206–211
climate considerations, 45, *48*, 49
in containers, 27, *27, 30*, 33, 37, 138, *138*
diseases/disorders, 114, 115, 116, 117
fertilizing, *60*, 67
harvesting/storing, *56*
insect pests, 144, 115, 116
for Italian-inspired gardens, 16
juglone susceptibility, 19
for Mexican-inspired gardens, 13
nutrients in, 9
planting tips, 81, *81*
from seeds/transplants, 73
staking, *81*, 139
watering, 89
Tomato tepees, 83, *83*
Transplants
buying, *102*
caring for, 82–83, *82–83*
for fall harvest, 53
planting, 14
vs. seeds, 73
Trellises. *See* Stakes, trellises, and cages
Tropical and subtropical fruits, growing tips, 11
Turnip, 212
climate considerations, 51
diseases/disorders, 114, 115, 116
insect pests, 113
nutrients in, 9
for partial shade, 142
Turnip, Swede. *See* Rutabaga

V

Vegetables, 146–213
as annual plants, 45
cool-season, 37, 48–49, *50–51*, 51, 52, *86, 92, 106*
deciding what to grow, 11
dwarf varieties, 27
easy-to-grow, *10–11*
for ethnic cuisines, 10, 12–13, *12–13*
front-yard worthy, 23
low-water crops, 89
moisture requirements, *15*
for partial shade, 142
in raised beds, 51
from seeds vs. transplants, 73
in traditional gardens, 20–21, *20–21*
warm-season, 37, 49, 51
weed-free crops, 105
when to plant, *50–51*, 51, 81
Verbena, lemon, **266**
in landscape, 23
Vines
planting tips, 81
supports for, 27
Violet, edible flowers, **261**
Virus, mosaic, **116**
Voles, 96, **121**

W

Walls. *See* Fences and walls
Walnut, juglone toxicity, 19
Watering, 83–93
conservation tips, 93
container gardens, 31, *33*, 37, 38–39, *38–39*
to dislodge insects, 101
for fall harvest, 53
outdoor seedlings, 82
plant diseases and, 77, 89, 92–93, 107, 115
as site-selection criterion, 19
smart practices, 92–93, *92*
when to water, 39, *86*, 87, 107
See also specific types of crops

Watering tools/systems
automatic timers, *38*, 91
basin irrigation, 89, *89*
drip irrigation, *39*, 32, 90, 91, *91*
furrow irrigation, 88
Gator Bags, 87
hand-watering, 88, *88*, 101
sprinklers, 89
winter hose care, 93
Watermelon, 213
diseases/disorders, 115
nutrients in, 9
Water stress, symptoms, 87, *87*
Weed control
disease control role, 103
for fall harvest, 53
integrated pest management, 98–99
methods, *96*, *104*, 105
mulch, 97, *98*, 105
pest-prevention role, 107
for specific weeds, **118–119**
tilling, 20
tools, 105
Weeds
common, **118–119**
diagnosing problems, 97
overview, 105
prevention strategies, 107
Wind damage, protecting fruit trees from, 47
Window boxes, support for, 31
Wireworms, 113
Woodchucks, 121

Z

Zones, U.S.D.A. Hardiness
defined, 44–45
planting for specific zones, 45, *46*, 47
zone map, 276
See also Climate and seasons
Zucchini. *See* Squash, winter and summer